Student Freedom
in
American Higher Education

LOUIS C. VACCARO
and
JAMES THAYNE COVERT
Editors

Teachers College Press
Teachers College, Columbia University

© 1969 by Teachers College, Columbia University
Library of Congress Catalog Card Number: 69:16222

The quotation on page viii is reprinted from *An Introduction to Medieval Europe 300–1500* by James Westfall Thompson and Edgar Nathaniel Johnson. By permission of W. W. Norton & Company, Inc. Copyright 1937 by W. W. Norton & Company, Inc. Copyright renewed 1965 by Edgar Nathaniel Johnson.

Manufactured in the United States of America

Foreword

An almost identical incident brought the majority of delegates to the 1968 national political conventions to their feet. In each case, a "representative" of the political establishment at the podium had just delivered a blistering condemnation of the licentious, long-haired, bearded, dirty, obscene, anarchistic, barefooted, hippie, "pseudo-intellectuals" causing chaos on our streets and on our campuses. We have come to expect that kind of personal harangue at the podium. We can even, in our better moments, point to it as a good example of the freedom of speech and public assembly that are deep in the guts of the American system. Yet, the instantaneous and tumultuous assent of the crowds—assembled to nominate a candidate who must lead an America torn by racial, social, economic, and generational strife—was, for me, a really frightening phenomenon acted out in Miami, and repeated in Chicago.

Your reaction, as a reader, may reflect the concern of the delegates about the young which must have motivated their support of the podium diatribe. On the other hand, you may share my concern about the simplistic attitudes of the delegates who accepted the diatribe against youthful dissenters with no apparent ability or desire to sort out the differences, even the mutually exclusive motivations and styles among them.

This collection of essays, edited by Professors Vaccaro and Covert, speaks to the range and complexity of this critical issue. The Editors' Introduction states clearly the essential dilemma which every citizen, every parent, every administrator, every faculty member, and every student must try to keep in focus as we learn to live effectively with a generation which is at the same time activist and "cop-out." The editors ask us to consider that "Today's students are seeking, on the one hand, increased influence in areas of policy formation hitherto controlled by faculty or administration; on the other hand, they are demanding a lessening of the bonds of authority that have traditionally governed their personal lives." In one sense, they are asking that the university extend its "authoritative voice," that it speak responsibly, even morally, to specific urban situations, to specific wars, to specific economic investors. And in holding this position, they demand a part, sometimes seemingly a controlling one, in determining the character of the "authoritative" moral voice. On the other hand, they are demanding that the university drop the *in loco parentis* role in their personal lives, desist from determining and sanctioning their moral behavior.

It is my own conviction that the young activists will remain active and grow daily more responsible as we are prepared to deal with both aspects of this problem. Deeply underlying the sometimes traumatic behavior of both student actors and adult critics is our mutual inexperience in decision-making in areas in which we are allowed and compelled to live with the consequences of our decisions.

The value judgments within this area represented by the authors of these essays display, on a kind of "mini-scale," the same kind of range, difference, and even polarity of view, which, I believe, characterizes the dissenters themselves. Dean Farris maintains that "the very essential matter of teaching and learning [demands that] one must teach while the other learns." Professor Vaccaro, in contrast, reminds himself and all adults that we, too, "need to stop, to look, to reflect, and perhaps to take up the search again," to *learn* again with our students.

The essays as a whole provide both a historical and a sociological context for the reader, together with a range of value commentaries against which we can examine our own prejudgments and muddlements. All of us, both professionals and laymen in education, must face both our rigid prejudices and our painful confusions about this critically important fact of American and international life if we are to meet our own decision-making responsibilities and their consequences for today and tomorrow. Because these essays help the members of the body politic at large to confront these issues soberly, I hope that they evoke in you, the reader, a response that will both confuse your prejudices and clarify your confusions.

Jacqueline Grennan, President
Webster College

Contents

Editors' Introduction	vii
The Campus Environment and Student Freedom Edward B. Blackman	1
The New Student Subculture and the Search for Meaning Louis C. Vaccaro	31
Social Role Limitations of the Student as an Apprentice Theodore N. Farris	39
Student Governance and the Issue of Student Freedom Robert M. Crane	49
Academic Freedom for Students: Some Thoughts on the Current Debate Mary Jo Hall	63
A Student's View of Freedom in the Multiversity Diane Keane Driessel	73
The Political Involvement of Students: Where Freedom Begins and Ends R. J. Snow	85
Student Rights and Academic Due Process Louis C. Vaccaro and Thomas E. Wolf	105
Religious Commitment and Student Freedom on the Church-Related Campus Sheridan P. McCabe	115
A Campus Sexual Revolution? Robert Hassenger	125
Student Freedom and the Development of Creative Education Douglas Kent Hall	147
Student Movements: East Asian and American Patterns John Blewett, S.J.	155

Editors' Introduction

Anyone even remotely familiar with American higher education today must be aware of the seemingly new force that is presently stalking the collegiate quadrangles across the country. This rising force can be referred to as "student activism." While it may focus on various issues or "causes," it is a single force in that it represents a general movement to expand the role of students in the affairs of higher education; and although its effects are sometimes difficult to discern, it is sure to have a widespread impact on the larger society. More specifically, this new activism centers on the fundamental question of student *freedom*, which has both a positive and a negative application. Today's students are seeking, on the one hand, increased influence in areas of policy formation hitherto controlled by faculty or administration; on the other, they are demanding a lessening of the bonds of authority that have traditionally governed their personal lives.

As one might expect, this quest for more freedom is not always happily met by faculty or administration. Although it is true that these other principal forces residing in academe, i.e., the faculty and the administration, are but former students themselves (who freely chose not to leave the relatively peaceful ivy-covered halls of higher learning), a major gap of understanding exists between them and the "new breed" of students. Many college and university officials view the so-called student revolt with mixed emotions although some regard it with outright alarm and others heartily cheer it on either from the sidelines or within student caucuses. To most teachers and administrators the phenomenon is of such perplexing proportions that a total commitment either for or against student activism is as improbable as it is unacceptable. One thing is certain: the specter of continued and increasing student protest is forcing an interesting *rapprochement* between faculty and administration who for centuries have regarded each other as natural adversaries.

Then, of course, there is another aspect to consider. The faculty and administration have traditionally found it necessary to defend higher learning from societal encroachments, particularly concerning *faculty* freedom. Now the problem is *student* freedom, a new shibboleth that may be less intelligible to the general public. Although certain agencies and organizations—governmental and private—are intimately involved in higher education, most of the general public are not; and they are no doubt bewildered and possibly perturbed by the growth of what must seem to them irresponsibility and insubordination among students. Because the larger society is apparently unable to discern between the "good" and the "bad" operating in student activism, its major impulse is to reject it.

Gone are the "good old days," bemoan many, when a docile college student was only interested in such things as sex, status, and security. And while it may be that today's student is still interested in these things, it is also readily apparent that he is concerned about other facets of American life, e.g., civil rights, poverty, war, and drugs. All of this goes to show that, if nothing else, higher education has enabled students to get into more intelligent trouble. Yet, were the "good old days" as good as we remember? History reveals that virtually every generation had to contend with some form of student radicalism. Robert de Sorbon complained that the thirteenth-century students at the University of Paris were more interested in gambling than studies; and the "town and gown" riots have been a customary feature in most college or university towns for centuries. The remarks of one medieval observer about the antics of university students have a modern ring:

> They are so litigious and quarrelsome that there is no peace with them; wherever they go . . . they disturb the country, their associates, even the whole university. Many of them go about the streets armed, attacking the citizens. . . . They quarrel among themselves . . . [and] rush into conflicts from which armed knights would hold back. Their compatriots come to their aid, and soon whole nations of students may be involved in the fray.*

Nevertheless, a good case can be made that student activism today is different in both quantity and quality of protest; and while it may vary greatly throughout the country as to specific issues and the intensity of demands, the fundamental problem exists and must be recognized. It matters little whether student demands have escalated into open rebellion at a major urban university or are still simmering beneath the surface at a small liberal arts college in rural America; the fact remains that this challenge must be understood and met squarely. It is for this reason that the following essays are brought together.

This study does not purport to provide definitive answers or solutions; rather, it presents an array of views by individuals closely associated with college and university life in order to delineate significant issues, to expose certain tendencies and characteristics of students, and in general, to offer the reader some mature and dispassionate insights concerning the question of student freedom in American higher education.

In the first essay, Edward B. Blackman, Assistant Dean of University College at Michigan State University, discusses the general problem of today's student quest for freedom and the environmental factors of campus life. This picture is reenforced by Louis C. Vaccaro, Vice President for

---

* As quoted in J. W. Thompson and E. N. Johnson, *An Introduction to Medieval Europe, 300–1500* (New York: W. W. Norton & Co., Inc., 1937), p. 735.

Editors' Introduction

Academic Affairs at the University of Portland, who evaluates and interprets some of the basic ideas that are shaping this emerging student subculture. Following this there are two essays that provide the historical setting of the student's relationship to the university as an institution. Theodore N. Farris, Dean of Students in the School of General Studies at Columbia University, points out the traditional limitations on the student as an "apprentice," while Robert M. Crane, Professor of Education at the University of Illinois at Chicago Circle, explores the historical connection between student governance and student freedom. Bringing the issue into its contemporary context, Mary Jo Hall, Director of Federal Relations at the University of Oregon, offers some discerning thoughts on recent student strategy in the struggle for expression and academic freedom. This is followed by Diane Keane Driessel's revealing essay. A graduate student at the University of California at Berkeley, Miss Driessel might be regarded as "an angry student," and she writes with verve and bluntness about student ideals and life at a "multiversity." R. J. Snow, Assistant Professor of Political Science at the University of California, Santa Barbara, then provides a penetrating analysis of the concept of student freedom and its legal and political implications. Louis C. Vaccaro speaks from the viewpoint of a university administrator and Thomas Wolf as a lawyer, as they discuss "due process" of the law as it relates to the settlement of conflict within the academic community.

The next three essays offer some important corollary studies. Sheridan P. McCabe, Director of the Counseling Center at the University of Notre Dame, probes the crucial relationship of religious commitment and student freedom with special emphasis on the church-related school; Robert Hassenger, who is Assistant Professor of Sociology at the University of Notre Dame, offers a critical, documented assessment of the so-called sexual revolution on American campuses and how it may have influenced student life; and Douglas Kent Hall, author-poet and former Instructor of English at the University of Portland, discusses the need to reevaluate the methodology of university education with a view toward establishing a more creative atmosphere. Finally, the last essay, by John Blewett, S.J., former Academic Dean of Sophia University in Tokyo, Japan, presents a comparative survey of Chinese, Japanese, and American higher education and the parallels that exist on the question of student freedom.

Not all of the authors whose writings appear in this book would agree with each other regarding the specific problems flowing from today's student activism, let alone the possible solutions. This is as it should be. Each, however, would agree with the fundamental proposition that to remain ignorant of or indifferent to this challenge presently confronting American higher education would be disastrous. And the contributors, as each brings the reader a personal, up-to-date observation of the college scene, collectively provide a dimensional study and an expertise that is sorely needed.

It is sincerely hoped that this volume will awaken educators, laymen, and students to some of the pivotal features of contemporary student activism as well as serve as a valuable guideline for further study of the academic and social milieu of today's collegian.

L.C.V.
J.T.C.

EDWARD B. BLACKMAN

The Campus Environment and Student Freedom

Edward B. Blackman is presently Assistant Dean, University College, Michigan State University. The author of numerous articles, he is active in the American Association for Higher Education.

"The fathers have eaten sour grapes, and the teeth of the children are set on edge." So runs the ancient Israelitic proverb. Moreover, Jehovah "visits the iniquity of the fathers upon the children, upon the third and upon the fourth generation." The Olympians in fifth-century tragedy often displayed the same inclination, as the family histories of Oedipus and Agamemnon demonstrate. While it is fruitless to cry out against God, as Job, for all his eloquence, discovered, it is easy and tempting to blame an older generation for the evils of this one: war in Vietnam, the unequal position of Negroes in American society, painful poverty in a land of affluence, Congressmen who find rats in slum tenements a source of amusement, excessive materialism that borders on bloated satiety, callousness to cruelty, self-centeredness to the point of moral indifference.

Proverbs and deities aside, ghosts do in fact stalk the earth; and the collective acts of prior generations do in large measure give shape to the character of the current age. The bewildered parent wonders whether an excess of permissiveness has produced children who defy his wishes and deny his values. A "Tired Liberal," John Fischer, patiently explains that in his youth youngsters were no strangers to poverty, that they knew from personal experience what hunger meant; and that now, having tasted the bitter fruits of a prolonged depression and a devastating world war, they feel no guilt in the barbecue, the thick steak, the suburban home, the station wagon, the country club, the power boat, and the summer home.

And he counterattacks by asserting that the young rebels of today know what they are against but not what they are for, that they are too dogmatic to compromise, too bitter to trust, and too naive to know that working with Communists in organized causes results in shattered hopes and abandoned goals.[1] But will the rebels listen to Fischer any more than to the subdued reasonableness of Walter Lippmann? Apparently not. In response to his restrained comments about generational differences and the eternal value of wisdom—"the capacity of judging rightly in matters relative to life and conduct"—Rita Dershowitz, an associate editor of *The Yale Alumni Magazine*, writes that Lippmann's "wisdom" is not relevant to her life ("relevant" has become the greatest catchword of our time); that her experiences are different from anything that has ever occurred before (apparently there are still some new things under the sun); that the old values don't hold true any longer, and this makes hers an exciting generation (an observation calculated to make a middle-aged man somewhat envious); that her generation is the first one to have a real choice of "self-imposed poverty" (perhaps her education is deficient in a knowledge of monasticism).[2]

The radical youth of the thirties (many of whom are now the tired fathers of the sixties) were essentially optimists, typical products of the eighteenth-century Enlightenment: pass some Social Security laws, require employers to bargain collectively with unions, get the unemployed back on the payrolls, tighten a bolt here and turn a wheel there—and the "system" would respond to the wisdom of the New Deal, and a better America would come to birth. But the radicals of the sixties have a dark strain of neo-Calvinism in them: man is basically evil, and so is the world in which he lives. Why prescribe remedies for a better world? Man's condition reflects a kind of hopeless determinism.[3] Moreover, one cannot place trust in those who belong to an older generation, and communication with parents is all but hopeless. Worst of all, the older generation is warped with hypocrisy about war (to burn a piece of paper in time of war is a grave crime calling for five years in prison and a $5000 fine but to kill is heroic), sex, drink, drugs, abortion, religion, capital punishment, poverty, civil rights, and morality in general.[4] When young, our elders naively trusted to partisan politics and legislation to right the evils of a wicked society, and they still do. Because we know better, we don't join established political parties; we

[1] "Letter to a New Leftist from a Tired Liberal," *Harper's*, 232 (March 1966), 16–28.

[2] "To Mr. Lippmann," *Harper's*, 235 (October 1967), 46–47.

[3] For a total rejection of the Enlightenment view of progress, see Carl Oglesby, "The Spanked and the Unspanked," *Saturday Review*, 51 (May 20, 1967), 76–77, 93.

[4] For a sweeping condemnation of the evils and hypocrisies of society, see Phillip A. Luce, *The New Left* (New York: David McKay Co., Inc., 1966). This book contains the SDS Port Huron Statement of 1962, a giant cry of despair at the "crimes of the Establishment."

avoid ideologies. Alienation, despair, and a sense of futility are our lot.[5]

The activists do not say so, but the hypocrisies of NSA, SNCC, SDS, and the campus groups which form today and disappear tomorrow are so often extreme in their cynicism and in their statements of "facts" (as they pour out their cries of despair in letters to the editor or foul a free press with their underground newspapers or grind away at dilapidated mimeograph machines) that one must wonder whether honesty has a place in the strange lexicons they habitually employ. Posed together, NSA and the CIA make something less than an attractive picture. So does the activists' strange and recent equation of Student Power, which, according to a former officer of SDS, means total student control of the university and employee roles for faculty and administration,[6] and Black Power, which now, although a confusing term, stresses pride in blackness, voluntary segregation, identification with Africa, and occasional overtones of possible violence if demands are unmet. As for the other groups who have discovered all the four-letter words in the dictionary and derive some sort of self-titillation from publicly displaying them in the apparent belief that people over thirty are unfamiliar with them, who can but pity the waste, the stupidity, and the remoteness from reality? For those who allegedly cherish honesty and despise hypocrisy, what a swift descent from idealism are the deliberate use of the word that offends, the slogan "Che lives," the elevating of Castro to the role of savior, and the adoption of his beard as a symbol of opposition to "clean politicians." [7]

Often the bitterness springs from alleged pressure to go to college and succeed there. And such pressure indeed exists in most middle-class homes. "You live from exam to exam"; "The pressure is always on"; "If you don't go to college these days, it's over and I mean over"—these are all student comments at the University of Illinois, quoted by Nicholas von Hoffman.[8] In Stephen Walton's novel, *No Transfer*, a certain number of below-average students are publicly decapitated. Independent spirits that they are, the rebels resent the pressure and find campus life lacking in intellectual stimulation (especially when final examinations approach), the administration totally devoid of the most elementary knowledge of how to oversee the affairs of the university, the faculty uninspired, the courses unrelated to the important concerns of our day, and their fellow students dull clods.

What to do? For the relatively moderate, there is activism in its several forms. For others, there is marijuana; for the more daring (or more

---

[5] See Irving Kristol, "What's Bugging the Students?" *Atlantic Monthly*, 216 (November 1965), 108–111. The extreme activists view with contempt all presidential candidates in 1968.

[6] Carl Davidson, "University Reform Revisited," *Educational Record*, 48 (Winter 1967), 5–10.

[7] See Luce, *The New Left*, p. 14. Luce asserts that more recently China has replaced Cuba as the mecca of the New Left (p. 60).

[8] Nicholas von Hoffman, *The Multiversity* (New York: Holt, Rinehart & Winston, 1966), p. 141.

despairing) there are LSD and the other hallucinogenic drugs; Haight-Ashbury lures the footloose to the land of hippies, lollipops, fancy-colored balloons, jelly beans, and flower people. The "love-in"—saturated with bitterness and self-righteousness—becomes a beer-drinking festival that often terminates in violence. The venereal disease, the malnutrition, the mental disturbances have been treated at a nearby San Francisco clinic. But in October of 1967, the clinic closed; the exhausted doctors withdrew; the colder weather made life in the streets less fun (and less profitable, for panhandling had become a way of life for some)—and many of the hippies announced that they would head south or home or back to school. All of this would have little to do with campus life were it not for the estimate that about half of the denizens of Haight-Ashbury were Berkeley dropouts. After the departure of the original hippies, a new generation of dropouts arrived—this time dropouts from home and high school. Paul Coates, reporting on this later group, wrote that "the typical hippie is 16, of average intelligence, and has experienced V.D. He frequently smokes marijuana and at least occasionally takes LSD or STP. He comes from a middle-class home and his parents earn $10,400 a year. He doesn't drink and rarely smokes tobacco. His 'bag' (or, if you come from the outside world, his purpose) is to do nothing." [9]

The reopening of the clinic in early 1968 helped spark a revival of Haight-Ashbury as a hippie center. But the new inhabitants are younger, most have never been college students, some work in the clinic, others have passed civil service examinations and deliver the mail. For all present concerns, the hippie is no longer either a college student or a former college student, and he need not be taken seriously in a chapter on students.

But not all dissidents who feel that they cannot go home again or that they are victims of a world they never made seek Nirvana by fleeing from reality or "dropping out" or "turning on." The haven for many who seek identity off the campus is often the Peace Corps, VISTA, working in civil rights groups or hospitals or playgrounds or other poverty programs. In any case, one must face with honesty the question of the validity of their accusations and the quality of their reactions against a society which in their eyes so sadly lacks integrity.

When a great nation makes war, when some men grow wealthy while others go hungry, when possessions take precedence over humanity, when men fight and die in the streets of cities for rights which are demanded by some and denied by others, the "campus environment" knows no barriers, physical or psychological. Like so much of the rest of the world, the United States is in many ways hypocritical, callous, and arrogant. A student requires no great perceptivity to see, nor need he be deeply sensitive to care.

To the activist student, his country is engaged in a massive war which begins to approach genocide, a war that the nation's leaders cannot explain

[9] Paul Coates, *Los Angeles Times* report, reprinted in *The Lansing State Journal*, September 19, 1967, p. A-7.

and from which they lack the capacity to disengage themselves. In the midst of plenty, so fully displayed at each moment in the mass media, he knows there are slums in which poverty, hunger, disease, and crime play their grisly roles on a crowded, warped, meaningless stage. He knows the curse of the black skin, the corruption in high places, the lust for power and political office which would repel the voters in a less callous nation.

In such a time and place, the theater of the absurd becomes the voice of reason, and the desire to separate oneself from the standard-bearers of an earlier age is easily intelligible. If the activist often seeks to shock, he also seeks to divorce trash from truth. For some the long hair, the beard, and the sandal emphasize the separation and at the same time create a symbolic badge of identification with others of like views. When the activist seeks "thrills" in unusual ways, he may simply be asserting what most older people know: Whether God is dead or not, much of what He is presumed to have revealed is not now alive. And so the zealous search for pleasure replaces many traditional values [10]—pleasure that need not be, but so often is, harmful to the mind, and even fatal to the body. Geoffrey Gorer once said: "Mankind is safer when men seek pleasure than when they seek the power and the glory." [11] The activist may misunderstand them, but he knows these are good words—better, say, than H-bombs, ICBM's, Sputniks, escalation, kill-ratio, B-52's, and the speeches of four-star generals who are always "doing a good job" (even though it is apparent to anybody who can read a newspaper that their competence is open to question).

The dates of history usually fail us when we would mark the birth or the death of a national mood. But hope and idealism came to life among the young of America on that frigid day in January 1961, when John Kennedy, hatless and handsome in his youthful vitality, proclaimed in his Inaugural Address: "Let the word go forth from this time and place, to friend and foe alike, that the torch has been passed to a new generation of Americans. . . ." Prophetically he announced that the tasks he undertook would not "be finished in the first 1,000 days, nor in the life of this Administration. . . . But let us begin." He spoke of the "struggle against the common enemies of man: tyranny, poverty, disease, and war itself." And he boldly added: "I do not shrink from this responsibility—I welcome it." Finally, the idealism in one of the last passages: "The energy, the faith, the devotion which we bring to this endeavor will light our country and all who serve it—and the glow from that fire can truly light the world." When John Kennedy fell dead in Dallas in November 1963, a different word went forth: not only was the Presidential apostle of youthful idealism gone; he was the victim of an act that lacked motive or meaning—an act, in short,

---

[10] See Mervin Freedman, "Post-Industrial Generation: Roots of Student Discontent," *Nation*, 200 (June 14, 1965), 639–643; and Kenneth Keniston, *The Uncommitted: Alienated Youth in American Society* (Harcourt, Brace & World, Inc., 1965), pp. 81 and 351–353.

[11] Quoted in John Poppy, "The Generation Gap," *Look*, 31 (February 21, 1967), 26–32.

that was absurd. And some symbols departed as others arrived: the Pedernales replaced the Charles; Texas and Lyndon Johnson ascended the mountain and discovered a great "cause" in Vietnam. When the American casualty figure passed 100,000 in late 1967, who could still speak rationally of idealism? The influence of the military-industrial complex, against whose combined threat to the nation President Eisenhower had warned in his farewell address, rose ever higher as the power and prestige of Lyndon Johnson declined among the older generation even as it had earlier died among the younger. The divisiveness created by the war helped persuade President Johnson not to stand for reelection.

Only those who are self-righteous, superpatriotic, or morally crippled can be surprised and outraged that some students seek through acts of nonconformity, acts that are usually minor and innocuous, to announce their repudiation of a world which is more evil than it need be but less easily improved than the nonconformist usually supposes. A few students who despair wholly of improving the evils they identify are sometimes disposed to turn to a complete and absolute individualism for salvation. In this kind of paradise, freedom, individualism, laissez-faire, indifference to earlier concerns, hostility to parents, teachers, and others who exercise authority, disdain for social welfare legislation, and the enthronement of Ayn Rand as the reigning queen of never-never land reflect a desperate turn from left to right, from concern to indifference, from reality to fantasy —a respectable form of flight into extreme self-interest.

Thus it is that events which seem at first glance so far removed from the secluded study, the quiet library, and the sober classroom of the campus push past the boundaries, invade the inner precincts, and demand the attention of the sensitive student. They seem to create in students a determined preoccupation with the present which makes the postponement of action—be it pleasure, correction of social evils, or modification in campus mores—unacceptable. For such students, the classes are dull or too far removed from current problems, the universities are too big, the teaching is pedestrian or precious, the bureaucracy is stifling, the parietal rules appropriate for children, the requirements and demand for grades destructive of intellectual curiosity and student freedom.[12] The intensity of juvenile emotion and the bitterness against on-campus customs and rules demonstrate clearly that in reality the off-campus influences have created the necessary preconditions of frustration and anger. Thus, reaction to on-campus courses and methods of instruction and grading bears little or no relationship to the magnitude of the issues. To study the campus environment of our day without prior analysis of the larger world would be to ignore most of the influences that give shape to that environment, at least that segment of the campus world which is caught up in the spirit of activism. The strictly on-campus forces which influence student behavior in

[12] See Nevitt Sanford, "Unrest in College," *School & Society*, 95 (April 15, 1967), 246–247; and Harold Howe II, "Our Colleges Aren't Ready for Today's Students," *Saturday Review*, 48 (May 15, 1965), 77–79.

significant ways are discussed later; we will find that although important and in some ways almost revolutionary, they are easier to identify, classify, analyze, and resolve—usually through an enlargement of student freedom in personal affairs and mutually developed arrangements for increased student participation in the governance of the college or university.

Those who read sensational newspaper accounts of campus life will respond with astonishment—either admiration or abhorrence, depending on their bias—to the news that a whole generation of students has turned its back on old values. But is it a whole generation? Exact figures are either difficult to secure or defy belief when available. The whole matter is further complicated by the fact that sociologists have identified a variety of student subcultures. Martin Trow and Burton T. Clark refer to four such groups: the students who come for an education; those who come for vocational preparation; those who seek fun and games; and, finally, those who are nonconformist, creative, and activist.[13] Other writers have chosen different names. But no matter: the different groupings are not mutually exclusive but overlap in different ways and on different occasions; most students share a large number of basic similarities despite the individual characteristics that identify them.

The usual estimate of activist students at Berkeley is higher than at any other place, but is vaguely said to be well in excess of 15 per cent. One Harvard student places the figure at his university at 10 per cent.[14] A national survey, defining an activist as anybody who has taken part in at least one demonstration, places the national average among freshmen at an astonishingly high 15 per cent.[15] And a Harris survey finds that two-thirds of all college students sympathize with both the causes and the tactics of the activist.[16] No doubt there are problems here of terminology and definition. The 10 to 15 per cent estimate for activists seems reasonable enough for many large campuses; and no doubt the number of tacit sympathizers is high. But the Harris findings must be treated with great caution since the percentages are known to vary so greatly from one cause to another and even from one season of the year to another on the same campus. At some of the smaller, more conservative colleges, the activists are almost nonexistent. And, inevitably, there are issues of so inflammatory a nature that they can bring together almost the entire student body in a demonstration

---

[13] The Trow and Clark article on four student subcultures continues to circulate in mimeographed form. An excellent summary of these very helpful categories appears in David Gottlieb, "College Climates and Student Subcultures," in Wilbur Brookover (ed.), *The College Student* (New York: Center for Applied Research in Education, 1965), Chap. 6.

[14] David M. Gordon, " 'Rebellion' in Context: A Student's View of Students," in Robert S. Morison (ed.), *The Contemporary University: U.S.A.* (Boston: Houghton Mifflin Company, 1966), pp. 292–314.

[15] "Education Notes: Current Freshmen," *New England Association Review*, (Winter 1967), pp. 41–42.

[16] Robert F. Wagner, Jr., "Students Speak for Action," *Saturday Review*, 48 (October 16, 1965), 82.

against a president. Thus, while figures on activists may be useful, estimates regarding sympathizers are subject to too many variables to be precise.

The problem of definition may be somewhat simplified if we think of an activist as one who participates in virtually every cause that comes along—a kind of professional agitator or demonstrator. The student who becomes involved only on occasion and only in selected issues should probably not be included in estimates of activists. Except for smaller schools known for their liberalism and permissiveness—Antioch and Reed would be examples—activism is more likely to appear in a larger school than a smaller one, an urban school than a rural one, a university than a college, a distinguished school than an average one, a secular school than a church-related one, a school whose students come from homes of above-average income, education, liberalism, and permissiveness.[17] Many writers assert that excessive permissiveness in the home unfits the young person for subsequent encounters with such less permissive authority figures as schoolteachers, professors, policemen, and employers. How little we understand about these matters is apparent from the confident assertions of other writers that children who are products of permissive homes are more secure and self-assured than others and thus better prepared to face difficult interpersonal relationships later on.

Why should adults devote so much time, attention, and concern to activists, who constitute a relatively small percentage of the total campus population? In part because their demands—accompanied often by demonstrations or civil disobedience and always by persistence and enormous self-assurance—are virtually impossible to ignore. In part because they are articulate, sensitive, concerned, and gifted in their ability to point the finger at evils in the larger society and at obsolete rules and procedures on the campus—evils and rules about which adults themselves are often confused, over which they often agonize as much as any student, and about which they feel guilt and inadequacy. In part the concern of the informed, reflective adult grows out of the knowledge that small, influential groups often speak unwittingly for a majority of their age, give shape to their time, determine the tone of their era—usually in ways that are not recognized until historians point them out long after the events. Finally, adult concern sometimes is born of the recollection that seemingly radical views in the thirties have become conventional American law in the sixties—Social Security and savings bank insurance and regulatory agencies, and federal aid to the states and to colleges and hospitals and schools for a great variety of purposes, laws to ease excessive unemployment, control of national fiscal policies, civil rights laws, laws enlarging the areas of freedom for extremists of the right and left, laws offering procedural safeguards for criminals or alleged criminals. Who is to say with confidence that the views regarded

[17] See C. Robert Pace, "Perspectives on the Student and His College," in Lawrence E. Dennis and Joseph F. Kauffman (eds.), *The College and the Student* (Washington, D.C.: American Council on Education, 1966), pp. 76–100.

as extreme in the sixties may not become the conventional wisdom of a later age? Indeed, one must face the fact that societal attitudes toward sex behavior, drink, drugs, abortion, capital punishment, and many other values of long standing may be undergoing some kind of revolutionary change and that some of the changes will seem routinely conventional to a later generation. One finds it more difficult to contemplate the possibility that students will seize and control universities, with their billions of dollars worth of physical plants and endowment assets, to say nothing of their varied ownership among the states, municipalities, private corporations, and churches. That professors and administrators would ever regard their youthful students as their employers is virtually unthinkable (despite medieval Bologna and the aspirations of SDS). The claims of the most radical students have made timely Plato's condemnation of democracy as a state in which everybody believes himself to be equal to everybody else and thus children regard themselves as equal to their parents, teachers, and political leaders!

Some may regard the activist student as the victim of a general malaise that seems to afflict so much of the modern world; and surely such a view is not devoid of truth. On the other hand, one may be much more specific: there are strong demands for the right to lead one's private life with fairly complete freedom from outside interference, even when some aspects of the private life depart from traditional moral views.[18] And there are other demands, less dramatic but of great significance in the long run, having to do with some substantial degree of control over campus governance. The words "student freedom" have meaning for both areas, and both require separate, but occasionally overlapping, analysis.

Other observers, many of them business executives, regret the unfavorable "image" of a business career that prevails among students and the reluctance of many able students to take positions in the world of business, industry, and finance. The reasons are clearly the other side of the coin from the desire for personal freedom; the business world demands conformity, promptness, hard work, self-discipline, a variety of inhibitions on behavior, lack of freedom to travel and explore and do the unconventional.

For the student, freedom lies both in areas already discussed and in numerous others: sex, drugs, drink, integrated dating, new art and music, new codes in dress and personal style, independence of the authority of parents, teachers, clergy, employers, and the government. Frank talk about taboo subjects is often a surface manifestation of the passion for freedom. The love-in, the be-in, the happening, and other acts that bewilder adults may be ways of ridiculing the values of the organization man.

While the "privatist ethic" holds that it is no proper concern of gov-

[18] For an attack on this demand for moral freedom, see Herbert Stroup, "Privatist Ethic and Self-Fulfillment," *Christian Century*, 81 (August 19, 1964), 1031–1033. For a defense of privacy, see Keniston, *The Uncommitted*, p. 73.

ernment authorities what a person does in such matters as sex, drink, and drugs so long as he hurts no one else,[19] there is also corresponding and even more intense feeling that such private actions are no business of the dean of students' office either and that any concern or penalty on the part of college authorities is an intolerable infringement on personal freedom. The student who holds to the privatist ethic generally fails to realize that somebody may well be hurt even in a wholly private act. Parents are hurt by the pregnancy of a daughter; family are shocked by the drug addiction of a son; innocents die because motorists are intoxicated. Thus the private act is not always really a private matter at all. The "double jeopardy" claim that a student, having been punished by the police for some offense, must not be placed in double jeopardy by being subsequently disciplined by the college authorities is specious. A bank teller who steals from a grocery market will be punished by the police and the courts but he will almost surely lose his job at the bank as well. As long as men are judged in part by their character, which is likely to be always, the man who breaks a law will face not merely double jeopardy but multiple jeopardy, for he may find that many aspects of his life are adversely affected.

While the word "teach" has historically included moral as well as intellectual instruction, and although colleges have been deeply concerned about character building as well as training the mind, many students now say that the colleges have historically gone beyond their proper bounds (or, if not, the student today is older, wiser, and more mature than in the past). Although there exists no shortage among those who consider the students wrong and many of their views dangerous (especially Whitney Griswold and David Truman),[20] most observers who write on the subject—and their numbers have climbed literally into the hundreds in the last two or three years—are much more disposed to have a cautious sympathy for these newer student views, as perhaps portending a moral revolution—a revolution hastened by war, the pill, TV, and other technological or medical or world developments, but probably inevitable in any event because of the current inadequacy of ancient faiths. One must add that the faculty have long since abdicated the field of personal values in favor of growing professionalism and have cheerfully turned over the tasks of discipline to deans. Many faculty, moreover, seem to derive some kind of vicarious excitement from the student rejection of traditional values, perhaps because the faculty themselves no longer accept the traditional beliefs but have hesitated to discuss these matters openly.

[19] See Kenneth Keniston, "The Faces in the Lecture Room," in Morison, *The Contemporary University*, p. 341. Morality is a private matter in Stephen Walton's *No Transfer*. Privatism is also a search for the development of one's own code; see *School & Society*, 94 (November 12, 1966), 395.

[20] The late President Griswold of Yale held the view that morality *is* the concern of the university; see "Moral Values and Our Universities," *NEA Journal*, 54 (January 1965), 8–10. David B. Truman at Columbia University shares Griswold's view; see "Morality of College Youth," *School & Society*, 42 (October 3, 1964), 258–259.

A certain "filtering down" process is in progress, leading to greater demands for freedom in small, church-related colleges. The demands are milder: freedom from compulsory chapel or required religion courses; the right to dance or go to the movies or use cosmetics or smoke or do some of the other things whose denial has over the years made some small church-related colleges havens for the intellectually inadequate, the dogmatists who regard minor forms of social recreation as having vast moral significance, and those who, for whatever reason, prefer to remain distant from the world of reality.[21]

Important changes in Roman Catholic colleges are too new to be evaluated, but the direction is clear enough and is related to other major developments within the larger framework of the Church. Ultimate control of the institution, curriculum, faculty, student mores—all will move in a more secular direction. In some places, the movement is already well underway. But a letter from President Hesburgh to new Notre Dame students is too delightfully blunt to omit. He writes:

> Beyond the normal griping, if anyone seriously believes that he cannot become well educated here without a car or girls in his room or one really thinks that his personal freedom is impossibly restricted by curfew, or state laws, or drinking. . . . then I think the honest reaction is to get free of Notre Dame.[22]

Yet not even major concessions to the privatist ethic by college officials make the student happy. The malaise remains. As indicated earlier, some students leave to serve in various social causes until they "find themselves" and return. Others are far less likely to return, for their departure has been to the drug-ridden Eden of the hippie, that pseudo-happy world in which nobody cares about the problems of society or even very much about himself because contact with reality is either lost or only feebly maintained.

The student who leaves the campus, whether for some constructive activity or for some Haight-Ashbury, is at least consistent. The environment is intolerable, and he abandons it to those who lack his sensitivity or wisdom. But there is a very large group of other student activists who not only do not leave the campus, but who exhibit a painful desperation in their search for a world that makes sense. They begin with a few simple assumptions: the God of their elders is dead; so are many of the values for which He was a

---

[21] The most recent book on the subject suffers from a large measure of blandness, but is the best we have: Manning M. Pattillo, Jr. and Donald M. Mackenzie, *Church-Sponsored Higher Education in the United States* (Washington, D.C.: American Council on Education, 1966).

[22] Quoted in Stroup, "Privatist Ethic and Self-Fulfillment." Many books have recently begun to appear in a reappraisal of the Catholic college and university, especially of the changes since the Second Vatican Council. A careful and recent book is Robert Hassenger (ed.), *The Shape of Catholic Higher Education* (Chicago: University of Chicago Press, 1967). See also *The Chronicle of Higher Education*, November 22, 1967.

symbol. The churches are middle-class, bourgeois, comfortable, fearful of controversy, shunning both the pieties of the past and the great problems of the present. The parents, as we have seen earlier, are too old and too remote from current concerns to engage in a helpful dialogue. With such initial assumptions, one might reasonably expect a simple atheism, a repudiation of old values, hedonism as a current philosophy of life, and an assertion of some new and radical ways of living and enjoying whatever pleasures life may be capable of offering.

While some students do respond in this way, the overwhelming majority of the dissatisfied engage in no such total repudiation of significance. On the contrary, they desperately search elsewhere for substitute philosophies of life. A minority, with Allen Ginsberg as their *guru*, have turned to the Orient for Nirvana or some lesser form of peace of mind.[23] Others, a decade after Kerouac, decide to "hit the road," or "see America," or simply "find themselves." Some turn to Zen; others to some form of existentialism. A few look for a new faith in Dr. Leary's drug cult. Some become—and these are the students who often embody the worst possible features of their own stereotyped views of their parents—campus politicians, as busy in student government as professional politicians are at the real thing, playing their anti-administration game with a cynicism and dishonesty that would bring a blush to the cheeks of Machiavelli. Some join groups like SDS and SNCC, rarely aware of the extent of extreme leftist infiltration into the leadership, the presence of various shades of Communists,[24] the ambiguous but increasingly menacing significance of the Black Power slogan. A student who sees a connection between Black Power and Student Power may be honestly seeking for answers or for meaning, but he is a pathetic victim of his own ignorance.

More important for faculty who cherish higher education, who are dedicated to instructing young people, and who sympathize with the current confusion of the activist are the students who are deeply concerned about such matters as—to use their own favorite terms—the search for identity, alienation, relevance, individuality, meaning, warm human relationships, knowing professors better, and, most of all, developing for themselves some philosophy of life, perhaps a private utopia.[25]

For the student who denies the existence of meaning yet searches for it with desperation, one can feel only compassion. The teacher or adminis-

---

[23] Perhaps, too, they have been influenced by the Beatles, other popular musical groups, and Hollywood personalities seeking peace of mind in India. For brief comments about Maharishi Mahesh Yogi as well as the musical contributions of Ravi Shankar, see *The National Observer*, December 11, 1967, p. 20.

[24] See Russell Kirk, "Politically Ignorant College Students," *National Review*, 17 (May 18, 1965), 423. The best material on Communism is in Luce, *The New Left*; Luce himself was once a member of the Party.

[25] See Keniston, *The Uncommitted*, pp. 231–253; and Mitchell Cohen and Dennis Hale (eds.), *The New Student Left: An Anthology* (Boston: Beacon Press, 1966).

trator who responds with scorn or rejoices in the irony forfeits the opportunity to educate. The activist student is no Monsieur Mersault (Camus' *The Stranger*) eating his eggs from the pan, smoking his cigarette, sitting on the balcony, going to a movie, sleeping with a girl, visiting the ocean on his day off, and regarding the death and funeral of his mother as an interlude in boredom. For Mersault there is no meaning, and even the prison priest can find no ground on which to conduct a dialogue. In the mood of the Psalmist, the student asks: "What is man, that thou are mindful of him?" But unlike the Psalmist, for the activist student there is usually no answer in faith. Job in all his misery can curse the day on which he was born, yet retain his faith in a living God. The student's reverence for life can be destroyed by an impolite clerk, a half-hour wait, an eight o'clock class, or the front page of the daily paper with its inevitable assortment of disheartening news items.

To this kind of student, the sensitive faculty member, whatever his private beliefs, may well have something of large consequence to say. Robert S. Morison has observed, "The students not only expect to be instructed—they positively demand to be endowed with a sense of direction and a conviction that life is worthwhile, all served up with an intimate personal friendliness rarely found even among blood relatives." [26] Few will find salvation, but some will discover a pragmatic meaning and others will learn that the good life is possible even without a guidebook.

But it is, after all, the presence or absence of meaning that makes all the difference. Whether the fruit blooms or withers on the vine, whether the bird sings or falls into solemn silence may depend almost wholly on whether life has significance. If life lacks meaning, so do all the seemingly important decisions we must make. To a sensitive, active, concerned, involved adolescent, confronting the eternal dilemmas of the student—courses, a major, courtship and choice of mate, commitment to a career, aging parents who offer love and money accompanied by subtle intimations of guilt, increasing frequency of illness, and approaching death—there is no time in life when the reassurance that meaning is at least possible counts more heavily.

While the goals of the activists are communal rather than personal, their concern for meaning is genuine, their disillusionment with the past is only occasionally a posturing. One expects to see them with a beard and other outward signs of invisible grace—symbols of estrangement from the old and identification with the new. The serious activist, quite prepared to demonstrate or employ techniques of civil disobedience, is genuinely angered by what he sees as evil in the larger society and as stupidity in the college student handbook. He will demand from administrators answers to campus concerns and, failing to get them, he will seek to effect change through organized techniques: petitions, editorials, letters, demonstra-

[26] Morison, *The Contemporary University*, p. x.

tions, sit-ins, underground papers, pressure groups, violence, seizure of buildings. His successes come with increasing frequency, especially as his militancy grows and his organizations move to the left.[27]

These students believe, so very many of them, that life has meaning if one can only find it; that utopia can be realized if men will but strive to create it. Rejecting purpose, they seek purpose. Doubting values, they seek values. Rejecting authority, they want closer relations with faculty members who will act unofficially as judges, advisers, and comforters.[28] Demanding independence from parents, they feel little twinge of conscience at accepting money from home. Proclaiming their capacity to manage their own lives and demanding that the college mind its own business, they turn eagerly to the dean of students or their parents or the college and community doctors when the police arrest, when the money runs out, when pregnancy occurs, whenever help is needed. *Time* magazine states; "Never before have the young been left more completely to their own devices. No adult can or will tell them what earlier generations were told: this is God, that is Good, this is Art, that is Not Done." [29] And Britain's Leslie Paul asserts: "The relations of the generations may become the central social issue of the next fifty years, as the relations between the classes have been for the past half-century." [30]

While these inconsistencies and ambiguities must be discussed if one is to understand these students, they may constitute no reason for despair. Emerson said: "Whoso would be a man, must be a nonconformist." And he added a few paragraphs later: "A foolish consistency is the hobgoblin of little minds, adored by little statesmen and philosophers and divines." At least these students are free of that kind of conformity and complacent consistency. At least most of them know that they don't know. It was Socrates who observed that the oracle at Delphi, in declaring him to be the wisest of men, meant only that he knew nothing and knew that he knew nothing, whereas other men thought themselves wise.

At the same time, one cannot ignore the often obvious fact that students of this kind suffer from an excess of self-pity, so that lamentation for the evils of the world becomes a "noble" reason for shirking one's obligations. Often they are indolent, and they have not yet learned the lesson, so difficult for young people to accept, that the acquisition of knowledge is hard work. In another age, hard work and pleasure were not incompatible, and for some students in our day they are not. But for students who have rejected yesterday's notions, one must insist repeatedly that introspection

---

[27] See Richard R. Renner, "Student Unrest in U.S. and Latin American Universities," *School & Society*, 93 (Summer 1965), 294–295.

[28] See especially Freedman, "Post-Industrial Generation."

[29] "Man of the Year," *Time*, 89 (January 6, 1967), 18.

[30] Quoted in *ibid.*, p. 23. Keniston, *The Uncommitted*, p. 156, calls alienation a refusal to accept adulthood. On pages 228–231, he describes parents as "squares" in the eyes of their children.

can become morbid and that ongoing "bull sessions" about the meaning of life can be a pseudo-intellectual substitute for real intellectual work.

To an adult, perhaps one of the most interesting characteristics of these students is their easygoing tolerance of nonconformist behavior by their colleagues. "I wouldn't do that myself," they often say, and then add quite matter of factly, "but it doesn't bother me that he (or she) does." [31] Even serious nonconformity or breach of traditional codes does not result in loss of acceptance among the activist students—perhaps because they are far from convinced that the breach is really morally wrong. Protagoras and Gorgias would find this kind of relativism congenial but unoriginal; for the philosophy is an ancient one and expediency is no stranger to it. If the breach is a total amorality, it becomes a far more serious matter; and at least one writer has compared the more radical activist students to the Nazi hoodlums of the thirties.[32]

Much of the foregoing seems to confirm what many writers, as well as many students (activists and nonactivists alike), insist is the case: the gulf between the generations is so wide that communication about important matters, usually meaning personal matters, is difficult and frequently impossible. Yet significance of the generational gap is minimized by von Hoffman, denied by Ian Thompson, rejected by those engaged in the famous Vassar study (including Mervin Freedman and Nevitt Sanford), and given an interesting interpretation by K. P. Cross in a publication emanating from the Center for Research and Development in Higher Education at Berkeley. This last study shows that where two colleges are markedly different from one another, the students at either college are much more nearly like their parents in their positions on all controversial matters than they are like the students at the other college. Of course, the Cross study may not be universally applicable, and Vassar is in many ways a special case. In any event, most investigators are convinced that the alleged generational gap is real, that it is far more significant than the usual misunderstandings between one generation and another, and that it is very likely to produce enduring changes in the moral codes of our society.

In the moral code of any society, sex occupies an important place. Although sensational articles about widespread sexual promiscuity appear now and then in the popular press, observers closest to students hold much more restrained views. Fred and Grace Hechinger, in reporting that almost half of all American women marry before their twentieth birthday, see early marriage as an escape from confusion about sexual values. They go on to deplore staying-out privileges, weekends off campus, and other aspects of

---

[31] Keniston, *The Uncommitted*, associates alienation with tolerant acceptance of deviant behavior.

[32] Prof. Charles Susskind, University of California, quoted in Max Geltman, "The New Left and the Old Right," *National Review*, 19 (June 13, 1967), 632.

the new "social freedom."[33] Nevertheless, the larger universities in increasing numbers allow women as well as men to observe any hours they please, to have visiting privileges, and to live in off-campus apartments by the age of twenty or twenty-one. Freedman and Sanford conclude from the Vassar study that there is no more promiscuity today than a generation ago, that promiscuity is in fact very unusual, that there has been no real increase in premarital sex except among those who are engaged or consider themselves deeply in love.[34] Much of the sensationalism is the product of a misunderstanding, for the breakdown in sex codes, if there is one, prevails among the high school students, rather than those in college. *Senior Scholastic* reports that teenage marriages have increased 600 per cent since 1940 and account for half the marriages in the United States today; that 40 per cent of all brides in the United States today are between fifteen and eighteen (not many of whom could be in college); that almost half the brides among teenageers are pregnant; that within five years divorce will terminate half the marriages in which the bride is eighteen or less.[35] The rather startling and disheartening information about high school teenagers must not becloud what Freedman and Sanford have found among college students: little promiscuity, intercourse when engaged or in love, frequent and heavy petting involving some genital activity, about 75 per cent of the girls graduating as virgins, and early marriage to avoid violation of respected sex codes. The evidence should alarm only those who believe or expect that premarital chastity will in our day enjoy universal respect and observance.

Aristotle called happiness man's highest good, the ultimate end which all prior means and ends aim at. Is the activist happy? Despite the occasional triumph over the administration, the relaxation or abolition of a rule, the generosity of parents and the modest expectations of faculty, enlarged freedom in behavioral decisions, the hang-loose ethic, libraries and laboratories and dormitories which are often strikingly attractive and beautifully furnished, the activists constitute a rather grim generation of young people. And the hippies are total pessimists. Their jelly beans, kite flying, balloons, and flowers are a bitter and extreme form of satirizing the meaningless morality of a society from which these people have dropped out. While exact definitions of terms are shunned by almost all writers on this subject, a hippie must be regarded as an activist who has given up and withdrawn, the battle lost and the enemy triumphant. Whatever else he does, an activist remains on the campus and continues to be active.

Arno Karlen sees his successors at Antioch as grim and self-critical.[36]

[33] *New York Times Magazine*, April 14, 1963, pp. 22, 120–122.

[34] Mervin B. Freedman, *The College Experience* (San Francisco: Jossey-Bass, Inc., Publishers, 1967); and Nevitt Sanford (ed.), *The American College* (New York: John Wiley & Sons, Inc., 1962), Chaps. 6 and 11.

[35] "Sex, Morality, and the 'Turned-on' Generation," *Senior Scholastic*, 90 (May 12, 1967), 6–11, 23.

[36] Arno Karlen, "Antioch College," *Holiday*, 41 (June 1967), 46–48, 108–118.

David M. Gordon sees the Harvard student as serious, hardworking, competitive, both eyes fixed on the graduate school.[37] Kenneth Keniston regards alienation as the executioner of good humor. The so-called underground newspapers produced at dozens of colleges and universities undertake, with words and cartoons, to ridicule the administration, faculty, "normal" students, and the outside world with a humor which customarily vacillates between idiocy and vulgarity, overlaid with a self-pity that renders the frequent striving for wit a sorry exercise in juvenile graffiti.

The activist, like many other students and like many faculty members, believes the universities are too large. In *The Uses of the University*, Clark Kerr says of the University of California:

> The University of California last year had operating expenditures from all sources of nearly half a billion dollars, with almost another 100 million for construction; a total employment of over 40,000 people, more than IBM and in a far greater variety of endeavors; operations in over a hundred locations, counting campuses, experiment stations, agricultural and urban extension centers, and projects abroad involving more than fifty countries; nearly 10,000 courses in its catalogues. . . . Over 4000 babies were born in its hospitals. It is the world's largest purveyor of white mice, it will soon have the world's largest primate colony. It will soon also have 100,000 students—30,000 of them at the graduate level; *yet less than one third of its expenditures are directly related to teaching.*[38]

One recoils from the term "knowledge industry," but it is obviously appropriate in some cases. And pain, sadness, and irony reside in the observation that

> the undergraduate students are restless. . . . There is an incipient revolt of undergraduate students against the faculty; the revolt that used to be against the faculty *in loco parentis* is now against the faculty *in absentia*. . . . The students want to be treated as distinct individuals. . . . A few of the "non-conformists" have another kind of revolt in mind. They seek, instead, to turn the university, on the Latin American or Japanese models, into a fortress from which then can sally forth with impunity to make their attacks on society.[39]

Except for some minor blurs—student anger is largely directed against the administrators rather than the faculty, who in some cases side with the students—Kerr's observations are astonishingly prophetic.

The curriculum, often rejected as irrelevant, is supplemented by so-

[37] David M. Gordon, " 'Rebellion' in Context."

[38] Clark Kerr, *The Uses of the University* (Cambridge, Mass.: Harvard University Press, 1963), pp. 7–8.

[39] *Ibid.*, p. 103. Kerr was probably the first writer on this topic to anticipate that student activism would move to increasing bitterness, more frequent confrontations, violence, and the attempt to capture universities.

called free universities. Apart from San Francisco State College, where the free university has had more recognition and formal organization than elsewhere, the work that goes on in a free university consists of courses taught by almost any student or faculty member who has some pet axe to grind or pet peeve that requires catharsis. With some notable exceptions, the quality of instruction is inferior, the instructors inadequately trained and self-appointed, the students irregular in attendance, the subject matter either trivial or sensational or, when worthwhile, available through regular class instruction by qualified professors. Yet, however much one may properly criticize the inadequacies of free universities, and they are many, the existence of such institutions on or at the edge of many campuses says eloquently that for some students the formal curriculum is far from satisfactory. The free university does have a place on our campuses as an extra-curricular study opportunity without formal credit. And one must assume that what happens within the forty to sixty free universities in America will eventually be reflected in both curriculum and instructional methods within the official courses.[40]

Disillusionment accompanies the failure of adult liberals (often one's own parents) to give active support to students protesting racial injustice and war. The narrow bread-and-butter concerns of labor unions and their loss of interest in large social issues have alienated the youthful leftist from the unions.[41] Attacks on the academic bureaucracy are frequent and bitter—and, until recently, largely ignored by administrators.[42] The SDS Port Huron Statement is pretty blunt: "They [students and faculty] must wrest control of the educational process from the administrative bureaucracy."[43] One wonders how long it would be before the faculty who did the wresting of control were themselves branded as administrators?

Nor does this exhaust the catalogue of student grievances. The activist seeks the elimination of the philosophy of *in loco parentis*, as we have seen, and the substitution for it of simple rules governing minimally appropriate behavior and protecting university property and procedures. Student records,

---

[40] Louis Menashe and Ronald Radosh suggest that the "teach-ins" may have created the model of the free university; see *Teach-In: USA* (New York: Frederick A. Praeger, Inc., 1967). But the "teach-ins" were usually a sharing of ideas between students and regular faculty members. The San Francisco State program is described by Herbert Wilner in "Zen Basketball, Etc. at San Francisco State," *Esquire*, 68 (September 1967), 98.

[41] See Cohen and Hale, *The New Student Left*.

[42] It is difficult to understand why the concern of the academic world for the complaints and increasingly irresponsible behavior of the students engaged in leftist activism has been so belated. This neglect is further reflected in the incredible failure of professional academic journals in the field of education to deal with the problem until recently; even in the last few years only a few professional journals have followed the issues with consistent interest and frequent articles. Almost all our knowledge comes from the reporters for popular magazines and newspapers—certainly dependable in large measure but lacking in sensitivity and employing journalese which obscures rather than clarifies the events occurring at more and more campuses. News stories about colleges and universities reveal almost invariably a deep and hostile bias against students and professors in the nation's newspapers and popular magazines.

[43] Cohen and Hale, *The New Student Left*, p. 223.

he feels, should be reduced to the absolute minimum, excluding at all times references to political, religious, or other controversial opinions—and, at graduation, the files should be cleansed of references to such things as minor offenses resulting in police actions. For most students little more than a record of grades should be retained. Many deans would agree.

The vehemence of cries for certain changes, openly called "demands" in many places, increases each year. One demand is for the publication of ratings of professors and courses, compiled from student checklists. This policy is already in effect at many schools. According to Martin Meyerson, the same students who wish to grade the faculty are often the most outspoken in their insistence that grading of students be abolished.[44] The abolition of grading in a large institution is virtually impossible, and those who demand it are either naive or indolent or mischievous. In any event, the incentive produced by grades, despite the pressures which grades produce in some students, is indispensable. When, in addition to the insistence that grades be abolished, the activist student calls for optional class attendance, he is in effect asking for the elimination of incentives, evaluations, and, ultimately, of studying—unless, of course, he is willing to make his attainment of a degree contingent on the passing of a series of rigorous comprehensive examinations at the end of four years or at any time he cares to present himself for examinations. But if such a proposal has appeared, it has been well concealed.[45]

More valid is the demand for due process in matters of student discipline—defined as the right to a hearing, to confront one's accusers, to offer evidence, to summon witnesses on one's own behalf, to have legal or other counsel, to have a stenographic record of "the trial," and similar safeguards associated with courtroom trials. In legal cases involving students and colleges, the courts now regularly insist on due process on the part of college authorities. A substantial body of legal literature has in the last few years grown up in connection with this kind of problem.

In a pamphlet called "The University and Due Process,"[46] James A. Perkins, President of Cornell University, expresses concern lest the day come when administrators and faculty spend more time in court than on the campus because of the rising frequency of student suits. He cites a few examples: A student sues when dismissed from the Merchant Marine Academy for disciplinary reasons. In a suit in Iowa a student claims he is a victim of discrimination because, as an out-of-state student, he pays higher fees than a native of Iowa does. A law student at Rutgers sues because his article was not accepted for publication in the *Rutgers Law Review;* he

---

[44] See Martin Meyerson, "The Ethos of the American College Student: Beyond the Protests," in Morison, *The Contemporary University,* p. 285.
[45] See Karlen, "Antioch College." He concludes that independent study is more "independent" than it is "study." He says students hate standards and judgments. Howe advocates voluntary attendance at classes, "Our Colleges Aren't Ready for Today's Students."
[46] Washington, D.C.: American Council on Education, 1967.

claims, among other things, that his right to free speech under the First Amendment has been breached. Parents of students denied admission sue the university on grounds of inadequate interviewing by the admissions officer. Perkins insists upon the right of an educational institution to make qualitative and judgmental decisions—decisions which often do not lend themselves to replicas of court cases.

Another area of dispute, far from new, concerns censorship of student newspapers and other publications. Editorials, news stories, and cartoons which anger public officials, prominent alumni, and university administrators are traditional—and so is censorship. It is customary for a faculty advisor to serve the paper as a resource person in legal matters and as a censor of content. Enlightened universities are disposed to allow their papers virtually complete freedom—limited only by civil laws on obscenity or libel and the like. But the issue is very much alive, and cases of censorship, often needless and absurd, abound. One of the most unpleasant in recent years concerns the effort, ultimately successful, of Barry Goldwater to destroy a president who took a tolerant view of the university newspaper's attacks on him. The episode is widely known, but those who might wish to read about it will find an account by David Mallery in "Mountain University." [47] Universities claim that their financial subsidies to the newspaper give them certain censorship rights. In a few universities, the newspapers have incorporated independently, relying on subscription and advertising income to support them. Even where the university provides subsidies, however, it is difficult to understand how, in a relatively free society, college administrators are so easily intimidated that they practice censorship.

Similar in almost all its implications is the matter of inviting controversial speakers to address student audiences on campus. Many shrewd administrators will prevent the appearance of a controversial speaker by invoking or creating bureaucratic intricacies. But equally shrewd students will present the speaker in a local church, theater, backyard of a fraternity house, or off-campus public building. Those universities that have placed no restrictions on speakers have discovered that there are no ill effects on the students and no repercussions from outsiders if they carefully define and redefine the proper role of a university. At my own university, we have had addresses before large audiences in one year, 1966–67, by Dr. Timothy Leary, the late American Nazi leader, George Lincoln Rockwell, several Communists, and other similarly controversial speakers. Former critics have become accustomed to the occasional appearance of this kind of outsider. Whether any student has suffered serious character corruption is impossible to say; but after all, the writings of these men are in books and their words and actions appear often in the mass media. To attempt to isolate college or university students from controversial speakers, however repugnant, seems fruitless, needless, and alien to the true character of a university. As such

[47] Mallery, *Ferment on Campus: An Encounter with the New College Generation* (New York: Harper & Row, 1966), Chap. 4.

speakers appear more frequently, perhaps the large crowds they now attract will dwindle to a size commensurate with the importance of their message. Some ground rules regarding the right to question the speaker or the subsequent appearance of an equally effective person on the other side of the issue should not be difficult to establish.

Only a few years ago, student government seemed on the wane on the large campus as interest shifted to the residence hall or fraternity. Today, the demand for powerful student government with elaborate committee structures has again arisen. Accompanying this rebirth of interest is the insistence that all college rules be written down, that there be no "unwritten laws," that a constitution or set of bylaws of some kind be established and meticulously administered. Where these developments have occurred, the resulting legal documents are still too young to be evaluated. But it is not too soon to say that they are extremely legalistic, detailed, and often difficult to understand because of their complexity. If taken seriously and followed as intended, they will modify student relations with faculty and administrators toward a somewhat formal, cold, contractual basis. Many students will claim that this is the situation that exists now but that the contract shifts at the will of the administration—thus they have everything to gain and nothing to lose. In fact, many student complaints have been successfully resolved through the use of these new judicial and legislative procedures.

Most interesting of all is the demand of the activist, in which he enjoys the tacit support of many other students, probably the vast majority of them, for participation in faculty governance by sharing in the work and decisions of faculty committees on interviewing and hiring faculty, promotions and tenure, curriculum and selection of books, and allocation of resources in the broad sense. There seems at this point to be no desire to share in determining individual salaries or cost of individual buildings. On more than half the campuses of the United States the student already has some measure of power in these areas, but often the power is so hedged in by rules and restrictions that it is more apparent than real. What student activists want now is real power, and in recent months the slogan "Student Power" has completely conquered many college groups and even penetrated many high schools. Like Black Power, it holds forth the promise of mutually advantageous cooperation, while at the same time, and surely not by accident, it constitutes an ambiguous and ominous threat. Activist white students, like Negroes, may numerically be some kind of minority, but any further resemblance is imaginary. The "blank check" endorsement of Black Power by NSA in the summer of 1967, with its rather obvious approval of the use of violence to achieve desired ends, raises the most serious questions about the integrity of the activists, their understanding of the purposes of higher education, and their acceptance of the democratic process.

Anyone who reads the article, "University Reform Revisited," by SDS officer Carl Davidson in the Winter 1967 issue of the *Educational Record* (a document which circulated in mimeographed form for months before it appeared in print), will conclude that the SDS, probably the NSA, and perhaps other student groups are prepared to employ tactics that can only be labeled Nietzschean and Marxian in their total disregard for ethics, their determination to seize control of colleges and universities, and their doctrine that breaking up meetings by shouting and singing, boycotting classes, employing clandestine methods to achieve one's goals, and infiltrating all campus organizations, are appropriate techniques, clever and effective and even amusing. Davidson is asking for complete student control of the institution, apparently to transform it from an instrument of academic power to one of political power. These methods have been used successfully in other parts of the world, but perhaps they go too strongly against the American tradition to win support here. No thoughtful American will complacently witness the destruction of the American university, and even bewildered and intimidated administrators may discover that a no-nonsense approach to the Davidsons of the campus will expose some paper tigers and allow everybody else to get on with the necessary tasks of education.

A new spirit of strong disciplinary response to student violence is here and there visible. But faculty support of administrators is too often lacking, and administrations are far from consistent. Negro presidents of Negro colleges in the South have generally reacted punitively against the student, probably because the white legislators who support these schools have given them no alternative. San Francisco State College has been consistently permissive; but the physical violence and generally chaotic atmosphere there seem to bear little relationship to the life of the mind.[48] The administration at San Francisco State has yielded on virtually every issue that has arisen with the exception of the abolition of ROTC. There is no reason to suppose that San Francisco State will fail to follow the example of so many other schools which have at least made ROTC voluntary. The University of Wisconsin has moved from a permissive to a "tough" line, and both legislators and the citizenry applaud this change at Madison even as they do those elsewhere in the country.

Inevitably, moral issues arise. Should a university already deeply involved in secret defense work under government contract and offering ROTC courses decline to admit recruiters for Dow Chemical and for the military establishment? How far may a university go in disciplining students who employ violent or semiviolent techniques in protesting a war they oppose but feel powerless to affect through normal governmental channels? The same dilemma exists on issues of civil rights, where Congress has made clear its intention to reduce rather than increase appropriations for improving the lot of the Negro. In short, if the issue is a moral one, if the cause being pursued seems just, if the normal avenues of a democratic society appear to be blocked beyond repair, what recourse is there except enforced obedience or violent resistance? For all those in authority, whether in government or in academia, it is essential that the channels exist and always be open. It is essential, too, that those in authority have the ability to provide the

[48] *The Chronicle of Higher Education*, November 22, 1967.

protesters with reasons rather than slogans for the acts the students deem objectionable. Such behavior on the part of administrators would be not only democratic and equitable, but also prudent and pragmatic.

At Rutgers (and at almost every other large northern university), the demand swells for the admission of far more Negro students, even though many of them may lack conventional credentials. S. M. Miller has prepared a small pamphlet for the Ford Foundation called "Breaking the Credentials Barrier," [49] which pleads for the use of new kinds of credentials, recognition of nonacademic talents, and the creation of "second chance" colleges. The demand for more Negro professors will be more difficult to satisfy, for all universities are looking for such men, and there is probably not a single unemployed Negro professor in the country. To lure them with high salaries from Negro colleges presents other kinds of problems. The highly selective universities of great prestige will probably have to limit Negro enrollment to students who have at least a reasonable chance of success. But the publicly-supported university may well feel a moral and legal obligation to admit Negro students in large numbers, offering them maximum counseling, tutoring, and remedial courses, providing financial assistance to those who need it, and encouraging the Negro student to progress from wherever he is when he arrives to the farthest point he can reach. Some universities are already responding favorably, but the ultimate success of this plan will depend on faculty willingness to modify grading standards and to offer credit for some nonconventional forms of achievement outside the classroom.

There are at long last some calm and wise voices being raised in response to the cacophony of half-educated juveniles who have recently discovered that the world is not perfect, who somehow believe that their parents are responsible for all the accumulated ills of mankind, who believe that in extirpating evil one may employ any means, including harming people, holding hostages, seizing buildings, copying secret files, and even overthrowing the Establishment (whatever that is). It has been argued that only educated, trained, disciplined minds, not posturing crybabies who in defeat plead for amnesty, will be needed to make an evil world better. The lead article in *Barron's* for May 20, 1968, is, as one would expect, a conservative analysis of the Columbia seizure. Yet liberals will sympathize with much that Robert Hessen has written there. Although SDS had only about 150 to 200 members in a university of 17,800 students, careful advance planning, shrewd choice of targets (a gymnasium opposed by Harlem Negroes and Columbia's connection with the Institute for Defense Analysis), a desire to see the shedding of some blood as a symbol that the revolution had begun—all of these, though failing to produce a revolution, did prove that universities (and other institutions) are vulnerable to sudden seizure.[50] Even the liberal

[49] The pamphlet appeared in March 1967.
[50] The role of SDS, having only relatively recently attracted the attention of many writers, needs careful study. *Time* magazine for May 24, 1968, estimates that SDS has 35,000 members, of whom 6000 pay national dues (p. 52). *Time* chooses to minimize the "conspiracy theory" attached to SDS by many observers who see

Progressive (December 1967) finds it difficult to determine what the students really want (if they know what they want) when, as at Wisconsin, they engage in violent demonstrations. Perhaps universities will have to enter the fray with clean hands; the university without defense contracts and without ROTC units can decline easily enough to permit Dow or military recruiters to come onto its campus. But if the university has dirty hands—defense contracts, ROTC units, suspicious faculty units overseas—it might as well get its hands a bit dirtier. When one experiments with chemical and biological warfare, surely recruiters on campus seem a rather mild addition to a corrupted conscience. Students in large numbers are revolted by the fact that places of learning and supposedly open research and free intellects have sold their souls. Most students do not know it, but George Washington and many other presidents have urged the formation of a National University; Congress has invariably rejected such bills.[51] A National University, whether it had any students or not, could have the best brains the government cared to buy and the best research hardware available. Thus, if the National University carried out military and secret research for the government, real universities could return to the world of the intellect, the life of the mind, the free pursuit of truth, and, above all, freedom.

The techniques of Che Guevara, Frantz Fanon, and Regis Debray serve as models for those who believe that the seizure of a university like Columbia or Paris may lead to the seizure of a nation. History has known periods and places where revolutionary students have triumphed, if joined by workers or farmers or some other large group, and if the police and the army also defected. (The kind of establishment that succeeds the one recently overturned is wholly unpredictable, however.)

It is at this point that disillusioned middle-class white activists from permissive families join hands with black militants who are convinced that only force will work. And it is at this point that an educational institution needs a faculty government and a student government to establish channels for resolving difficulties or, preferably, for enacting overdue reforms before a crisis arises. Too often the members of the faculty, either too busy with their own professional work or too annoyed with the administration for a variety of petty grievances, ignore student protests and the problems of the administrator—until violence jeopardizes the entire enterprise.

The combined activities of middle-class whites and revolutionary blacks are puzzling. In an article in *American Education* the typical activist is

---

the 250 campus chapters as engaged in close cooperation and long-range planning. *The Chronicle of Higher Education*, January 15, 1968, describes the growing militancy of SDS. Almost all schools engaged in IDA activity have become targets. Thomas Hayden, a founder of SDS, told a *Chicago Tribune* reporter that the goal is not peace or civil rights but control of the universities. Carl Oglesby told *The New York Times* that the goal is revolution. Dotson Rader, present at last fall's conference to plan the Columbia University seizure, told *The New Republic* that the IDA issue was a pretext only. (All of this appears in *The Chicago Tribune*, May 25, 1968, p. 12.)

[51] John S. Brubacher and Willis Rudy, *Higher Education in Transition: An American History, 1636–1956.* (New York: Harper & Row, 1958), pp. 217–219.

described as "a bright, stable, successful, and highly principled fellow from an advantaged background." Activists are determined to master frustrating conditions rather than to conform. They have "a will to change the social environment, a tendency to explore the inner life," and a willingness to take risks. They have "permissive and affectionate" parents with high occupational status who are well educated. Studies show that activists are usually liberal arts students. They show signs of "romanticism" and are interested in social service projects. They resent lack of control over their own lives.[52]

This description rings true in some instances but sounds phony in others; for students seem both idealistic and cynical, humanitarian and selfish, kind and callous. So we face again the imponderables of definition, of conflicting social science research, of the obvious incompatibility of some of the idealistic traits with the conspiratorial resort to violent and revolutionary techniques without regard for human dignity or ethical conduct. The complaints of the Negro, on the other hand, are as clear and obvious as can be, and their resort to violent methods in the Black Power program is, whether one approves or not, at least understandable.

The Black Power movement [53] is not primarily a student phenomenon, but it is, in the middle of 1968, a major force on almost every large campus and on many smaller ones. Their demands are for more black students, often for so many additional black students that administrators, with the best will in the world, may find insurmountable practical difficulties in trying to respond favorably. Moreover, as we have seen, these students are to be admitted regardless of their academic credentials; in short, the admissions office will discriminate in favor of the black applicant to atone for discrimination against the black man since 1619. Other demands include more black professors, more courses in Afro-American history and culture, more reading of black authors, black coaches, black cheerleaders, black clerical workers in larger numbers, separate living quarters for black students (either wholly separate buildings or at least separate floors).

Fortunately, these demands are made by what is still a minority, but the majority obviously walk in fear of being called Uncle Tom and of ostracism from their own, and increasingly, on campus after campus, the Negro speaks with one voice (though one must assume that many do not do so with complete freedom). There is still very much we do not know about this movement, but we do know that rising Negro militancy in the streets and the legislative halls for remedial action to reduce poverty and discrimination has its counterpart among Negro students in campus activism. Thus far, most schools seem ready to make great changes in their admission standards, to provide remedial courses, to increase the number of Negro students and Negro professors (if one can find the latter). The collective feelings of guilt are striking in the reactions of administrators and faculty, as they are, too,

---

[52] Eric Van Loon, "Who Are the Activists?" *American Education*, 4 (December 1967–January 1968), 2–4, 28.

[53] For the birth of the slogan "Black Power" and a condemnation of its extreme forms, see Martin Luther King, Jr., *Where Do We Go from Here?* (Boston: Beacon Press, 1967), Chap. 2.

among American businessmen. But the underlying hostilities are apparent as well when townspeople or the police exhibit their feelings in response to open housing demands or riots. It will surprise few observers if administrators resign in large numbers in the years immediately ahead, for the problems are extraordinarily complex. Feelings of compassion jostle against the desire for rational dialogue with students, black and white, who are too bitter to be patient, too passionate to be easily satisfied. The granting of one demand is followed almost always by an immediate and more extreme demand. To hold intact the house of intellect under these circumstances may prove impossible.

Some administrators think it can be done if we will abandon some rigid notions from our past experience and show flexibility in meeting new situations. Those who until recently directed affairs at San Francisco State followed such a philosophy, but they failed. And those who administer Merritt College near the Berkeley campus display a detached, somewhat amused tolerance of student behavior, but such an attitude almost surely exceeds the capabilities of most present administrators and faculty to change their conceptions of appropriate conditions for living, teaching, and learning.[54]

The question of sincerity is vital at this juncture. Students announce that they lack confidence in what administrators say, that there is a massive "credibility gap," as the journalistic phrase has it. On the other hand, administrators have sound reasons for distrusting students who defend their extreme ultimatums, confrontations, and violence with the plea that they are so overwhelmed by the evils of the world that they simply cannot restrain themselves and must destroy the established order. In efforts to defy and damage the established order, the student activist of the extreme left does not hesitate to lie, cheat, steal, employ violence, and display in maximum measure the worst qualities he attributes to adults.

One must take very seriously the opinion of George Kennan that one must spend time at the university learning and reflecting before one can be ready to act with intelligence.[55] No activist should ignore John Gardner's comment that the student who thinks the world is evil and wishes to repair the damage had better get an education first, for only the skilled, the trained, the educated can correct the wrongs and right the evils. One can view with contempt those who have abandoned nonviolent for violent civil disobedience and then whimper for amnesty when apprehended.[56]

[54] Edward H. Redford, "Profiting from Activism," *Junior College Journal*, 38 (November 1967), 7–12.

[55] George F. Kennan, "Rebels Without a Program," *New York Times Magazine*, January 21, 1968, pp. 22–23.

[56] The best, single, compact survey currently available is "Violence Hits Schools, Colleges," *U.S. News & World Report*, 64 (May 20, 1968), 36–44. Especially informative is the interview with Dr. Logan Wilson, President of the American Council on Education. This remarkably well-informed man urges faculties to awaken to the very real dangers they face, and he favors the tough policy of expulsion of serious trouble-makers. The article also contains brief summaries of events at Columbia, Northwestern, Stanford, Southern Illinois, Roosevelt, Cheyney State, Princeton, **Trenton, and Denver.**

The Campus Environment and Student Freedom

From the activist, the campus official must learn that we as a nation have been too long complacent about evils such as poverty and war and discrimination that can under the right circumstances lead to revolution and that, in any event, are so inhumane that a decent human being must recoil whenever he contemplates them. From the activist we must learn that the manner in which we teach and the courses we offer and the rules we impose are often obsolete or unimaginative or oppressive—and that, once again, reform is long overdue, though these are matters which should inspire less bitterness.

From the campus adult community the activist must learn that knowledge is neither cheap nor easy to come by, that long years of hard study and postponed fun are required, that respectful behavior does not make a Negro an Uncle Tom, and that the most violent candidate for student office is not necessarily the best choice. The activist must learn that feelings of alienation are normal and even desirable, for such feelings indicate that the student has discovered that the values of his family and home town are not universal and is acquiring a more cosmopolitan view of life. The activist who bemoans his identity crisis must be assured that identity is not a fixed object in space to be pursued like the Holy Grail, that identity is for everybody a problem involved with changing and conflicting roles, changing values, growing and maturing, and discarding this and adding that. To be satisfied that one has found his identity, full and complete and for all time, is to be intellectually dead. The activist must learn that there is no democracy in knowledge, for some people know more than others; that there is no virtue in playing at anti-intellectualism and that such games can end in disaster; that even people over thirty are beset with doubts, have their own inner crises, are familiar with the world's ills; that the pursuit of material things is not virtuous among blacks and evil among whites; that the world's population is not made up of two classes, angels and devils; that the problems are intricate, the solutions often defying the best efforts of the wisest men. We must assure the activist that we value the constructive gadfly, the protest against censorship, against the banning of a controversial speaker, against unfair or obsolete practices and customs. Is it too much to expect that the activist will discover that calling all non-activists "jocks" is morally equal to calling all liberals "commies"?

At some point in time, the ultimate responsibility may have to fall upon our judges, men who will issue the warrants, hear the evidence, and protect the universities (and society) from destruction. It is not without significance that two of our most prominent judges have recently taken a thoughtful but tough-minded approach to these problems. They make it clear that no organized society can tolerate prolonged violation of law, violence, terror, seizure of private property, or revolution.[57] If campus administrators had the strong support of their faculties, they would probably be able to resolve

---

[57] See Charles E. Wyzanski, Jr., "On Civil Disobedience," *Atlantic Monthly*, 221 (February 1968), 58–60; and Justice Abe Fortas, "The Limits of Civil Disobedience," *The New York Times Magazine*, May 12, 1968, pp. 29, 90–98.

these issues without sitting at the feet of judges to learn elementary lessons in jurisprudence.

No one can read an article like this without being uncomfortably aware of the enormous amount of writing already done on this topic, the seemingly inept quality of much of it, the contradictions and ambiguities in both facts and feelings. One must regret the absence of clear categorization, lucid description, controlled judgments. Perhaps it is too early for clarity. Surely it is too early for dogmatism.

Nevertheless, there are a few matters about which this writer does feel fairly certain, and these have appeared in the last few pages in a consideration of what the activist and the administrator may learn from each other. One may feel somewhat confident about the wisdom of the advice offered by men like Kennan and Gardner. One may take it as fundamentally true that the use of evil means in pursuit of a righteous cause will corrupt the man who employs the means so that, should he achieve his good end, he will be a changed and evil man, destroyed by his own habitual techniques—a truth recognized as early as Plato's earliest dialogues. No one with historical perspective will say that violence and revolution are never justifiable. But the same perspective will teach that a form of government like that of the United States is a rare and fragile phenomenon in the history of man, containing within itself a variety of techniques for orderly change. The black man may understandably succumb to the temptation to use violence because the existing channels do not work—the Congress will not provide the massive quantities of money that are needed and those with political power would rather explore space and an empty moon or fight a remote and evil war against a people who have never harmed us than spend the same money for solving the problems of the Negro. The billions of dollars required to restore cities, to educate Negroes, to provide a guaranteed annual income for everybody will never become available, in the judgment of this writer, without fighting in the streets, the burning of large portions of cities, and massive fear among white people to venture out of their homes without arms—a terrible picture of the future. But if the Congress and the American people so will it, they can prevent it. The seeming indifference, if not hostility, of the President and the Congress to the Watson Report, the so-called Kerner Report, and the march of the poor on Washington offers scant reason for optimism, however.

The use of violence and the planning of revolution by white students lack any shred of moral justification. The students in this group, to judge from the few this writer has observed, are seemingly mentally disturbed and may need to be treated as such.

Among all of us—black and white, rich and poor, parents and children, employers and employees, students and teachers—there is a crying need for recognition of our common humanity and our common end, for honesty and integrity in our mutual relations, for compassion and assistance in our human limitations, for the courage to carry forward the daily tasks that give to the life of each of us whatever significance it has, for the decency to reject pride in a white skin or a pretty face or a substantial bank account or a position of authority. Most important, if we are somehow to begin anew to build a civilization in which the good life is generously extended to all who will take it and in which the inevitable shortcomings of man are tolerated as nearly as possible with charity and understanding, then, above all, the need is for forgiveness, for we have all sinned.

SELECTED BIBLIOGRAPHY

Barbour, Floyd B. (ed.). *The Black Power Revolt.* Boston: Porter Sargent, Publisher, 1968.

Cohen, Mitchell, and Hale, Dennis (eds.). *The New Student Left: An Anthology.* Boston: Beacon Press, 1966.

Davidson, Carl. "University Reform Revisited," *Educational Record,* 48 (Winter 1967), 5–10.

Dennis, Lawrence E., and Kauffman, Joseph F. (eds.). *The College and the Student.* Washington, D.C.: American Council on Education, 1966.

Fischer, John. "Letter to a New Leftist from a Tired Liberal," *Harper's,* 232 (March 1966), 16–28.

Friedenberg, Edgar Z. "Polite Encounter Between the Generations," *New York Times Magazine,* January 16, 1966, p. 73.

Hoffman, Nicholas von. *The Multiversity.* New York: Holt, Rinehart & Winston, Inc., 1966.

Howe, Harold, II. "Our Colleges Aren't Ready for Today's Students," *Saturday Review,* 48 (May 15, 1965), 77–79.

Katope, Christopher G., and Zolbord, Paul G. (eds.). *Beyond Berkeley.* Cleveland: The World Publishing Company, 1966.

Katz, Joseph, and Sanford, Nevitt. "Causes of the Student Revolution," *Saturday Review,* 48 (December 18, 1965), 64–66, 76–79.

Kauffman, Joseph E. "Student Personnel Services," *Educational Record,* 45 (Fall 1964), 355–365.

Keniston, Kenneth. *The Uncommitted: Alienated Youth in American Society.* New York: Harcourt, Brace & World, Inc., 1965.

Kerr, Clark. *The Uses of the University.* Cambridge, Mass.: Harvard University Press, 1963.

Kristol, Irving, "What's Bugging the Students?" *Atlantic Monthly*, 216 (November 1965), 108–111.

Luce, Phillip A. *The New Left*. New York: David McKay Co., Inc., 1966.

Mallery, David. *Ferment on Campus: An Encounter with the New College Generation*. New York: Harper & Row, 1966.

Morison, Robert S. (ed.). *The Contemporary University: U.S.A.* Boston: Houghton Mifflin Company, 1966.

Stroup, Herbert. "Privatist Ethic and Self-Fulfillment," *Christian Century*, 81 (August 19, 1964), 1031–1033.

LOUIS C. VACCARO

The New Student Subculture and the Search for Meaning

Louis C. Vaccaro is presently Vice President for Academic Affairs at the University of Portland. Author of numerous articles, he also edited *Toward New Dimensions of Catholic Higher Education*.

We have long been convinced that the transition from adolescence to adulthood is both difficult and stormy. But there is growing agreement among observers of the contemporary scene that the experience of today's younger generation is more difficult and stormier than has ever been the case in the past. The frequent instances of value conflict, alienation, and pervasive despair that seem to occur among young people in our society with increasing regularity lend support to this view. Most observers would also agree that the problem is more intense on our college and university campuses than in society at large. Where once the "collegiate way" provided comradeship and psychological support for youth and their values, there is now increasing evidence of alienation and value conflict. Where once values were stable and consistent, the norm of today seems to be doubt, moral relativism, and confusion.

De facto, the campus has become a place where young people explore value conflicts—and the "collegiate way," which once characterized college life, has been replaced by a totally different campus ethic. Clearly, there is a new mood among today's young people. They have cast off, once and for all, the adult ethic. They no longer wish to conform to the "adult view of reality." Moreover, they regard such a view as out of touch with the basic human values that they see as necessary for the fostering of "the good life"; they are striving to shape something that we might properly call "the new student subculture"—a cultural subsystem based on views, values, and anticipated outcomes different from those of their elders.

But all this conflict and striving are not really new to academe. Those who know the historical development of campus life in this country are aware of the student activism of the mid and late 1800's. The noted educational historian, Frederick Rudolph, has catalogued this period of turbulent, and sometimes violent, student activity and described the incidents that led to many of the academic and curricular reforms of that time. Professor Rudolph's contention, which he documents well, is that the most effective barometer of what is going on at a college is the extracurriculum.[1] During this early period in the development of American higher education, student concern resulted in the introduction to the campus of intercollegiate athletics, fraternities, literary societies, and other extracurriculum. Professor Rudolph's analysis indicates that what is happening among today's students is neither new nor abnormal. One might also contend, however, that today's student activism is nevertheless more pervasive and far reaching than what occurred earlier. It is not limited solely to the campus although it reaches its greatest height and intensity in institutions of higher education—the very institutions where presumably the most liberal and well-educated reside. More specifically, some social analysts are saying that the current concern and activism on campus will inevitably lead to large-scale changes in the structure of society as well as in most, if not all, institutions of higher education.

It is not necessary that one be a social psychologist or even a trained observer to recognize the widening gulf separating the "adult" from the "nonadult" in contemporary society. Differences in dress, manners, language, and the like constantly remind us that a new culture is in the making. The builders of this new subculture subscribe to no tradition, no rules, no pattern, except that they proclaim the right to be! It would be a superficial approach to contend that the reason for such activity on the part of youth is that they no longer think that the adult ethic is meaningful or relevant. Such a proposition naturally leads to further questions: Where does the point of relevancy break down? What is it that youth wants that the adult, if he ever wanted it, no longer wants? And what are the underlying reasons for the changing value systems being formed? Without attempting to oversimplify, I am suggesting that the "relevancy break" occurs because adults have stopped seeking and searching and as a result have stopped developing a system of values. They have stopped going through the process of value questioning, choosing among alternatives, and forming their own self-commitment. Thus, the adults implicitly reason, their own values are "right," necessarily practical, and much better than youth's, since young people, because they are still searching, presumably have not found "the values."

The younger person, on the other hand, claims that the adult has "sold out"; that he lives by expediency rather than by high principles. Youth sees the adult as having abandoned the very core of the good life—he

---

[1] Frederick Rudolph, *The American College and University—A History* (New York: Alfred A. Knopf, 1962).

is living the "unexamined life." In short, the adult feels he cannot search forever while the young person claims that to stop searching is to cease to be.

One source of these two divergent views is the difference in the perspectives of youth and adults on material wealth. What their parents experienced during the Depression is not and never was "real" for youth; therefore their parents' enjoyment of affluence is not understood by the young people, and actually turns them against the adult world. To demand of young people strict adherence to the values of their parents is to deny them the one value they see as all-important—personal freedom. This is the critical value upon which a whole new subculture is beginning to develop. Real freedom to the young person does not so much mean freedom from physical discomfort as it does freedom from prejudice and ignorance. Describing the different motives and values of the student activists, Paul Jacobs and Saul Landau write:

> In their personal life style, their aesthetic sense, many in the Movement reject affluence and its associated symbols. The ambition to escape from poverty is no spur to action in their lives, for many are children of America's post-Depression *nouveau* middle class. Their parents are the once-poor scholars who head rich academic institutions: the ex-union organizers who run their own large businesses; the former slum dwellers who develop segregated real-estate tracts; the families once on the WPA who live in suburbs—all those who have made it. But their parents' desire to own, to accumulate, to achieve the status and prestige which go with material wealth, are meaningless goals to the children. To them television is not a wonder but a commonplace and they see the $5,000 a year their parents spend on the analyst as too high a price to pay for the loss of human values.[2]

If economic poverty was the concern of their parents, today's youth are more interested in overcoming the ravages of psychological poverty, a characteristic that is ascribed to many who have become economically affluent.

The hippie movement is the most extreme form of youth's rejection of the adult or "straight" world. The hippie's advice to "drop out" is a plea to all those who are "hung up" in the structure to examine their system of values and discard those that stifle the spirit, shrink the mind, and make slaves of man. The only way to do this is to "get outside" of oneself so that a total appraisal and examination can be made of one's values. What is more, the student who has "dropped out" and joined the hippie colony (or any offbeat group) see the campus as the most glaring example of a withering spirit. They reason that the one place where "community" and shared values could be effectively achieved has sold out for a set of values tied to commercialism, excessive bureaucracy, and bigness—all the wrong values! Thus, the search for a new culture, for the ideal state, seems the

[2] Paul Jacobs and Saul Landau (eds.), *The New Radicals: A Report with Documents* (New York: Random House, Inc., 1966), p. 5.

only solution for the disenchanted young person. He will seek knowledge, ideas, and community in a truly "free" gathering of persons dedicated to similar values; all under thirty, preferably. There will be no problem if all are dressed identically and have similar hair styles, mannerisms, and language. At least the style and sameness will be devoid of commercialism, phoniness, and affluence. Furthermore, society's dropout sees as necessary the total rejection of all values and forms of activity built on the profit motive and pure commercialism. The "system" which has been allowed to develop in American society, and which is seen as wrong, is aptly described by a young college student in the recently published book, *To Make a Difference*. This is what Timothy Earle relates about his early education and how it was tied in with society's values:

> Another consequence of the systematic tyranny of the school-business was that it was in the nature of things that, as I was an ignorant, unaware boy, I had to be told what I was and what I was to become. Thus it was determined as early as the grammar school years just what course of study I would follow. One aspect of the control which the state wields over the production of new citizens is seen clearly here. In my case I was informed that I possessed a scientific bent; I should take all the mathematics and science courses which were offered and thus prepare myself for college and eventually for a well-paying job in industry. In short, industry (or government) needed scientists; I possessed the ability to become one and I was free of any commitment other than the vague desire to go to college. Therefore, I would become a scientist in order to fulfill the expressed need. After all, it was they who were paying for all the educational machinery.[3]

The young person realizes he will have less and less opportunity to actively change his value commitments as he grows older and settles into a routine of business or professional life and the raising of a family. He knows that the time to question and act is *now*—when actual opportunities exist for him to discard nonrelevant values and choose those that are more meaningful. He has the freedom—in the sense that he is not hamstrung by economic, social, or political threats—and believes he must assume the responsibility to live out that freedom if he is to really grow "more human." To "cop out," to defer on the difficult decisions, is to ascribe to the system.

In a sense the adult realizes that the ideal state is not achievable and he settles for something less. The young person is not yet ready to give up. He is idealistic enough to keep searching. In fact he believes searching is an essential part of the good life.

Since most adults operate in the larger society and school is the place where the proportion of youth to adults is highest, the young person who is seeking answers to the fundamental issues naturally gravitates to the campus. Because of what he has read and heard about the liberal thought

---

[3] Timothy Earle, "At Stake is a Chance for Survival," in Otto Butz (ed.), *To Make a Difference* (New York: Harper & Row, 1967), pp. 95–96.

on many campuses, he views the college and university as an ideal place to search for answers. If it is possible to communicate with adults anywhere, it should be possible on the campus. Hence, the university forms the focus of this search for a new culture. There, reasons the eager new student, commercialism, bigness, and materialistic values do not form the basis for activity and life. He will be free to examine, question, and build his own personal system of values. Indeed, if he so chooses he can select the academic profession as a career and spend his life "seeking." Except, as he soon discovers, such is not always the case. The young person is constantly learning, from first-hand lessons in achieving adulthood, that freedom is a difficult concept to live out. It is not sufficient that rules and codes guarantee certain freedoms—the difficult task is actually to perform a truly free human act. It is one thing to have such freedoms guaranteed; it is quite something else to develop the personal integrity to choose freely among alternatives. To leave behind the security and comfort that result from not having to choose or commit oneself is difficult indeed. But the immediate rewards of participating often motivate young people to leave the sidelines in order to test the boundaries of new-found areas of freedom—ideas, sex, drink, and so forth.

On the campus, as in the larger society, many subcultures operate and compete for a person's allegiance. Martin Trow and Burton T. Clark have identified four student subcultures in today's university: "collegiate," "vocational," "academic," and "nonconformist." [4] It is in the nonconformist subculture that the student seeks a distinctive identity—one that is in keeping with his own temperament and experience. The authors contend that this subculture "provides some intellectual content and meaning to the idealism and rebelliousness generated in adolescence in some parts of American society." [5] It is increasingly evident, however, that even within the same campus community there is conflict among the various types of subcultures. Moreover, those who subscribe to the nonconformist subculture are, in increasing numbers, defecting from the colleges and universities to find a "purer" and truer experience in a less "straight" setting. The freedoms are always more attractive on the other side of the fence. This is exemplified in the increasing popularity of nonadult subcultures on the fringes of university campuses and other places such as the Haight-Ashbury district in San Francisco.

Many of the activities that take place in such settings would be outlawed in the "straight" world and on the campus. Smoking pot, sex parties, LSD trips, and the like are all geared to provide new vehicles for achieving the highly prized but elusive experiences of "community" and "oneness" (which have little relationship to the huge numbers of people characterizing mass society and the multiversity). Due to the increasing pressures of aliena-

---

[4] Martin Trow and Burton T. Clark, "Determinants of College Students' Sub-Culture," *The Study of College Peer Groups* (Berkeley, Calif.: Center for the Study of Higher Education, University of California, 1966).
[5] *Ibid.*

tion and aloneness, and the increasing disfavor into which organized religion has fallen, the young person reaches out in any way available to achieve some relief from the agony of his pressure-ridden life. The results of such reaching, through the use of alcohol or mind-expanding drugs, are usually euphoric—but they are short-lived. They provide no lasting relief from the agony—the hell—of aloneness and alienation experienced by increasing numbers of young people. Another reason why many students are defecting from the campuses is that they see little relationship between what is being taught in classes and what is happening in the world. One answer to this "hang up" is seen in the growing interest in the "free university" movement on many campuses. Here again, if such a movement progresses we will see some fundamental changes occurring in the curriculums and structures of many colleges and universities.

One should not underestimate the power of student concern, thought, and activities. It is more realistic to expect changes in higher education to occur as a result of student activism than of faculty concern and action. It is no secret that the most conservative constituency in a university is the faculty—those who have arrived and already have the union card (which allows them to limit the "arrival" of others). Again, the majority of professors on today's campuses grew up in a world very much different from the world of today's student. Therefore it would be foolish to expect relations between faculty and students to be smooth and devoid of value conflict. Likewise, the very values of the institutions themselves often conflict with students' values. In a provocative talk to university faculty and administrators the past president of Students for a Democratic Society described what he considers the reasons for student discontent on today's campus. In describing the students' hopes and anticipations, Paul Potter said:

> The experience of students in universities has had a great deal to do with their disaffection. Somewhere earlier they had already begun to understand that much of what they were supposed to cherish and emulate was sham. The jolt of the college experience has been for many, however, the event that brought discontent to the surface. That reaction may stem partly from the fact that many of us had high expectations about what college would mean. There was an excitement about finding an intellectual and personal seriousness in universities which we frequently had not found in high schools, and there was a sense that college offered independence in directing our education and lives that had previously been missing. There was a vague yearning for something in college that we had begun to sense was missing from our backgrounds.
> The reality of universities was, to a great extent, the opposite of what we had hoped for. In the place of intellectual and personal seriousness was substituted the academic grind of large classes, intense competition for grades, exams that were irrelevant and intellectually damaging, and an environment in which the chief academic occupation seemed at times to consist of learning how to beat the system and "psych" out professors and exams. In place of personal independence in shaping life and education were substituted numerous requirements characterized mostly by dullness and massiveness, the confining and

degrading existence of dormitories and their regulations, and the general recognition that less personal freedom was extended in the university than there had been in the home. Independence, university-style, meant isolation in an environment that was essentially callous to personal needs. For most, it was the the first encounter with the full inflexibility of mass bureaucratic organization, the first experience with the rat race and a system of external pressures and deadlines that substitute for internal initiatives or concerns, the first invitation to take on the barb of hipster, to ask questions that you really didn't care about, to "bull" your way out of situations that were embarrassing or threatening. If on occasion, students found good teachers or exciting classes, it did little more than underscore their sense that the rest were bad or useless.[6]

It is interesting to speculate what the behavior of today's youth would be like had not the United States within the last fifty years been involved in a depression and a couple of world wars and committed itself to universal free secondary education. Surely the liberal ethic which sprung phoenix-like from the Depression–World War experience has had much to do with creating a favorable climate for the emergence of an articulate and vocal student subculture on our campuses. And the situation and environment of the campus itself has had much to do with fostering the present critical mood of many of today's students. Again, Paul Potter relates how the university experience has led to the present discontent of today's brighter students:

> Perhaps the most difficult thing to assimilate, however, was the phoniness of the presentation of the university experience. Most institutions insist on clothing themselves in liberal rhetoric, for whose benefit it is difficult to say. They begin with applauding the virtues of liberal education, continue with much ado about the importance of the student assuming his educational responsibilities as an adult (the conclusion is difficult to avoid that adults are people who have learned to function well in such systems), and end with a system of junior residents who, the students soon learn, write regular reports that are kept in some central place; house mothers, who are most frequently caricatures of mother surrogates; counsellors, who help the misfits adjust; and disciplinarians, who mete out justice in a system that students soon learn is arbitrary, although somewhat manipulable with the aid of parents or through effectiveness as a hipster. On the whole, colleges seem to try to present themselves as permissive and mildly parental when in fact they are neither. The tired and elaborate rationalizations for keeping things as they are, are soon seen as just that.[7]

It is neither easy nor wise to attempt to explain away or ignore such analyses as these. To claim, as do many critics of student activism, that they do not have the support of the majority of students in our colleges and universities will not help either. It is significant to learn that the majority

---
[6] Paul Potter, "Student Discontent and Campus Reform," in Knorr and Minter, *Order and Freedom on Campus*, p. 72.
[7] *Ibid.*, pp. 72–73.

of those who do criticize and demonstrate in our colleges and universities are intellectually superior to the average student and come from families that have offered them every opportunity. They are not criticizing the establishment because they have not had opportunities or a share in life's material blessings. They are criticizing, demonstrating, and searching precisely because they have shared in such a life, and found it wanting. They should be applauded for the hope they exhibit in their continual search for meaning.

All this being said, the question of what will come of such student discontent and searching remains. On the one hand, it is too easy to say that the totality of our lives will be affected by such a movement—it is almost a cliché. And yet, many still fail to take seriously what is being said by the younger generation. We have become defensive about our values, and it is painful to have to be told (by nonadults, no less) that much of what we do, of what we stand for, is wrong. This is not to say that the nonadult is 100 per cent on the side of the angels. It is only to say that we need to stop, to look, to reflect, and perhaps to take up the search again—to recapture some of life's hope, by admitting that we are fallible; by saying that we do need to continue to search for the good life; perhaps even by admitting that we are not really aware, after all, of what the good life is. This will take some doing.

SELECTED BIBLIOGRAPHY

Clark, Burton R. *Educating the Expert Society*. San Francisco: Chandler Publishing Co., 1962.

Freedman, Mervin B. "Impact of College," *New Dimensions in Higher Education*, No. 4. Washington, D.C.: U. S. Office of Education, 1960.

Goldsen, Rose K., et al. *What College Students Think*. Princeton, N.J.: D. Van Nostrand Co., Inc., 1960.

Sanford, Nevitt. *Self and Society: Social Change and Individual Development*. New York: Atherton Press, 1966.

Sanford, Nevitt (ed.). *The American College: A Psychological and Social Interpretation of the Higher Learning*. New York: John Wiley & Sons, Inc., 1962.

The Study of Campus Cultures. Boulder, Colo.: Western Interstate Commission for Higher Education; Berkeley, Calif.: Center for the Study of Higher Education, University of California, and Committee on Personality Development in Youth, 1963.

THEODORE N. FARRIS

Social Role Limitations of the Student as an Apprentice

Theodore N. Farris has recently assumed the position of Dean of Students in the School of General Studies at Columbia University.

In the decade of the 1950's observers of the American scene complained about the noninvolvement of college and university students in the political and moral issues of the day. Articles in the popular press complained of the insensitiveness of students to everything but their own career prospects. But it is difficult to recall the mood of this period now, when hardly a day goes by without a report of the involvement of college students in a strike, march, rally, or protest meeting. The civil rights movement, the Peace Corps, the sexual revolution, and the war in Vietnam are all partially responsible for the change from noninvolvement to radical activism on the part of college students. Of course, many students are still not involved in political activism, but the temper of those who are not is largely tolerant or even supportive of those who are. The student of today sees every area of action as rightfully subject to his review and will often maintain that he has the "right" to seek to enforce his views on those in the student body, faculty, administration, and outside political systems who do not agree with him. The swing from student noninvolvement to the student strike in which activists jump into trenches in front of bulldozers or march on the Pentagon is another of the familiar pendulum swing-changes in American life that involve a 180 degree reversal of attitudes toward such countries as Japan, Germany, and Russia, and opinions on such matters as the United Nations, birth control, Negro rights, and legalized gambling.

Today, the shibboleths are "student power," "student rights," and "student demands." What is surprising is that student demands are usually treated symptomatically on the basis of recommendations of social psychologists, sociologists, and political scientists. Clearly, practitioners from all of these disciplines have significant and useful things to say about the problems for the university posed by the demand for student power. When the Berkeley crisis ripened and Chancellor Edward Strong resigned, the Regents quickly picked a sociologist as Acting-Chancellor, sensing that at least he would have some theoretical basis for taking practical action to stabilize the situation. Since the Berkeley crisis, social scientists have given extensive consideration to the dynamics of student movements.

Unfortunately, when students themselves discuss student freedom, student power, or student demands, they frequently do so without knowledge of any of these studies or of the history of higher education, and with little or no understanding of the role of the university in society. The discussions are characteristically carried out on a level of rarified philosophical abstraction, with many moralistic a priori assumptions smuggled in.

It is not the intention of this article to attempt to solve the many problems posed to university administrators, boards of trustees, or the political establishment by the demands of students for student power. Nor is the intention to attempt to tell students how they might organize to achieve power more effectively. The purpose of the discussion is to offer clarification of the essential matrices or parameters within which the various groups compete for power in the university. No resolution of the problems of power within the university can ever be permanent. The constantly changing conditions of society make a final solution neither possible nor desirable. Yet even temporarily satisfactory solutions can be found only if the accommodations reached by students, faculty, and administrators are consonant with the social roles demanded of them by the needs of the larger society. The failure of any person or group to whom power has been apportioned to serve the needs of the larger society for which the university exists will result in pressure to reallocate the power so that a more functional accommodation can be reached. While it is quite clear that students' current demands will result in some substantial reallocation of power, it is equally clear that students will not get all that they demand, because if they did, the university would simply cease to function as an instrument of education, as a system for apportioning status, as a center for research, or as a system for the preservation and transmission of the cultural heritage. Its essential functions would be threatened.

One important feature of the present unrest in colleges seems to center around student demands for the control of most areas of student life, usually under the rubric of parietal rules. Parietal rules, as many administrators are privately inclined to admit, are really concerned not so much with protecting the student and nurturing his moral growth as with public relations with the community, the parents, the legislature, etc.[1] The problem of reaching some accommodation between the demands of the students and the requirements of public relations, while irksome to the administrative authorities, is

---

[1] This point is emphasized in an article by David Riesman and Christopher Jencks, "The War Between the Generations," *The Record*, Teachers College, Columbia University, 69 (October 1967), 1–21.

probably the easiest problem to deal with through more liberal administrative procedures. This is only the old conflict of "town and gown," which had its origin in the medieval universities, where students' conduct was frequently at odds with the moral and political standards of the surrounding burghers, the church, and the political authorities. Problems of this sort of conflict were resolved by various devices, including student jails, student courts (presided over by the faculty), and special sanctuaries. The offensiveness of students to the surrounding town has a long and honorable history. So does student insolvency, drinking, carousing, wenching, and exemption from military service and secular courts. The goliard, the wandering, hell-raising inebriate of the medieval university, is an archetype who has descendants in the student subculture of every institution of today worthy of being dignified by the term "major university." The problems posed by student conduct have never had more than a temporary solution, and survival of the university as a viable institution does not require that they ever be solved. Some sort of uneasy truce is all that is required. An administrator today who is worried about student conduct, student sex, student dress, and drugs, would do well to reflect that he is not likely to solve any of these problems and that the university will continue to flourish perhaps as much because of as in spite of his failure.

When we leave the area of student life and parietal rules to consider the other demands of the student power movement, the problems are not so easily accommodated by patchwork and inaction. Student demands for power over the curriculum, degree requirements, and hiring and firing of faculty strike at the very heart of the functioning of the university in its essential relations to the external sociopolitical structures. Students also make dysfunctional demands on the internal social system of the university and attack the status and roles of the faculty, which have been the matrices for the preservation of academic freedom and the transmission of learning. Academic freedom would be without substance if every faculty member depended on the students for his tenure, for his license to teach, for his approach to his subject, and for his apportionment of time between teaching and research. Nor is it to be hoped that society at large would be willing to grant academic freedom to professors who could function under such a system. The structural threat to academic freedom posed by student demands for power over hiring of faculty and determination of curriculum also threatens the student's own freedom and the special role traditionally accorded to the university of awarding rights, privileges, and immunities. If students are allowed to make this kind of determination, one may well ask why they need to come to a university in the first place, and the society would rightfully question why a degree from such an institution should confer any rights, privileges, or immunities.

What is being suggested here is that the proper functioning of a university in its duty to transmit and expand knowledge, and to confer status by the granting of degrees, requires that certain actors perform certain roles in certain ways, and that without this division of roles the system cannot function. Stated simply, the student is not a professor and the professor is not a student. The student may one day be a professor and the professor was once a student. But some indelible change is required before one becomes the other. The role of each is defined by certain constraints upon action, and the constraints for each are different. The student is in some way an apprentice, the professor is in some way a master. In the essential matters of teaching and learning, one must teach while the other learns. Student demonstrations, opinion, and manifestos to the contrary, there are proper and definite limits imposed on the student in his role as an apprentice, and these limits have nothing to do with student freedom in the essential areas of student life (parietal rules, sex, etc.). The student who chooses to ignore his role as an apprentice does so to his own detriment and, unhappily, to the detriment of the institution of the university.

The origin of the student's role as apprentice lies in the medieval guild. The university as an institutional invention of the Middle Ages was a blending of several institutional ideas: the Roman joint-stock company evolved into the eleemosynary trust; the merchants' and craftsmen's guilds; and the cathedral schools. Apprenticeship was a common feature of the guild system. From the very beginning the student in the university had a role analogous to that of an apprentice and the professor a role analogous to that of a master. Apprenticeship has been defined as

> in law, a contract by which a person called a master who understands some art, trade or business, undertakes to teach the same to another person, commonly a minor, and called apprentice, who, on his part, is bound to serve the master, during a definite period of time, in such art, trade or business. . . . The contract need not specify the particular trade to be taught, but it is sufficient if it be a contract to teach such manual occupation or branch of business as shall be found best suited to the genius or capacity of the apprentice. . . . The duties of the master are to instruct the apprentice by teaching him the knowledge of the art which he had undertaken to teach him, though he will be excused for not making a good workman if the apprentice is incapable of learning the trade, the burden of proving which is on the master. . . . The master must not abuse his authority, either by bad treatment, or by subjecting his apprentice to menial employments unconnected with the business he has to learn; but he may correct him with moderation for negligence or misbehaviour. . . . An apprentice is bound to obey his master in all his lawful commands, take care of his property, promote his interests, endeavor to learn his trade or business and perform all the covenants in his indenture not contrary to law. . . . A master cannot delegate to another the power to chastise his apprentice, as his authority is a personal one.[2]

Students in the medieval university also were exempt from fealty to a feudal lord and had varying degrees of exemption from secular authorities,

---

[2] *Encyclopedia Americana*, 1943 ed., I, 97–98. Reprinted from the 1943 edition of the *Encyclopedia Americana* by permission of the publishers, Grolier Incorporated, New York.

particularly in the matter of debts, and some degree of exemption from even the authority of the bishop, though this varied from time to time. In the earlier years the faculty had some power to express their displeasure with town reactions to the university by literally decamping to another town where they might be better treated. The mere threat of leaving might be enough to change the attitudes of the town authorities and secure a respite from the persecutions of the burghers. Unhappily, this tactical device disappeared with the invention of the printing press and the accumulation of library collections.

In spite of all the changes that have taken place in higher education since the development of the medieval university, in the liberal arts college and the university of today there are certain continuing features. Today's institutions are still in the business of granting rights, privileges, and immunities—in other words, *status*; they are still providing both liberal education and professional training, and they are simultaneously attempting to transmit the cultural heritage and expand knowledge. And the colleges and universities of today still come into conflict with the civil authorities and the communities in which they exist because of their claims of academic freedom and because of the conflicting value systems of their student population and the society at large.

Perhaps more important than the conflict between the component parts of the university and the civil and economic power structure of the nation is the conflict between the student body and the faculty and administration for control over the internal governance of the university. This also has a history behind it just as has the town and gown conflict, but it is only in very recent times, particularly since the Berkeley crisis, that the demands of students for power have taken an ideological form.[3] It is the present ideological nature of the student demands that poses serious questions for the academic community. It is not the fact that these demands are made, but that they are made on the basis of a new democratic ideology that has strong appeal to many people within the academic community. The students claim that adherence to democracy requires that they be allowed to advise in the hiring and retention of faculty and in the establishment of a curriculum and in the allocation of the financial resources of the institution. Rating systems for faculty and courses have also had widespread trial at many institutions with various degrees of support from faculty and administrators and with varying degrees of success.

The task of correlating demands of students for internal power within the university with the function and purposes for which the university exists is one of the most serious of the many problems facing the university today. The chronic financial crisis of higher education is likely to receive more administrative attention, but the demands of students for power in academic decision-making will also certainly receive increasing attention

---

[3] Nonideological student action to force curricular reform has a record of success in American higher education. An early instance of this was the move to make courses in science and mathematics count toward the B.A. degree at Harvard in 1827.

because the way such demands are dealt with affects financing. The reaction of the taxpayers of California to the Berkeley crisis shows quite clearly that the community outside the university is ultimately very much interested in how demands for student power are resolved. The victory of student power can prove quite hollow if the financing of the university by the state is seriously curtailed by reaction in the polling booth, the legislature, and the coordinating superboards that determine fund allocation among different institutions. Financial support from alumni and business and philanthropic foundations is also affected by student power demands, and unfortunately usually adversely.

In attempting to resolve the many problems that the demands for student power entail, one should remember that the problems did not arise yesterday, although their ideological formulation is of recent origin. The subordination of the student to the professor in medieval universities did not originate through a mere whim of the teachers. It was arrived at after quite a different system had been experimented with. Student control of the university, of the curriculum, and of the terms and conditions of teaching was tried in the Middle Ages at the University of Bologna and eventually abandoned. The students at Bologna who governed the university were by no means comparable to the students who clamor for power today. Rather they were the sort who would have been able to exercise student power with restraint and circumspection if this were possible considering the nature of the university as an institution. The Bolognese students were in large part mature civil servants, already occupying substantial and responsible positions. They administered the university fairly well but eventually turned the control over to the city because it was too time-consuming. The city also found the task too difficult and turned the management of the university over to a lay board.[4]

No one would maintain that simply because student control was inappropriate in the university of the Middle Ages it is still inappropriate today. But it is here suggested that there are sufficient common features between the roles played by students and professors currently and those played by their medieval counterparts to provide some guidance on appropriate role conduct. Since we are here concerned with student roles, nothing will be said about professorial roles, although such a discussion would also be fruitful.

There are appropriate limitations on student roles rooted in the nature of the university that have been present since its beginnings and that are likely to endure for some time, for their foundation is not only historical but also sociological and psychological—in the process by which teaching and learning take place. These limitations on student roles and the possi-

[4] See W. H. Cowley, "Some Myths About Professors, Presidents, and Trustees," *The Teachers College Record*, 64 (November 1962), 159–171. Cowley attributes the temporary success of Bolognese student power to the relative maturity of the students and the fact that many of them had positions of responsibility in the civil service.

bilities of autonomous action within these roles arise from the fact that the student is an apprentice and the professor is a master. There is a possibility of a wide variation of style and conduct so long as the essential role is preserved by each party to any interaction. The relation of the student to the professor is in some sense always subordinate and the relation of the professor to the student is always in some sense superordinate; and this is the case whether the attitude of the student toward the professor is characterized by fear, hatred, churlishness, admiration, respect, love, or ambivalence; or whether the demeanor of the professor toward the student is characterized by peevishness, spitefulness, contempt, concern, helpfulness, benevolence, love, collegiality, or indifference. The student who chooses to ignore the fact that he is subordinate in some very important ways to the professor does so at considerable risk to himself, to his own interest, and to the functioning of the university. This is not to say that role conflict may not have some long-range beneficial results in the macrosystem of education and society; but it is likely to result in some serious problems for the actors.

American colleges and universities exist for many purposes, and the motivations for attending them are also varied. Discounting for the moment such secondary motives for attendance as socialization, and mate-hunting, the three chief motivations of the students are: (1) to accumulate a body of knowledge, skills, and competencies; (2) to receive the award of the rights, privileges, and immunities appropriate to such knowledge and skills; and (3) to learn the social role appropriate to an individual in possession of such knowledge and such privileges.

The accumulation of knowledge, skills, and competencies implies a period of apprenticeship to persons who possess them already, or who are through some peculiar gift or talent capable of teaching the student apprentices how to acquire them (by art, by research, by practice, etc.). The student is not in possession of these competencies, or, in any case, is less so than the professor. If, at the end of a suitable period of apprenticeship, the student attains a suitable level of proficiency, as attested by various examinations, he is given the award of a degree which carries with it certain rights, privileges, and immunities. The right to confer this degree is a legally sanctioned function of the corporation of the university, granted in its charter from the state. It is possible for a student to attend an institution for a suitable period of time, and even to achieve a high level of competence in a field of knowledge, but to fail to receive the appropriate degree. As a result his status will be considerably lower than that of a person who has been awarded the degree, even though he may be the more competent of the two. Failure to achieve the degree is usually the result of some failure to fulfill the role requirements of the possessor of the knowledge or skill in question. It is not then sufficient to learn the subject matter taught. The student must also learn the role to which he aspires. The socialization process by which the student learns his role utilizes mimesis (imitation) and introjection (a process similar to that oral erotic stage described by psychoanalysts, in which the child introjects the feared, loved, and powerful parent into his psyche). The final examination for the degree that carries the highest reward of privileges and immunities, the Doctor of Philosophy, is interestingly enough termed the "oral." Here the *rite de passage* is specifically aimed at determining the degree of successful mimesis and introjection of the apprentice.

The reasons universities and colleges are run by faculties and not by students are that: (1) the student population is transient when compared with the faculty; (2) the students are not masters of the subject matter and therefore are not capable in the main of judging validly what they should be taught; and (3) the learning of the role of the master requires discipline and respect (perhaps even awe or fear) which cause the student to want to learn to imitate the master or to introject the master into his own psyche so that he then becomes a master himself.

In order to show that granting of student demands to participate in major decision-making in areas outside of student life would be dysfunctional for the system of higher education it is not necessary to return to the medieval University of Bologna. We have only to look at the universities of Latin America, in which the Cordoba system governs student behavior. In these universities the students are a disruptive element in the world of higher learning. By their strikes they can force the resignation of eminent scholars with whom they do not agree politically. Their power to force resignations prevents many able people who cannot afford the insecurity of a chair that rests on student whims from pursuing an academic career. Their conduct disrupts classes and scholarship and makes the university a battle arena for violently contending political forces. It also reduces the meaning of academic freedom to mere sanctuary from police and army troops (although the sanctuary is not always respected, as recent invasions of the campuses in Venezuela and Argentina have shown). Student power in Latin American universities prevents the dispassionate and sober consideration of issues so essential to scholarship. As a result many of these universities have become merely ceremonial institutions that award degrees of questionable worth, while providing a center for student apprenticeship, not to knowledge, but to partisan politics and guerrilla activity. The usurpation of faculty power and faculty rights by students in these universities has had disastrous consequences not only for scholarship but also for their usefulness as instruments for economic development and social revolution. It has turned them into creatures of the student. This is one possible result of student power and it warrants serious consideration by those in American higher education whose liberal democratic sympathy with the more sanguine demands of students leads them to ignore the historical evidence already available.

Although the case has been made that it is impossible for the university to relinquish complete control over essentially academic matters to the students without undermining the structure of the present system of higher education, it does not follow that many of the legitimate concerns of students over important curricular decisions should not be fed into the decision-

Role Limitations of the Student as an Apprentice

making process. Students frequently have valid complaints and criticisms about the irrelevancies of the curriculum, the assignment of rewards to the incompetent, and the general functioning of the university in its service to the larger society. Both faculty and administration would do well to listen to responsible student opinion, responsibly expressed. And they would do well to assist rather than hinder students in the formation of groups capable of representing critical student opinion.

Students will continue to win increasing control over the more personal aspects of their lives, but they are about to reach and in some places have already exceeded the limit of political control over the university that can be allowed them without endangering the system of higher education itself.[5] Of course, some more radical students are perfectly capable of taking, with full knowledge, steps that can damage the institutional integrity of the university. Their attitude is that the university is rotten and its rotteness should be exposed along with that of the rest of society. Faculty and administration who value the survival of a meaningful system of academic freedom have at hand adequate administrative devices to deal with this small minority, and only their pusillanimity is to blame if they fail to use these devices wisely and selectively to insure the survival of the university.

To grant the more radical demands of the students for university control would be ultimately self-defeating even for these student radicals themselves. The result would be a curriculum with no standards and degrees of no value, awarded to students of doubtful worth by a faculty of no distinction, in an impoverished institution. The *reductio ad absurdum* of the more radical demands of the student left shows clearly that they must be resisted. The student is still an apprentice, and when he attempts to usurp the role of master the university cannot function.

[5] Riesman and Jencks, *op. cit.*, also see student political control as a hollow victory, one that will lead to a "neo-colonialism."

ROBERT M. CRANE

Student Governance and the Issue of Student Freedom

Robert M. Crane, Professor of Education and Coordinator of the Psychological Foundations of Education Group, College of Education, University of Illinois at Chicago Circle, is a frequent contributor to professional journals.

"Governance," by most definitions, means management, control, direction over an institution; it is a process or art of administration, particularly the process of deciding and then implementing the decision. John Corson in *Governance of Colleges and Universities* defines "governance" as that art or process "with which scholars, students, teachers, administrators and trustees associated together in a college or in a university establish and carry out rules and regulations that minimize conflict, facilitate their collaboration, and preserve essential individual freedom."[1]

In order to define "freedom" one must know what it is *not*. In the very essence of freedom, if it is to be realized by every individual equally, lies willingness to agree to laws and regulations, to submit to some constraint, indeed to subordinate a part of one's personal freedom to basic authority. License cannot be misconstrued as freedom; rather, some minimal yet clear limits to freedom must be present. To the question of what freedom does mean, then, would come the answer that individuals who are free can consciously move, act, choose, and will. Governance limits freedom, subordinating all participants by their own agreement to those aspects of rule and order that are implicit in the institution—the "grouped individuals."

As these ideas are applied to student life, it becomes clear that the old adage of "reason doth prevail" should be adhered to. To have an institution and to keep it functioning, a certain structure and a set of laws

[1] John J. Corson, *Governance of Colleges and Universities* (New York: McGraw-Hill Book Company, 1960), pp. 12–13.

and regulations must obtain. Ideally, these are continuously redesigned as environments change and as it becomes clear that the more responsible an individual is, the more freedom can be granted him. Of necessity, guidelines must be given to every member of a college or university if equal freedom is to be made available to all. Through governance then, the basic laws are created from which guidelines for profitably functioning in a community can be drawn up.

The continuous nature of this revamping, restructuring process in higher education has not always been made clear to students. Worse than that, the propensity of men to resist, indeed to resent, change tends to freeze institutions, to cast them literally in a concrete form. This means that attempts to restructure the university are sure to meet with resistance, but such conflict is a healthy sign of institutional growth. To say that change and restructuring have not taken place in colleges and universities is to deny the obvious. To suggest that change has happened now and again is to speak of the snail's pace with which it has occurred. And to observe that at times of crisis, with great surges and thrusts, major recasting of institutional life has taken place is but to recall that invariably after every major war and economic depression, in times of social upheaval, American colleges and universities have also been directly affected.

Such great and obvious changes as the expansion of knowledge at a rate never before realized, the extension by electronics of man's learning and communicating power, and the goal of overall improvement of society in the immediate future, all have produced urgent needs. In particular, the present upheavals in higher education derive from increasing dedication to higher education for all able and interested Americans. This has activated movements to establish new institutions, particularly junior and community colleges, and to recast, enlarge, and experiment with the older four-year colleges, and graduate schools. Finally, to overlook the general self-conscious, self-critical, self-analytical nature and the sincere desire to improve of Americans in general and of academicians in particular would be a gross oversight.

Current student moods in the university, especially as they affect changes in attitudes and relationships within areas of governance and freedom, have arisen from a variety of causes, including the enormous growth of American colleges and universities since 1945, the required specialization of faculties and administration necessitated by increased knowledge and complexity of structures, the civil rights movement, the draft, and the Vietnam war, each and all of which have created a series of uncertainties for individuals. Children raised since 1945 have come into an impersonal world of electronics and automation; their needs for personalization, for individual involvement are intense and call for immediate satisfaction. New conflicts and controversies have occurred in the first half of the 1960's and have continued. Indeed they will continue until full recognition is given to how American students have changed and still more to how expectations have multiplied regarding the role colleges and universities should play in solving social problems. Many of the demands by students for more freedom and for "power" stem from these foregoing conditions; however, *the* greatest single factor that has caused so much unrest on the part of both students and faculty is the *urgency* for change both within colleges and universities and in the myriad services they now perform in society. The need for urgency has provided the sowers of distrust with fertile ground within the institutions or "establishments," within existing groups and organizations, and, more especially, between age and youth, that generation gap which always exists. The gap can be capitalized on when there are such large numbers of youth as now and when the political and social milieu is in such turmoil.

Higher education only very recently began to plan for change, shifting from the age-old "drift" process. Yet drift, or unplanned-for change, is still all too evident a process in many colleges and universities. Add to this the fact that students, indeed faculty, have not traditionally been directly involved in planning for change and the setting for some of the recent explosions is complete. Students have demanded more participation in governance, using methods from both the civil rights movement and the labor movement to assert themselves. This application of force to effect change is relatively new to higher education in America and has come into colleges from the political and social milieu outside of them.

In times of change like these, it is not at all unusual for small dissenting groups to be considered as typical by the news and image-making media. Recent presses for power by students come from but a few really, and although more may well join them when and where real inequities are found, more than likely most students will taper off when they have acquired some increased measure of participation. It is important to recognize, however, that most of the so-called activist students who now demand more freedom and a greater share of the authority and power in colleges and universities have been found to be, more often than not, the brightest ones, the most sensitive, articulate, and sophisticated ones.

Yet it would be naïve to overlook the resurgence in this country of subversive elements, including the widely announced expanded activities of the American Communist Party. Extremism for its own sake also has become much more blatantly displayed in the issues of governance and freedom. Historically, students have been known to advocate dissolution and revolution instead of evolution as a method of change. Their variability, versatility, and volatility qualify youth as adventurers. They have advocated nihilism, atheism, agnosticism, existentialism, and theism, to say nothing of all the other "isms." Interestingly enough, few of these characteristics are new or different, for the forefathers of many of the young were also the same. The rebelliousness, the restlessness, the incompleteness of youth give the real hope for the future. If students, the young, were apathetic and listless, then society could well be on the down side of the hill. Students want to be included in the deliberations and decisions that affect their lives, and they need to be or else they will be completely unprepared for living in the educated and technological society that has evolved.

Several guidelines are here advanced for clarifying the confusions that now exist in areas of governance and freedom. Later these will be juxtaposed with the historical and analytical aspects of governance and freedom.

First, the focus in every college or university today simply must be on the student: how he learns and what, how he is taught and where, how he lives and learns out of class. The clearest possible definition and continuing redefinition of the role of the student in areas of governance and freedom must of necessity be determined jointly by regularly enrolled students and the faculty.

Second, the model of the student set before the public must be a serious, sensitive, and capable person and attention must be given to his needs and drives. More especially, this student should be accepted by the faculty as a colleague, or a companion, in learning.

Third, at all possible points of contact between student and faculty, both established and informal, clear and open lines of communication must be initiated wherein the modus operandi is listening to one another, caring about what each has to say, considering each other's proposals for solving issues and problems, and jointly assuming a shared authority and responsibility for the academic community.

Fourth, a continuous educational program must be kept in the public view to illustrate the goals of learning in an open, controversial, conflicting, and indeed sometimes confusing yet honest set of circumstances. Order can and does arise from thoughtful, critical analysis and striving toward better understanding, the objective weighing and balancing of alternatives, and the acceptance of fair-minded solutions.

Fifth, teaching and learning can be viewed as restrictive and authoritarian, as absolute and hierarchical, or as liberating, self-developing, and enriching. If the latter course is chosen, negotiation and mediation processes enter, and knowledge becomes the real basis upon which conflicts are resolved. It is hardly conceivable that healthy human beings can be encouraged to maximum functions by mere assimilation of factual data, by vicarious or indirect actions, or through little or no application of all of learning to living.

These are exciting years in American higher education. When unrest and rebellion *are* leading to changes, *are* renewing relevancy and meaning to higher learning, *are* keeping colleges and universities close to their publics, then a free society can hope to be kept on its toes and ahead of all those forces that strive to put it in chains. Issues of governance and freedom ought always to be debated. Shared responsibilities and consultation are the best ways to carry forward the American traits of optimism, philosophical positivism, and faith in and hope for the future. These are both personal and national traits worthy of keeping alive at all costs.

Some of the present-day confusion over rightful roles, privileges, and responsibilities, the power and authority conflicts, have evolved to a large extent from the diverse lines of college and university history. To trace such vital issues and relate them to life on today's American campuses requires a brief review of the historical lineages and traditional patterns of colleges and universities.

About the earliest universities little is accurately known except that their beginnings—1100 to 1200 A.D.—were in Paris and Bologna. As so-called societies of masters and scholars, these people-centered institutions became, almost at their inception, diversified in purpose, idea, and scope. The University of Bologna became a strongly student-centered institution characterized by student guilds organized first for protection against the townspeople, later for protection against professors. At the outset, the professor lived entirely from the fees he collected from the students and was often put under bond to guarantee an education worth the money students paid for it.

The University of Paris, on the other hand, became a strongly faculty-centered institution, wherein the faculty guild predominated and students solicited their education from a simplified institutional source—the administration of the guild. Here, then, was the beginning of a core structure that later evolved into today's university in America, although research and service agencies and all related functions came later. Cathedral schools were evident in this beginning period, and were joined to the universities later to become what are now the colleges, with residential or living-learning centers as their primary units.

The earliest medieval universities had no fixtures, no laboratories, not even libraries. In all probability, they could not have passed any of the tests of the accrediting agencies of today.

> The mediaeval university was, in the fine old phrase of Pasquier, "built of men"—*batie en hommes*. Such a university had no board of trustees and published no catalogue; it had no student societies—except so far as the university itself was fundamentally a society of students—no college journalism, no dramatics, no athletics, none of those "outside activities" which are the chief excuse for inside activity in the American college.[2]

The influx of learning into Western Europe—chiefly through the Arab scholars of Spain, who introduced the works of Aristotle, Euclid, Ptolemy, and the Greek physicians, along with the new arithmetic and texts of Roman law—created a new knowledge that produced the learned professions in the twelfth century. Medical education began at Salerno, probably before the universities of Paris (1200 A.D.) and Bologna (1100 A.D.) were established, but since the University of Salerno was not a multipurpose institution like Bologna, it does not now hold so distinguished a place in the history and development of higher education as does Bologna.

[2] Reprinted from Charles Haskins, *The Rise of the Universities* (Ithaca, N.Y.: Cornell University Press, 1957), p. 2. Copyright 1957, by Cornell University. Used by permission of Cornell University Press.

As early as 1180 A.D. the colleges—residences for learning—had attached themselves to the universities; however, many disappeared from the Continent in later years, and the ultimate home of the college became Oxford and Cambridge, where it developed in the early part of the thirteenth century and became the central focus of British higher education. The university per se was (and is) but the degree-conferring body.

From this, it might be possible to conclude that the simplistic aspects of student life in the medieval universities, its spontaneity, even its bawdiness as it has become known through the student manuals, student letters, and student poetry, all precluded many problems of freedom and governance. Actual concerns about governance and student freedom were not reported upon, but certain incidents do bring to light the control of the master or the teacher, or vice-versa, through incidents of student wrath when all did not go well. Attitudes soon became set toward the courtesies of school life, especially reverence for the master. The cathedral college, where the master-to-subject relationship obtained, evinced the more protective, the more confined environment. This enclave existence, a highly structured and routinized way of collegiate life, gradually emerged from earlier forms as higher education grew. The possible exception was the strong urban and student-centered university, of which there were few.

Characteristic of the Middle Ages was devotion to form and substance, dominance of the letter of the law, indeed almost a regimentation of conduct that squelched, in the main, individual student initiative and creativity. Abject poverty was common in early student life. Most students' letters then (as now) were written to request more funds from home. Fears of failure, hard-heartedness of instructors, and overall problems of living and learning were characteristic of the student life of the Middle Ages. Thus the student of today and the student of the Middle Ages resemble one another very much: their needs, drives, desires, and accomplishments do not differ greatly; the change is in the means of satsifying those needs and in the environment.

Student governance and issues of student freedom have evolved as faculty and university solidified an organization and a system, developed traditions and a culture—a collegiate way of life—and above all, set standards for behavior related to the image of a gentleman, a man of intellect and reason, all of which seemed to be required by the needs of the times. The students were young, generally fourteen or fifteen, a motley crowd to be tamed and disciplined, to be acculturated and educated.

Age-old and often still persisting attitudes on the part of some faculty are reflected in the college and university structures, rules, and traditions. That students are inept and ill-informed, an ill-prepared lot, "pitchers to be filled" seem now to be attitudes most difficult to justify, just as the reverse would be—to assume that *all* students are right and good, able to learn on their own with but little guidance. However, if one were to err in one direction, take one extreme position over the other, the latter attitude would be much more logical than the former, at least in present-day American culture, for some simple but well-known reasons: public school systems from elementary school through high school have succeeded magnificently in the past fifty years; bare percentages alone record that in America between 60 and 70 per cent of the population has had twelve years of schooling. To assume that students come to college or university completely ill-prepared or to overlook that this electronic age has saturated their experience outside of school with much learning would be to underestimate student capacities. Most are well prepared to accept freedom within the framework of correlative responsibilities and authority.

But these comments have thrust the writer ahead of his story. Earlier, reference was made to the gradual assumption by the university of authority and responsibility for the student. W. H. Cowley pointed out that the universities of Bologna, Paris, and Oxford in mid-thirteenth century had large influxes of fourteen- and fifteen-year-old students, many of whom were poor, lived in most undesirable surroundings, created many disciplinary problems, and generated most difficult town-gown relations.[3] Students themselves first began group housing (like many other "firsts" in higher education), and these houses, not controlled by the universities, spread rapidly over the Continent between 1200 and 1400 A.D. Gradually, universities began to assume greater control over some of these facilities as they were given properties directly or were consulted by good-hearted landlords who were sympathetic to the lot of the poor, underprivileged students. From 1400 to 1800 many of these housing units continued, but few if any new ones came into being as more and more students sought their own living arrangements. Only Oxford and Cambridge seemed to survive as residential colleges. Much of this decline in college-controlled student housing occurred on the heels of the waning monastic systems of the Middle Ages. Although student governance and student freedom fluctuated in intensity of concern, the academic master-to-scholar, superior-to-inferior, ruler-to-slave images prevailed, for the limited access to knowledge, the dearth of books and materials, and the large numbers of students desiring to expand their knowledge contributed to a situation in which the demand exceeded the supply of education. Elitism, the creeping class distinction, and the low purchasing power of all but a few soon brought higher education into an era of exclusivity and virtually isolated it from the masses.

American Colonial colleges largely derived their patterns from the British colleges. Here again the master-to-subject, teacher-to-student, superior-to-inferior relationship became intensified. Early American colleges, originally charged with preparing clerics and a few doctors and still fewer lawyers, subsequently took on a variety of purposes. From the documents of these early colleges come clear descriptions of these changes in scope and purpose.

Early American colleges attempted to duplicate in every respect the

[3] See W. H. Cowley, "The History of Student Residential Housing," *School and Society*, 40 (December 1, 1934), 705–712.

colleges of the ancient universities, even to verbatim copying of the rules. The conditions of the old English and European universities were to be altered in America in only one way: in the form of the land-grant institutions, which still later in American history, became the "people's universities."

European universities and colleges were founded by mature scholars; similar American institutions were founded by communities. The mature scholar was late in coming to these community institutions, and they were staffed initially and primarily with itinerant young tutors. But to overlook the church's influence upon the expansion of American higher education would be negligent. The evangelical and expansionist purposes of the church in the movement West were assisted by the development of church colleges for perpetuation of the faith and expansion of church membership. Since the clerics were the chief Colonial Americans who had received higher education, they naturally assumed leadership, even in the developing state colleges and in the land-grant universities soon to come.

A number of years and another war transpired before the next major changes brought about the land-grant and "public" universities, which combined the purposes of the early colleges with comprehensive liberal arts and sciences and technical-vocational education. In fact, these additions changed the whole direction of the American university from higher learning for learning's sake to higher learning for more practical purposes.

Arguments about the pros and cons of student life, student controls, and more especially about "moral" supervision of students were rampant in early Colonial colleges. In many cases the adherents to religious and moralistic codes won out, and student life was strictly regimented. Although tied closely to residential living, the early American college system differed from the traditional British pattern, especially among those men who first supported education for women and who wished to universalize opportunities for higher learning, thereby offering more opportunities to children of yeomen and workers, farmers and tradesmen. This latter ideal had to be discussed for some years before implementation, simply because of a major contradiction in the environment: great and numerous opportunities existed for gaining personal wealth and social status through the westward movement, through pioneering and land acquisition, and through hard work. All of this and more too could be accomplished without an education. On the other hand, schooling, especially college-level work, meant an investment of time and literally restricting one's mobility and material gain when the prosperity of society at large was increasing.

As the West developed, the church expanded and played an increased role in higher education. In many cases the church became the symbol of and indeed reinforced paternalism, strict obedience, and overregulation of students. In fact, Colonial college governance denied any role to student opinion or to student voice. This made for situations of violence and overthrow at certain colleges, reports of which make the spine tingle! The history of early American campuses is replete with stories of student rebellions, presidents being tarred and feathered, buildings being burned, and real damage and personal harm inflicted upon individuals. Naturally, student life was to become tamed as the years went on and as students themselves saw the benefit of organizing into groups and establishing their own peer controls through various forms of governance. As the saying goes, when there is a vacuum, something will fill it; when there are human needs to be filled, some way of satisfying them will arise. So it was that students introduced their own elements of governance; namely, clubs, literary societies, living groups, and fraternities and sororities. These, together with athletics and a variety of "spirit-building" programs, came into existence through student initiative.

Concurrently, faculties and administrations were exchanging views, building facilities, and establishing institutions with varied purposes. They were continually involved in projects related directly to financial, legal, and public support of their endeavors.

At some unmarked point in history, and the literary societies could have been the spawning grounds for such, recognition was given the positive potential of the consultative role of students, of the effective assistance in control and overall institutional support they could offer. This undoubtedly led some colleges and universities (particularly Eastern ones) to delegate to students deliberately and constitutionally some direct responsibilities for governance of their own affairs. Often, student activities were separated specifically from the governance of faculty, who held full responsibility for academic and institutional affairs.

The particular way in which the student literary society or debating club (which often owned more books and printed materials than the early libraries) affected the early American colleges and the academic-intellectual growth of students is yet to be fully documented; however, John S. Brubacher and Willis Rudy have recorded some aspects of these groups:

> As time went on, these societies came to be the center of interest on the campus. "A new order of champions and hero worship developed." At most colleges, at least two rival literary societies appeared, and sometimes three. Between them the most heated rivalry existed. It was expressed in competition over the building of the societies' libraries, in the electing of honorary members, and in the recruiting of new student members. Rivalry was especially hot in debates between representatives of the contending societies and in the selection of student speakers for commencement or for the public displays of oratorical prowess which were referred to at that time as college "exhibitions." The literary societies commanded the kind of passionate student loyalty which was later accorded to fraternities and athletic teams. This is why such hectic efforts were made to raise money for the society libraries and for the furnishing of clubrooms. It also explains why such frantic electioneering went on during the campaigns for offices in the societies. The question of status and rank within the society interested many students far more than the formal curriculum. President Hitchcock of Amherst found the literary society elections "often as hotly contested as those for the various offices in our State and National governments." The im-

portance of this kind of activity as a training ground for a political career is obvious.[4]

Early eighteenth-century college life saw much development in student activity, including both organized groups and spontaneous ones. A brief description of the latter would have to include rowdyism, vandalism, and riot-rebellions of savage dimensions. But it is clear that well-ordered types of activity prevailed, with students seeking relief from academic pressure in drinking, food rioting, and general discontent. The faculty and administration exercised strict and explicit controls, however. Still later, athletics and social-fraternity groups displaced the literary societies. Academic work had become such a drag that these spirited activities were not only substitutes for but were actual escapes from the main enterprise of the college or university—formal learning for its own sake.

Student governance was tried on some campuses even before the Civil War in order to bring about greater order. So like the present was this period of social upheaval—as students pushed for more freedom, more democratization—that it deserves intensive study and commentary. After the Civil War, little or no student rebellion was in evidence, for student involvement in governance became real as their demands for freedom were somewhat realized, first, in changes in curriculum, particularly the elective system which introduced freer choice of courses; second, in the change in attitude on the part of faculty toward students, who accepted them more as young adults; and, third, in the introduction of the most important factor in calming and sophisticating campus life—coeducation. Three other influences, one of which has been pointed to previously, became further reasons for more governance, freedom, and sophistication: the development of athletics and fraternities; the introduction of special police forces, and hired policing proctors, preceptors, and residence staff; and, most important, the land-grant college movement, which established so-called people's universities all across the nation.

In 1937, W. H. Cowley delivered a paper to the Nineteenth Annual Conference of the National Association of Deans and Advisers of Men that relates the story of the introduction of a new dean into American higher education.[5] President Eliot of Harvard upon his election to office in 1869 began to implement his deep personal concern for professional education, especially graduate work. He began early to revolutionize Harvard and in 1870 chose a professor of history, Ephriam Gurney, to be a dean with duties similar to those of most deans today. This deanship was active until 1891, when President Eliot decided to divide it into two positions as a result of great growth due to the elective system he had established and the developing student problems incident to this increase in size. One dean became

---

[4] John S. Brubacher and Willis Rudy, *Higher Education in Transition: 1636 to 1956* (New York: Harper & Row, 1958), pp. 47–48.

[5] W. H. Cowley, "The Disappearing Dean of Men," *Secretarial Notes, Nineteenth Annual Conference of the National Association of Deans and Advisers* (Austin, Texas: University of Texas, 1937), pp. 85–99.

Dean of the Faculty of Arts and Sciences; the other, Dean of Harvard College. This latter division established a precedent for a dean of student life, an office that was to assume major responsibilities for the out-of-class activities of students both on and off the campus. Many, many functions, both by default and by design have since become the province of this office of dean of student life, more often titled dean of women and dean of men. In most institutions these officers were vitally concerned with the student's personal, social, recreational, and spiritual life, to say nothing of the efforts they made to establish guidelines, rules, and regulations within student governance and freedom areas.

Most recently, especially since World War II, through a very gradual movement, almost through drift, students have begun to assume more and more responsibility for their own affairs out of class, in some places even assuming functions and duties heretofore performed by the deans. The philosophy of some student personnel workers is interesting; namely, that they were in business only insofar as students needed them. Thereafter, when young adults assumed their naturally free and responsible roles, although they might not have achieved their majority, they would be allowed to take over the management of their own lives on campus and off. This has not always occurred, nor has it been the goal or purpose of some deans (and others) in higher education.

Student energies and drives, coupled with the explosive issues of these uncertain days, have caused rebellion of both individuals and groups against most authorities. To overlook the permissiveness in the child-rearing patterns of the past twenty-five years and the subsequent earlier achievement of independence, often with less than adequate self-preparation, would be fatuous. Natural tendencies to rebel and to gain self-identity have made deans of students and their staffs, presidents, chancellors, and faculty prime targets. At the same time it must be recognized that the life and death issues of the day create arenas for authentic leaders as well as for self-styled or puppet-like leaders to emerge. These so-called leaders may well become more militant, more oppressive, more parental than the individuals or establishments they are maligning. The natural generation gap is being oversold as the cause for confusion and misunderstanding. Granted, there *are* ills in society, grave injustices and evidences of neglect of human and natural resources that create serious needs and deficiencies in colleges and universities. Nevertheless, student energies must be redirected into constructive activities if strikes and power-grabbing for power's sake are not to be the only means for reform. If students hear only voices of dissent—not advice, counsel, and consent—if present negativeness and divisiveness proceed unaverted, chaos will prevail.

Even now, however, amidst the turmoil in American higher education and in international circles, there are signs of hope; in fact, there are models of individual and personal, as well as institutional, integrity and worth which can be looked to for assistance in the restoration of equilibrium. Such models must be continually before us.

About the future and its inevitable expanding of student freedoms and governance, this writer has this to say, based upon his years of experience as a member of the "deaning" profession of both varieties—those responsible for class-related and out-of-class activities: it is clear that the complexities of life today on American campuses are not amenable to being administration-run, Board of Trustees-run, State Board-run, or even federally run. All of these levels and agencies must be joined in a working unit dedicated to the best interests of the individual and society and of the generic university with its comprehensive goals. If academic life becomes a continuous power play and one group tries to consume the others, a university will not be maintained in any recognizable form. Rather, a hydra-headed monster with no assurances of which head will devour the other may well prevail. Freedom and governance then may be subverted, indeed contraverted and reverted, to an almost primitive status.

Evidence does seem to point to a need for a rebalancing of the institutions of higher education, a new channeling and leveling of their tasks, a continuous restructuring of their unique and peculiar functions. So it is also with the positions of deans of student life. More than likely the old images and even the positions of control—"Mom," the dean of women, and "Dad," the dean of men—will disappear, and in their places the concepts and functions of professional-services personnel will evolve. The care-and-feeding operations for students have become such big businesses that specialists have had to be employed. Such areas as counseling and health services, advising of organizations and activities, financial aids and assistance programs, residential counseling and housing management, police protection, and safety and security programs—all need specialists. But to ignore the coordinating and integrating functions that can be performed by top academic generalists concerned with overall campus affairs is to overlook a great need of higher education today.

With recognition of the minimal changes recorded here, it becomes clear that more and more weight must be given to the responsible role students can assume in governance and higher learning in America. Their freedoms and their rights, based on knowledge of the great privileges they have, will emerge in proportion not only to their demands, but also to their acceptance of full measures of self and group responsibilities and controls—self-governance of the highest form.

The present, much like the past, is asserting anew the need for redefinitions of democracy. This has given rise to some of the riotous and "power play" activities of late. Persons not truly devoted to the real tenets of democracy, of freedom, indeed of governance as a necessary ingredient of the foregoing, are involved. License and anarchy seem to be the only end goal or result of the present drives by these groups of students. In studying the student movements of today and books like *The New Student Left*,[6] *The*

---

[6] Mitchell Cohen and Dennis Hale (eds.), *The New Student Left* (Boston: Beacon Press, 1967).

American Student's Freedom of Expression,[7] *Freedom and Order in the University*,[8] *To Make a Difference*,[9] and *The American Student and His College*,[10] it also becomes clear that the time for involvement of students is long overdue if we are to ensure that the persons most directly served by the processes of higher education do become truly "our most important products."

So many times before in the history of American higher education students have had to rebel, yell out, and be counted in order for change on their behalf to be effected on college campuses. Now, however, students, often more mature and in fact better educated than ever before, are linking social, political, and international concerns with their concerns about higher education—all with an immediacy for change which mightily confuses issues, particularly academic ones.

The new urgencies for change are related to the rapid pace at which the "electronic age" and the "education age" have become one and the same—have literally become synonymous goals for the future. Also, the automation images have had the effect of depersonalization—because of widespread misuses, yes, but really more to the point, because of widespread misunderstanding of their value for the future. If we overlook the perilous and infectious strains of forces counter to the good life, such as war, conflicts in political, racial, economic, and personal ideologies, and the population explosion, we will contribute mightily to worldwide confusion.

The young adults, the college students inheriting not only these massive problems, but even worse, the archaic and often inadequate tools and institutions for changing these conditions, can become disillusioned and alienated, can drop out, not only from school but also from society and can so fear life, so dread responsibilities, so deny themselves healthy growth toward the good life that new escape mechanisms are developed. This, however, cannot, must not, and this writer asserts firmly, will not be the condition that will prevail.

As one views the exigencies of today's world, especially as they impinge upon the young adult, it is evident that every effort must be made to put older heads on younger shoulders, to engage the young adult in serious activity. Perhaps one of the real problems is that of not being able to know how to balance serious hard work with corresponding and equally necessary play. This says much for our needs to teach better the meaningful use of one's leisure time, to teach ways of real re-creation.

Also clear is the fact that the young, now that under-twenty-five-year-

---

[7] E. G. Williamson and John L. Cowan, *The American Student's Freedom of Expression* (Minneapolis: University of Minnesota Press, 1966).

[8] Samuel Gorovitz (ed.), *Freedom and Order in the University* (Cleveland: Western Reserve University Press, 1967).

[9] Otto Butz (ed.), *To Make a Difference* (New York: Harper & Row, 1967).

[10] Esther Lloyd-Jones and Herman A. Estrin, *The American Student and His College* (Boston: Houghton Mifflin Company, 1967).

olds make up half the population, will have to be given more responsibilities and tasks sooner than ever before in history in order to keep society, in fact the world, in step with the advances that have been made. To suggest that the needs for growth and change, for broad-based improvements in understanding the emotional, spiritual, and social life of man are not numerous would be to deny the most pressing problems of the moment.

It is the young, then, as always, who must take up the banners of adventure, of creativity, of service, of dedication, and of renewal. If this is done in a united and cooperative way with the middle-aged and with the older generation, real self-transcendence and involvement of the young in society can become a reality. The greatest need of the young, and indeed of all men, is to continually reestablish hope for, faith in, and allegiance to the goals of a free society, a society in which the necessary limits of freedom and control are known to and supported by all.

The educated society is the best known vehicle for accomplishing the good life, indeed for overcoming the ravages of distrust, the divisiveness and the imbalances sown by the pathological, the power hungry, and the negatively driven elements in the world. Full recognition must be made of values both realized and yet to be realized, of the advances made and yet to be made, of the opportunities given and yet to be given to individuals in a society based on maximized freedoms. All such values must continually be reinforced in and through systems of learning and living that give young adults a responsible role in decision-making and planning for the future. Then colleges and universities can be model communities that serve as examples of such freedom and governance, in full recognition that they too are incomplete and yet dynamic organisms—just as are the lives of men.

MARY JO HALL

Academic Freedom for Students: Some Thoughts on the Current Debate

Mary Jo Hall is Director of Federal Relations at the University of Oregon.

Readers of the University of Oregon's campus newspaper were pleased to learn in the fall of 1967 that, according to its student editors, their institution was more committed than most to the concept of student academic freedom. In a lengthy article in its orientation issue, the *Oregon Daily Emerald* enumerated area after area in which it said the University administration had clearly established a pro-student policy and provided proper safeguards for their protection.[1] These areas included freedom to invite and hear any speaker, due process in student disciplinary cases, a policy of noninterference with off-campus activities, no discrimination in admission, proper safeguards against arbitrary or prejudicial grading, and a free student press.

The student journalists observed, accurately enough, that there was a great upsurge in student self-expression on American campuses. They added that as students increasingly sought a larger voice in the determination of various campus and community policies, it became even more important to determine exactly what their freedoms and protections were. Few would dispute this, and partly because of the need for some clear-cut statement of student freedoms, the educational community gave a collective sigh of relief in August 1967 when the American Association of University Professors and nine other organizations issued the *Joint Statement on Rights and Freedoms of Students*.[2] Sometimes called the "Student Bill of Rights,"

[1] "Academic Freedom Covers Many Areas at University," *Oregon Daily Emerald*, September 19, 1967, p. 3.

[2] The *Joint Statement on Rights and Freedoms of Students* resulted from a conference held in Washington, D.C. on November 13–14, 1966, to discuss the academic freedom of students and to explore the feasibility of reaching a consensus on standards in this area. Representatives from ten educational organizations were

this document set out to enumerate those areas in which a consensus had been established on standards and procedures. It covered such thorny trouble spots as the use and content of student records, the maintenance of membership lists for student organizations, the disclosure of student views and beliefs to prospective employers, and other questions of this nature which had traditionally plagued faculty members and administrators alike.

One would think that a document as inclusive and carefully drawn as this would have put an end to a discussion that has raged intermittently since American educators first discovered the concept of *Lehrfreiheit* and *Lernfreiheit*, the freedom to teach and to learn.[3] Such has not been the case. And I suspect that even if all ten educational organizations represented in forming the *Joint Statement* ratify this draft at their next national conventions the debate over student academic freedom will continue for some time to come.

It could hardly be otherwise. While the concept of academic freedom for faculty members has evolved through traditions going back several hundred years and finally been interpreted in this century for an American audience by the A.A.U.P., similar attention has been given to this country's student freedoms only during the past twenty years. Some would even date this involvement as late as 1960 when the A.A.U.P. formed Committee S on Faculty Responsibility for the Academic Freedom of Students, or even later, in 1964 with the so-called Berkeley Revolt.[4] Not only has the concept of student academic freedom not yet completed a reasonable gestation, but the problem of formulating a general philosophy which can adequately cover the many viewpoints and experiences represented in some 2,200 American institutions of higher education is staggering.

---

included: The American Association of University Professors, the Association of American Colleges, the U. S. National Student Association, the National Association of Student Personnel Administrators, the National Association of Women Deans and Counselors, the American Council on Education, the Association of American Universities, Association for Higher Education, Association of State Colleges and Universities, and the American College Personnel Association. The statement was actually the work of seven individuals: Dr. Phillip Monypenny, University of Illinois; Dr. Harry D. Gideonse, New School for Social Research; Mr. Edward Schwartz, U. S. National Student Association; Dr. Peter H. Armacost, Ottawa University; Mr. Earle Clifford, Rutgers State University; Dr. Ann Bromley, Santa Fe Junior College; and Mr. Robert Van Waes, American Association of University Professors. Copies of the statement have been circulated widely and reprinted in many journals, including *College and University Business*, 43 (September 1967), 78–81.

[3] A thorough discussion of *Lehrfreiheit* and *Lernfreiheit* is included in Richard Hofstadter and Walter P. Metzger, *The Development of Academic Freedom in the United States* (New York: Columbia University Press, 1955), pp. 383–497.

[4] At least two of the earliest official statements on the academic freedom of students were issued by the American Civil Liberties Union. These included a pamphlet entitled "What Freedom for American Students?" which was published in April 1941, and "Civil Liberties of Teachers and Students" issued in February 1949.

The big debate thus far, of course, has centered on just what constitutes the academic freedom of students. The drafting committee of the *Joint Statement* tried to outline the general perimeter of their viewpoint in the document's preamble. It reads as follows:

> Academic institutions exist for the transmission of knowledge, the pursuit of truth, the development of students, and the general well-being of society. Free inquiry and free expression are indispensable to the attainment of these goals. As members of the academic community, students should be encouraged to develop the capacity for critical judgement and to engage in a sustained and independent search for truth. Institutional procedures for achieving these purposes may vary from campus to campus, but the minimal standards of academic freedom of students outlined below are essential to any community of scholars.

They continued:

> Freedom to teach and freedom to learn are inseparable facets of academic freedom. The freedom to learn depends upon appropriate opportunities and conditions in the classroom, on the campus, and in the larger community. Students should exercise their freedom with responsibility.

And turning to the institutionalization of these freedoms, the committee noted:

> The responsibility to secure and to respect general conditions conducive to the freedom to learn is shared by all members of the academic community. Each college and university has a duty to develop policies and procedures which provide and safeguard this freedom. Such policies and procedures should be developed at each institution within the framework of general standards and with the broadest possible participation of the members of the academic community. The purpose of this statement is to enumerate the essential provisions for student freedom to learn.

These sentiments are almost identical to earlier A.A.U.P. statements on the academic freedom of students issued in 1964 and 1965.[5] Yet, many faculty members and administrators are still shaking their heads over this entire area, and it is not too difficult to pinpoint at least four viewpoints which are undoubtedly represented somewhere on every campus in this country. To use the jargon of the psychedelic era, their particular "hang-up" can be lumped into one of four general types.

First, they find it difficult to reconcile statements of student academic

[5] See "Statement on Faculty Responsibility for the Academic Freedom of Students," *A.A.U.P. Bulletin*, 50 (Autumn 1964), 254-257; and "Statement on the Academic Freedom of Students," *A.A.U.P. Bulletin*, 51 (Winter 1965), 447-449.

freedom with the traditional precepts of academic freedom as applied to the faculty member. On the one hand, we are discussing such items as safeguarding the students against unnecessary room searches or establishing due process in disciplinary cases arising out of social activities. Or to cite an extreme example, we are trying to assure that no one gasps too audibly when certain well-known four-letter words are used in undergraduate literary magazines. On the other hand, we are dealing with "that freedom of members of the academic community . . . which underlies the effective performance of their functions of teaching, learning, practice of the arts and research." [6] This is not to say that the former areas are unimportant. But their significance can be questioned when placed in juxtaposition to the hallowed freedoms of the competent scholar to pursue knowledge and truth regardless of what authority might be offended. Who can blame the faculty member who balks at statements of academic freedom which include safeguards against institutions' prescribing the length of hair or dress?

Second, some concerns have arisen because of the apparent blurring of "academic freedom" to include areas which should more normally be called "individual freedoms" or "civil liberties." Until recently, there was a rather conscious distinction made between these areas in professional statements or articles dealing with the academic freedom and civil liberties of students in colleges and universities. In this context, the freedom of students to assemble to discuss or demonstrate on social issues off campus was termed a "civil or individual liberty." The freedom to take exception to a professor's data or opinions in the classroom became an "academic freedom." Such clear-cut lines are more difficult to draw in philosophies of academic freedom that expand the concept of the classroom to include almost any arena, on or off campus, which might offer the student opportunity for his intellectual or moral growth. Too, the American experience with academic freedom has been somewhat unique in that its essential ingredients are inextricably entwined with the constitutional freedoms accorded every citizen. Yet there are many who argue that the words "academic freedom" can only reasonably and practically be reserved for those special activities which take place in or through the auspices of an educational enterprise, that "community of scholars devoted to the discovery and propagation of knowledge." [7]

Third, some observers have expressed dismay over the fact that students appear to be agitating for academic freedom with different goals in mind than those which prompted their faculty counterparts many years earlier. The student newspaper article mentioned earlier serves as a good example of this particular point. Its authors noted that academic freedom for students was important because students were increasingly interested in exerting more influence in campus and community policies (nee politics). On the

---

[6] Ralph F. Fuchs, "Academic Freedom: Its Basic Philosophy, Function, and History," in Hans W. Baade (ed.), *Academic Freedom: The Scholar's Place in Modern Society* (Dobbs Ferry, N.Y.: Oceana Publications, Inc., 1964), p. 1.

[7] Phillip Monypenny, "Towards a Standard for Student Academic Freedom," in Baade, *Academic Freedom: The Scholar's Place in Modern Society*, p. 198.

other hand, the scholar's interest in such safeguards has been directly and primarily tied to his functions of teaching, learning, and researching within a chosen field. These goals are quite different, and it has been pointed out that when the doctrine of academic freedom is used as a special plea for the citizen-role of either scholar or student, then the entire concept is in jeopardy.

Fourth, and perhaps most important, there is considerable head-holding over what, for lack of a better word, could be called the "implementation" of academic freedom for students. These concerns arise because of the very dependent position of students, subject to the authority of the institution from which they hope to earn a degree. This discussion boils down to the essential point of whether or not the academic freedom of students is a shared right within the total community of scholars and, as such, is something that transcends the legal charters of individual institutions or the hesitancies of specific faculties and administrators.

There appear to be two rather strong and imminently respectable movements afoot in this area. On the one hand, we have those who subscribe to the position included in the *Joint Statement* that academic freedom, whether for students or faculty, is an inalienable right of the scholarly life. And as such, it forces a duty on every college and university, public or private, to develop policies and procedures that nurture and safeguard these freedoms.

Opposing this, we have those who discuss the fiduciary responsibility of the institutions and who claim that the nature and content of institutional charters establish a legal basis for the control of every aspect of student behavior. They argue that the college stands in the role of trustee or guardian for the students, who are in a sense its wards, and the recipients only of those freedoms which are granted them by the college. This viewpoint was explicitly stated in a recent controversy at Colorado State University, where the governing board rejected the draft of a new campus constitution increasing student powers and noted that students have "only the rights and functions . . . they are permitted to have by the Board." [8]

This does not mean that persons holding this opinion are necessarily opposed to academic freedom for students. But it does serve notice that they are operating from a different point of reference than the drafting committee of the *Joint Statement*. How this point is resolved may well be the most important part of the debate about academic freedom for students.

After this rather general introduction to the problem at hand, let us turn to what administrators call the "nuts and bolts" of the situation— an identification of what actually constitutes the academic freedom of students. At the risk of offending those readers who would prefer to see clearer distinctions made between academic and civil freedoms (and I place myself in this camp), it seems profitable to concentrate on those areas which have been included in the *Joint Statement* or developed through earlier pronouncements of the American Association of University Professors and the American Civil Liberties Union. These freedoms are generally identified

---

[8] See "National Association of State Universities and Land-Grant Colleges," *Circular Letter*, No. 27 (September 29, 1967), p. 14.

in reference to their physical location, i.e., freedom in the classroom, freedoms in on-campus student life, and freedoms during off-campus activities. At least this gives one some recognizable boundaries to visualize, which is useful in dealing with so amorphous a topic.

Freedom in the Classroom. This heading most often covers the protections that should be accorded students in their discussions with their professors, and coincidentally, by the establishment of proper safeguards against prejudiced or capricious academic evaluation. In this latter area, we have seen recommendations for, and often the creation of, special campus committees to hear student complaints about the grading process. Such committees have handled cases ranging from the certification of pass–no-pass courses as general learning aids to the actual changing of letter grades where student complaints have been verified. Recently, this particular set of freedoms was also expanded to include statements to the effect that professors should consider confidential any information about student views, beliefs, or political associations which they might acquire through the role of instructor, adviser, or counselor. This latter area has been quite a touchy one, partly because of the practice of many prospective employers (particularly governmental agencies) of gaining some evaluation of a student's reliability by querying his teachers about his participation in relevant classroom discussions. This question is still not entirely settled, as a close reading of the *Joint Statement* will show. It is noted there that "judgements of ability and character may be provided under appropriate circumstances, normally with the knowledge or consent of the student." Certainly the professor who is interviewed concerning a student whom he knows holds views contrary to the established mores of society will find himself hard-put not to reflect this knowledge during a character evaluation. And the caution against disclosing such information without the student's consent will obviously be impractical for interviews that take place during school vacations or that concern graduated or transferred students. More clarification will have to take place in this area before students can truly feel free to discuss, inquire, and evaluate openly in the academic setting.

Freedoms in On-Campus Student Life. Most of the standards of academic freedom considered by the drafting committee and included in the earlier A.A.U.P. and A.C.L.U. documents fall into this category. These areas are identified only briefly here and the reader is urged to consult the original texts to gain a full appreciation of the nuances involved in establishing procedures to protect on-campus student life. The areas include:

(a) safeguards on the content and use of student personnel, academic, or disciplinary records;

(b) protections for student organizations against infringements by the institution, faculty, or nonstudents;

(c) the right to support causes by orderly means which do not disrupt the regular operation of the institution;

(d) the opportunity to invite and hear any person of the students' choosing;

(e) the means to participate in the formulation or application of institutional policy affecting academic and student affairs, including explicit statements about the rules and responsibilities of the student government;

(f) the creation of sufficient editorial freedom and financial autonomy for student publications to maintain integrity as vehicles of free inquiry and free expression;

(g) proper procedures to guarantee due process in disciplinary cases, plus the publication of clear and reasonable standards of behavior expected by the institution;

(h) the right to remain on campus and in classes pending disposition of disciplinary actions, except in extreme cases;

(i) protection from unauthorized or unreasonable searches of student dwellings or possessions;

(j) freedom from any type of harassment, exclusion, or prohibition on the basis of race, creed, or national origin, except for religious qualifications which may be required by organizations or institutions whose aims are primarily sectarian.

Such a hasty listing can hardly do justice to the complexities involved in this aspect of student freedom nor to the thoroughness with which these areas have been discussed during the past few years.[9] There is still room, however, for improvement. Some debate has already taken place about the provision in the *Joint Statement* which suggests that institutions clarify "those standards of behavior which it considers essential to its educational mission and its community life." There is considerable feeling that such standards should only be concerned with the academic performance expected of the student body. Others feel that institutions of higher education have a mission to insist on patterns of behavior even more rigid or moral than those normally tolerated in the average American community. Certainly the students who consider themselves part of the "Berkeley phenomenon" would argue that no institution has the right to promulgate standards that touch on the political behavior or beliefs of on-campus student life. This promises to be one of the more interesting if troublesome compromises which undoubtedly will be formed during the next few years.

I personally suspect, however, that the drafters of the *Joint Statement* did not have this particular set of questions in mind when they included that rather open-ended provision. It would appear they were actually insisting that institutions stop using their disciplinary machinery in a capricious and arbitrary manner. Most students would agree that they feel much safer when it is clearly stated which patterns of behavior will be accepted and which

---

[9] Several articles in this area are of particular interest: Elinor Langer, "Students' Rights; They Should Have More," *Science*, 157 (August 4, 1967), 524–526; "More on Academic Freedom," *America*, 115 (September 17, 1966), 285–287; James Petras, "Politics of Democracy: The Free Speech Movement," *Phi Delta Kappan*, 46 (March 1965), 343–346; and E. G. Williamson, "Students' Rights and Responsibilities: Competing Concepts of Freedom," *National Association of Women Deans and Counselors Journal*, 28 (Winter 1965), 81–87.

will not. If a student is likely to be expelled for certain activities, whether in or out of the classroom, he has the right to know this beforehand. This makes sense in any learning situation. Too, a written standard provides a starting point for communication between students and their elders. The success of the Student Conduct Code developed at the University of Oregon during the past few years by committees of faculty, administrators, and students bears eloquent testimony to this point.[10]

Freedoms for Off-Campus Activities. A majority of the court cases that are cited in the literature of academic freedom have resulted from the off-campus activities of student and faculty. This is one of the few areas in which there is still genuine and widespread debate about what constitutes proper safeguards for the scholar and the scholar-in-training. This debate is shaped by the realization that members of the academic community are also citizens of other communities; yet, because of their special place in our society, they must assume uncommon responsibilities and be accorded uncommon safeguards.

The emotions, both on and off campus, which resulted from the latest round of loyalty oath cases have flared again because of the civil rights and Vietnam war activities of students and faculty. It is generally assumed that as citizens, students and faculty members should enjoy the same freedoms of speech, peaceful assembly, and right of petition as other citizens. Yet, both the academic community and the general public have on occasion urged either special privileges or special restraints for those persons living and working on this nation's campuses.

The problems facing the average student are even more complex than those which greet his faculty counterpart, partly because of his youth and partly because of his dependent situation within the institution. This is again an area where the *Joint Statement on Rights and Freedoms of Students,* while providing a useful starting point, has left considerable room for additional clarification and interpretation. The document states that students should enjoy the same rights as other citizens. It notes, however, that as members of the academic community, students are subject to those special obligations and responsibilities which that membership entails. This distinction, ambiguous enough when applied only to faculty members, is even more difficult to interpret in respect to the current college generation, with its youthful enthusiasm and idealistic emotions. To a student participating with his professors in a civil rights demonstration or an antiwar "teach-in," there is something noble and inspiring about this membership in the cutting-

---

[10] The University of Oregon has distributed a *Student Handbook* to all incoming students during the fall term of the past few academic years. One of the most comprehensive documents of its kind, the *Handbook* carries the full text of the so-called Student Conduct Code which is revised and enforced by joint student-faculty-administrative committees. Also included are the stated mandates of the major administrative committees on campus, the full text of the student government constitution, and the text of other policy matters such as content and use of student personnel forms. Copies of this document can be obtained by writing the Dean of Students, University of Oregon, Eugene, Oregon.

edge of society. But under the law, he has only the same protections or liberties as his noncollege neighbor. Yet, at what point is the political scientist (whether age seventeen or forty-seven) to be reproved for his opinions on foreign affairs or the sociologist to be chastised for his concerns over societal discrimination? For the student there is more involved here than just the legal maneuvers of the A.A.U.P. and the A.C.L.U.; it is possible for him to be subjected to double jeopardy, resulting in both civil sanctions in the courts and academic sanctions by his institution.[11] The *Joint Statement* is aware of this danger when it cautions institutions never to use their authority merely to duplicate general civil laws. It notes that "only where the institution's interests as an academic community are distinct and clearly involved should the special authority of the institution be asserted."

This does not, however, answer the question of whether or not the interests of academia are at stake when a student pleads the Fifth Amendment during Congressional hearings, is caught off campus using illegal drugs, or is arrested for leading a "filthy speech movement" parade downtown. All of these are areas in which civil court cases have been involved. They are also areas in which some institutions have compounded the punishment by asserting their "special authority" in one form or another.

There are many who feel that institutions have an obligation to provide the opportunity for political and societal involvement by their student body. But as Edward Joseph Shoben, Jr., Director of the American Council on Education's Commission on Academic Affairs, has noted, "for that opportunity to be genuine, it must involve no risks greater than those shared by all members of society." [12] Students who take advantage of this opportunity are appropriately accountable to the civil authorities if civil laws are violated, but they should expect no additional penalties to be imposed by the university. As Shoben has written, "the capacity for independent thought is developed only through its exercise in a context of the consequences of ideas and a chance to reflect upon these consequences. It is in this educational truism that the meaning of academic freedom for students basically resides." [13]

The academic freedom of students is one of those topics, like democracy, which is destined to reappear in various literary guises for some time to come. There has been and will continue to be enough debate just on those particular items included in the *Joint Statement on Rights and Freedoms of Students* to keep the subject unsettled and undefined for many years. In addition, there are many corollary matters that have not yet received much public scrutiny, such as the very special academic problems which face this generation of graduate students. This changing kaleidoscope of opinions

---

[11] A useful discussion of this point is contained in an article by Alan W. Johnson, "Double Jeopardy: A Misnomer; the Relation of the Student to the College and the Courts," *The Journal of Higher Education*, 37 (January 1, 1966), 16–23.

[12] Edward Joseph Shoben, Jr., "Academic Freedom for Students," *N.A.S.P.A. Journal*, 5 (July 1967), 29.

[13] *Ibid.*, p. 30.

and posturing is as it should be, though, in a strong and viable educational system, for as the roles and responsibilities of today's youth change, as they predictably will, so must the safeguards and protections.

There are darkening shadows observable, however, that distress those who still find pleasure in gentle rumination on the future of higher education and its practitioners. I, too, must admit some fears about trends clearly identifiable in the current generation. The cherished freedom of scholars to select their arena of study and to pursue its truths undaunted may soon atrophy in the present rush to identify "acceptable" thesis topics within ever-rigidifying disciplines. Clearly the battle being waged by the traditionalists and behavioralists in many disciplines has prompted a subtly creeping paralysis in the intellectual choices of tomorrow's teachers.

Also it seems that all too often there has been a tendency in recent years to redefine freedom as license. As a philosophically-minded colleague of mine once observed, "freedom is indispensable. But like good health, its value is largely determined by what you do with it." [14] The robust exchange of ideas is one thing. The disregard of those procedures and common courtesies which permit this exchange is another. A most significant phrase in the *Joint Statement* says that "students should exercise their freedoms with responsibility." It remains to be seen whether or not this admonition will receive the same attention as the rest of the document.

[14] For this observation I am indebted to Dr. Harold Stoke, New Boston, Sandisfield, Massachusetts.

DIANE KEANE DRIESSEL

A Student's View of Freedom in the Multiversity

Diane Keane Driessel, a graduate of Marquette University, is currently completing course work for the Ph.D. in Speech at the University of California, Berkeley.

The multiversity, like Topsy and the great urban sprawl, "just grew." Today's consequence is a frighteningly powerful giant that stirs restlessly in outgrown institutional clothing. A nervous nation has heard its voice in Berkeley, demanding freedom. The nation cannot be reassured until it understands the nature of this giant and its demands.

The multiversity may be defined in terms of its structure, purposes, and constituencies. A spokesman of the New Left, Paul Goodman, finds its structure top-heavy. There are too many administrators. The value judgment of how many is "too many" is probably related to the regard one has for academic administrators, and Mr. Goodman has little. In any case, compared to its academic polar opposite, the small liberal arts college, the multiversity has more of everything in the administrative hierarchy.

More significant than the increase in ratio of administration to faculty is the change in the distribution of power as a consequence of size. The small college can have a paternal president who makes hundreds of daily decisions, small as well as large. The Clark Kerr who supervised the spread of the University of California to almost a dozen campuses made no small decisions. Questions that loom large for the small college president, such as the hiring and firing of deans, may not have even merited his attention.

Power this overwhelming is seldom felt personally. The Oshkosh undergraduate may know his president's power by the presence or absence of a drinking fountain, a statue, or even the dean of instruction. If he becomes a graduate student at Berkeley, he will never know the signs and symbols of the president of the University of California, although the latter's power is incomparably greater.

The signs and symbols of power are there, but they are produced by several hierarchical layers. They are impersonal in that no human individuality can be attributed to them. In Berkeley one cannot say, "Yes, that's just the kind of silly parking regulation the old man would have made." When this exercise of power becomes impersonal, when rules become unresponsive to human needs, or the lumbering hierarchy is unable to respond flexibly to change, then the voice of Berkeley is heard. Its demands are for those freedoms that will eliminate "alienation" and the "Machine."

If presidents and chancellors and regents have become remote from the students in the exercise of power, then other structural organs have filled the gap by the acquisition of power. The academic department now makes decisions of academic life and death for the student. If it is large, like the English Department at Berkeley, it may have the same mechanical quality as the central administration. If it is small, like the Speech Department at Berkeley, the student may discover in it a saving influence through personal relationships with faculty and other students. This is an area where student demands for freedom overlap faculty demands for greater autonomy in academic decision-making. When the voice of Berkeley cries for the death of the "Machine," it often sees in its place the academic department, with its greater ability to respond flexibly to student and faculty needs.

The multiversity may also be defined by its purposes. An obvious and traditional purpose of any institution of higher learning is the preservation and transmission of the cultural heritage of our civilization. In addition, it is expected to acquire new knowledge. But the multiversity has grown beyond this function; it has become an agency of change as well. The new knowledge it acquires is likely to be used for the purpose of changing society. Few would deny that the convocation of physicists beneath Stagg Field during the agony of World War II changed human history.

In addition to effecting social change, the multiversity has become an agency of social criticism. Many middle-class Americans draw back in annoyance at undergraduates who presume to preach to America about Vietnam and civil rights. But if the university has the power to make major social changes, and it does, it would be an awful and soulless giant if denied conscience and moral responsibility. J. Robert Oppenheimer's sorrow, "The physicists have known sin," was the nation's hope, for it meant that the makers of Leviathan wanted to endow Leviathan and its users with their own sense of moral responsibility. In the same way, the social criticism generated by the multiversity is the nation's hope for future integrity. The activists sense the moral dimensions of the multiversity's ability to change society.

One of the reasons the multiversity is an uncomfortable giant is that these two purposes sometimes conflict with one another. It cannot transmit, criticize, and change the same aspect of Western tradition without at least suffering pangs of inconsistency. The great question of the modern university now becomes, what is to be preserved and what is to be changed? This is one function of social criticism in the multiversity. Criticism becomes an analytical tool. Those aspects of Western tradition that can withstand criticism are preserved. Those that cannot are changed. The recognition of this function prompted the classic "sifting and winnowing of truth" proclamation by the trustees of another multiversity, the University of Wisconsin, more than two generations ago.

As the multiversity grew to encompass its new purposes of social criticism and change, some old academic attitudes toward student freedom became inconsistent. The multiversity's new tool of social criticism has been turned on itself. In the name of consistency, the politically active student has demanded freedom from concepts like *in loco parentis*. In many cases the university has been afraid to give this freedom because the community at large was afraid. Granted, changes in dormitory regulations might give young university women the same freedom to make moral choices as that presently had by young telephone operators or stenographers who live in apartments. But what is the source of this inconsistent community fear? To find it, one must return to the liberal arts college.

The small college was frequently controlled by a religious denomination or greatly influenced by a limited cultural or socioeconomic point of view. This association gave the status of higher education to sectarian beliefs. The academic purpose of searching for and transmitting truth reinforced the claims to verity of the denomination that operated the college. Whether the beliefs taught were Baptist, Roman Catholic, Methodist, or Episcopalian, the college was sufficiently insulated to protect students from embarrassing contact with other value systems and to foster attitudes of parochial superiority.

In addition to this quality of insularity, the small college possessed other traits that reinforced traditional values. An example would be one mechanism it employed to maintain its consensus. Whenever a member of that small community shifted too far from the stance of his fellows, he was called an "eccentric." This kept freedom from becoming an issue, for an eccentric is not taken seriously. Too large a shift from center removed the eccentric from the community entirely. He left or was fired.

Thus the small sectarian college has been a child of a group with an insulated value system, and it has functioned to protect and perpetuate that system. As an institution, it generally could not afford, and usually did not want, the agony of self-questioning and searching. Because it functioned that way, generations of Americans have grown accustomed to thinking that this is the way higher education *should* function, that its primary purpose is to stabilize and perpetuate traditional values.

The multiversity raises freedom as a question in a way the self-contained world of the small college never could. It embraces not just Baptist, Roman Catholic, Methodist, and Episcopalian values, but Jewish, Arabic, Hindu, and agnostic as well. Thus, no one religious or philosophic stance can gain status by being The Answer to higher education's quest for truth. The multiversity does not reaffirm the superiority of one's personal beliefs, and it does not give those beliefs and values status. Those who look to the university for such support and reassurance do not find it. Their reaction to an institution that does not make moral judgments itself, but leaves its members to make these judgments as individuals, is apt to be that of hostility, fear, and confusion.

Furthermore, the research orientation and monetary resources of a multiversity generate activity that is regarded highly by society and that cannot be duplicated by the small college. The production of a linear accelerator, collaboration with the government on a lunar orbiter shot, or the direction of a billion dollar research institute are examples of projects that cannot be carried out by the small college that is the bastion of a particular value system. Thus, value-supportive institutions are made to look inferior in contrast to the multiversity. The implication is that since it takes neither money nor competence to advocate sectarian values, the institution incapable of selling quality-controlled items can always sell values. Consequently, the very presence of the multiversity undercuts the ethos of the small college in its support of traditional values.

Therefore a nervous nation puts pressure on university administrations to maintain traditional policies of *in loco parentis*, which attempt to restrict the realm of moral choices made by the undergraduate student. The moral choices made by the nineteen-year-old stenographer or soldier do not affect the average citizen and his values. But a multiversity that is officially value-neutral, and that strips the small college of its ability to give status and support to traditional values, is asking the private citizen to participate in the intellectual agony of moral decision and moral choice. The citizen who prefers a social inconsistency at the expense of a student's freedom is using that student's freedom as straw for the crumbling walls of his own value system.

If the desire to apply *in loco parentis* is inconsistent, the manner of its application is even more inconsistent. When the law makes differentiations on a sexual basis, it recognizes the earlier maturity of the female. For example, some states permit eighteen-year-old females to purchase alcoholic beverages while forbidding males to do so until they reach the age of twenty-one. There is no state in which the reverse is true. Another example is found in the laws regulating marriage. Most states permit eighteen-year-old females to marry without parental consent, but many require parental consent for the marriage of males under twenty-one. Contrast this with the way most colleges and universities apply the concept of *in loco parentis*. If housing regulations are taken as an example, one finds that females usually have to be older than their male fellows to obtain the freedom to live off-campus or in "unapproved" housing. Within the dormitory itself, the rules governing females are usually more stringent than those governing males. The tacit assumption underlying these rules that females have less "character" or less ability to make their own moral decisions is intolerable. The thrust of society in the twentieth century has been one that increasingly denies this assumption. The voice of Berkeley is clear in its demands for consistency and the freedom to make those moral choices that make responsibility meaningful.

Finally, the multiversity may be defined by its constituencies. Who are the members of the academic community, and where are the points of its articulation with society as a whole? One obvious constituency is the student population. The growth from a small college to a multiversity has changed the nature of this population in a manner that explains the intensity of student demands for freedom. The small college had a relatively homogeneous student population. Their generally white, Anglo-Saxon, and Protestant values were matched by a similarity in background and aspirations. The young men were usually there as part of the rites of passage into the social and economic structures of upper-middle-class life. The young women were sometimes there to acquire the professional credentials for a genteel occupation like teaching. They were just as likely to be there because it was an environment that offered a plentiful supply of the "right kind" of men. By and large these students had never participated in the adult patterns of marriage and earning a living. The comfortable circumstances of generous parents often meant that they were free from financial responsibility during the four years of college.

The students at a multiversity are not homogeneous. They vary greatly in age, knowledge, income, family background, and motivation. Some universities are dominated by graduate student populations whose ages range from twenty-two and twenty-three to the upper forties. These people, who are frequently married and almost always self-supporting, do not take kindly to old-fashioned paternalism.

Multiversity students also vary greatly in socioeconomic background. The graduate student in humanities with a degree from Yale, Harvard, or Princeton represents one end of the spectrum. The Negro boy who rides the bus from East Oakland to attend a university that presently charges less than $80.00 a quarter represents the other end of the spectrum. Add to this profound differences in cultural background. The heterogeneity of a student population that also includes the Israeli agnostic and the Coptic Christian cannot even be accounted for in traditional socioeconomic terms.

These physical and environmental differences all contribute to the most significant area of heterogeneity, that of motivation. Here, too, is the young man who wishes to signal his entrance into upper-middle-class life with a degree, and here, too, is the young woman who wishes to find a mate. They, however, are relatively scarce in the multiversity for two reasons. First, any small college can do the job of providing a degree and a mate. Second, the highly competitive environment of the multiversity makes earning a degree more difficult, and its heterogeneity makes an "undesirable" marriage more likely. If Junior goes to the University of California, there is a much higher probability that he will flunk out. If he does so, he will lose face in his community. If Sally goes to the local small college, almost anyone she might come home with could live next door. If she returns from Berkeley with a mate, it could well be one that lives in a "different" part of town, if ever seen in the town at all.

Because of the rigid entrance requirements and the stiff competition, the students at a multiversity are, on the average, smarter, more knowledgeable, and better educated than students at the typical small college. Because of the heterogeneity of the student population, they are more experienced in terms of marriage, earning a living, travel, and tolerance of others whose opinions or behavior they disagree with. In their ability to make informed and responsible choices they are one, if not two, levels removed from the nineteen-year-old file clerk, soldier, or mail boy. This is why the voice of Berkeley demands student freedoms that are at least the equivalent of the civic and personal freedoms available to the nonstudent.

Besides the student population, another obvious constituency of the multiversity is the faculty. They, too, are very different from their colleagues in the small college. A critical difference to the student and the institution is their research orientation. Most faculty members at a multiversity are hired, fired, or promoted on the basis of the quantity and quality of their contributions to scholarly literature. Since research takes time, they teach fewer courses and sometimes, unfortunately, spend less time on the courses they do teach.

On one level this is compatible with high quality students who are capable of getting basic information themselves. They need to be shown where the boundaries between the known and unknown are, and only those who participate in the process of the expansion of knowledge can begin to show them this. On another level, faculty research is incompatible with student demands for the elimination of anonymity and alienation. The professor whose office door is always open cannot engage in successful research. The scholar who tries to satisfy fully the demands of research and the classroom is very much like the man with two mistresses. He does not have the time or energy to do justice to both.

Another constituency of the multiversity is the administration. It has already been noted that the administration differs in size and in the extent of its power from that in the small college. Because of the extent of its power, an administrative organ like the Board of Regents changes the character of the administration as a constituency. The tenure of office for a University of California Regent is normally sixteen years. Some of the positions, however, are *ex officio* and limited to one's term in office. The Regents represent one way in which the multiversity articulates with society as a whole. When Governor Ronald Reagan and Max Rafferty sit on the Board of Regents, the state executive and legislative branches, and indirectly the people of California, become members of this constituency. Labor unions became members of this constituency when Einar O. Mohn was a Regent, and the establishment's power of money and influence is represented in the person of Mrs. William Randolph Hearst.

The extensive power of the Regents is often matched by their hostility to the university functions of social change and social criticism. They *are* the establishment, and if the establishment needs changing, they would be unlikely to admit it. When one asks people to judge justly in a contest in which they have a stake, one asks a great deal. Some student demands for freedom are directed against the power of the Board of Regents and would shrink the influence of this oligarchy that sometimes has vested interests. Most would replace it with a more democratic reorganization of the administration, one in which faculty members as well as students had a greater share of power.

There are other, less obvious, constituencies of the multiversity. The University of California staff is comprised of tens of thousands of people, whose occupations range from the clerical to maintenance to highly skilled technical jobs to teaching positions that are not "on the ladder." Demands for freedom by these staff members often approximate the arguments of labor unions. Publications like "The Employee Press" of the University of California at Berkeley and the "Stanford Faculty-Staff Newsletter" reflect their desire for participation in making policies and shaping conditions that affect them.

Some student demands for freedom have already been noted in describing the structure, purposes, and constituencies of the multiversity. But the voice of Berkeley cannot be understood unless this terribly general notion of "freedom" is seen from the students' point of view. Students have been educated in a culture where "freedom" was a shibboleth suspiciously like "God" or "Motherhood" in that it seemed to demand approval on the naming of its name. Americans have seldom withheld their verbal, financial, and military support when this name has been invoked. Some even prefer to use a different word, "license," to describe abuses of freedom, as if to say that all freedom is a "good thing" by definition. All of this merely emphasizes that freedom is an ideal prescribed by American culture.

Yet, if there is any exception to this general enthusiasm for freedom, it can be found in higher education. We seem more comfortable when speaking of freedom in the political sphere. It was Germany, not America, that fathered the application of freedom to the university in the conception of academic freedom, although academic freedom is only one of many kinds of freedom on campus. Thus, although communists can speak publicly elsewhere in North Carolina, this freedom of speech was not extended to Chapel Hill.

This represents a rather substantial ambivalence, if not outright contradiction in American commitments. Further, it is an inconsistency that spurs student demands for freedom in the multiversity. Attitudes can and do shape the issues confronting institutions, and students feel that freedom on campus has been jeopardized as a consequence of these inconsistent attitudes. Students are more concerned than faculty, not because the former are pushy and immature and the latter wise and disciplined, but because faculty members have a powerful organization, the American Association of University Professors, to provide a nationwide counterweight to offset the power of any community that might threaten their freedom. Part of the thrust of student demands for freedom is directed toward establishing nationwide instruments of power comparable to the A.A.U.P. or labor unions. The "New Student Left" recognizes that groups did not achieve "freedom" in American society until people like Sam Adams and Samuel Gompers organized effective resistance to established power.

This ambivalence in the application of freedom has become an issue in the multiversity for two reasons. The size and power of the multiversity has removed it from the control of small interest groups. The small college, when controlled by a group, could more easily be regarded as "private property." Most of our claims for freedom apply only in the public domain. We seldom if ever demand the full exercise of freedom of speech, religion, or the right to distribute pamphlets in our neighbor's living room. The second reason also has to do with size. The very fact of small size tends to create a much higher degree of consensus in the liberal arts college. When there is consensus, the presence or absence of freedom cannot be satisfactorily demonstrated. Only difference and dissent can illuminate the boundaries between freedom and control. The multiversity has the heterogeneity that provides dissent, and it is more easily seen as a public institution where public rights apply.

Trying to categorize any object of human aspiration as general as "freedom" may be attempting to divide the wind. Nevertheless, it is possible to find different kinds of freedom demanded or obtained in the university. Those civic freedoms which are not proper to the campus alone, such as freedom of speech, freedom of press, and freedom of worship, are an obvious kind. Because institutions of higher education have been in and out of the public domain to greater and lesser degrees, depending on whether or not they were private or state institutions, this civic freedom has had an ambiguous status on campus. Even the public university has sometimes been a kind of halfway house between the public marketplace, where a question of freedom of speech is decided in court, and a private home, where the owner can say, "Not in my house you don't."

Student demands for freedom on this level approximate those of the nation at large, and do not usually exceed them. What the Free Speech Movement wanted at the University of California at Berkeley was court resolution of issues concerning freedom of speech, and not decisions made by administrative fiat, as by the owner of a private home. In this sense one might view the increase of student radicalism on campus as a stage in the democratization, or perhaps socialization, of the university that has been authoritarian and capitalistic in terms of its corporate management structure.

Another kind of freedom demanded by students is personal freedom. This covers areas of choice like dress, residence, and social activities. This, too, has become an issue in the multiversity because it has outgrown the paternal and private confines of the small college. It has also become an issue because when members of the multiversity exercise the function of social criticism one of the things they look for is inconsistency. Student demands for personal freedom are based on the premise that most of these restrictions are inconsistent both with the nature of the academic community and with general patterns of personal freedom in society. These demands are best understood by comparing traditional restrictions on personal freedom with those imposed on people of a similar age who are not enrolled in a college or university.

Perhaps there were instances in the nineteenth century of employers insisting on the right to determine their employees' place of residence and to legislate the hours of their coming and going. There are none now. The nineteen-year-old with an I.Q. of 90 who was unable or too lazy to earn good grades in high school and unable or unwilling to go on to college, who now works only 35 to 40 hours a week, has all the dimensions of personal freedom that our society provides. This is not the case with this young person's intellectual polar opposite. The nineteen-year-old with an I.Q. of 125 who works a total of 50 or 60 hours a week in class, in the library, at a part-time job, and at study is often told where to live and when to come and go, and can be subjected to annoying indignities, such as having his dormitory room inspected for disorder or searched for contraband liquor. If college and university administrations continue to reject demands for personal freedom made by this student and others like him, they are in a rather ludicrous position. For then they assume that members of their select community have less intelligence, capacity, or self-control than those unable or unwilling to be students.

A third kind of freedom in the multiversity is that traditionally prescribed by the name "academic freedom." Some aspects of this, too, articulate with student demands for freedom. Graduate students who are also teaching assistants are directly concerned with academic freedom in the classroom. These people, as well as almost every kind of university employee (and large percentages of students are employed by the university), are affected by the requirement of a loyalty oath. Part of academic freedom is related to the freedom of speech guaranteed all citizens. The initial German conception of academic freedom included two areas: the freedom of the professor to profess, and the freedom of the student to hear controversy and inquire freely. The power of the American Association of University Professors and the lack of a comparable student organization has led to the lopsided development of academic freedom in the United States, although in the spring of 1968 the organization recognized the imbalance by approving the *Joint Statement on the Rights and Freedoms of Students*.

A final kind of freedom is the general kind from which this categorization has, in a sense, tried to escape. Freedom generally means freedom from control, from rules. The nation has been disturbed by student demands for freedom because it fears that students want freedom from all controls. This is not the case. Indeed, students do want the elimination of many rules and a general reduction of the number of rules. Yet their motivation is no wild urge to indulge in riot and license. After all, rules on campus are an addition, not an alternative, to the rules of society as a whole. The demand for minimal rules stems from the nature of the multiversity. Any rule assumes some common denominator about the persons to whom it will apply. Large numbers of specific rules assume a large degree of homogeneity in the population affected by them, such as was the case in the small college. The heterogeneity of the multiversity means that there is no such thing as a "typical" student. There is not even a "typical" undergraduate. When the rules assume more homogeneity than actually exists in the student population, they become damaging.

The necessary consequence of the heterogeneity of the multiversity must be the diffusion of power in rule-making. When rules are made by those structures that embody a more homogeneous population, such as a department, the rules are more likely to be fair. When people who live with the rules participate in making them, the rules are more likely to be fair. This explains student demands for increased power for structures like the academic senate and for representation on such bodies.

The necessary consequence of students' acquiring critical skills in the multiversity is that they direct these skills toward their immediate environment—the multiversity. Higher education, like the society it serves, is feeling the pains of being scrutinized. The voice of Berkeley is turning back on society and the multiversity those standards which they both profess, namely consistency and moral responsibility.

SELECTED BIBLIOGRAPHY

American Council on Education. *Spotlight on the College Student.* Washington, D.C.: The Council, 1959.

Benezet, Louis T. "Student Leadership: Dilemmas of Loyalty," *Educational Record,* 35 (October 1954), 275–280.

Daily Californian, The. Published on weekdays during the university year by Associated Students of the University of California, Berkeley. This is one of the best sources of articulate student opinion at the University of California, Berkeley. In addition, it provides both immediate and long-term reactions of students to issues associated with student freedom.

Falvey, Frances. *Student Participation in College Administration.* New York: Teachers College Press, Teachers College, Columbia University, 1952.

Freidson, Eliot. *Student Government, Student Leaders, and the American College.* New York: United States National Student Association, 1955.

Hofstadter, Richard, and Metzger, Walter P. *The Development of Academic*

Freedom in the United States. New York: Columbia University Press, 1955.

McGuire, Edward D. "The Role of the Student in College Policy Making," *The Personnel and Guidance Journal,* 38 (January 1960), 378–384.

Stanford Daily, The. Published on weekdays during the university year by the Associated Students of Stanford University. This, too, is a good source of articulate student opinion. It further provides a valuable contrast to *The Daily Californian* in that Stanford University is a medium-sized and private school. Thus where arguments in these two newspapers converge on major issues of student freedom, it is possible to begin to identify invariant trends.

Stretch, Bonnie B., and Peleaz, L. C. "Autonomy and Student Co-Government in the University of Uruguay," *Comparative Education Review,* 7 (October 1963), 166–172.

R. J. SNOW

The Political Involvement of Students: Where Freedom Begins and Ends*

> R. J. Snow, who recently completed a postdoctoral year at the Center for the Advanced Study of Education Administration, University of Oregon, is presently Assistant Professor of Political Science at University of California, Santa Barbara.

President Charles J. Hitch of the University of California, successor to Clark Kerr, said recently, "Universities are not often comfortable with the surrounding society. They cannot be and should not be, because they are agents and harbingers of change." He added, "If you find a university that is not striking some sparks, you can assume that it is dead."[1] Especially since 1964 even those who expose themselves most casually to news reports will be aware that in the matter of spark-striking, as in other regards, university campuses have been among the liveliest places in the entire country.

The sparks ignited in the Free Speech Movement in Berkeley in 1964 may never have cooled fully. The FSM, as it has become known, has been followed by additional free speech and political activities among students on the Berkeley campus. The most widely publicized were the 1966–67 anti-Vietnam War demonstrations which culminated in the disorders at the Oakland Army Induction Center and the 1968 "Vietnam Commencement," which honored those who had opposed the war policy and would have graduated from the University of California except for having been drafted, having flown the draft, or being suspended. In retrospect there

---
* The author expresses grateful thanks to Professor David Gardner, Assistant Chancellor, University of California at Santa Barbara, for reading and suggesting improvements in an earlier draft of this chapter. Professor Gardner, however, bears no responsibility for the final product.
[1] *University Bulletin: A Weekly Bulletin for the Staff of the University of California*, 16 (October 2, 1967), 1.

seems a basis to argue that the spark of large-scale student activism has spread to other American campuses from Berkeley since 1964 to ignite such additional campus conflagrations as those at the University of Wisconsin, Howard University, Roosevelt University, the University of Chicago, Northwestern, Stanford, Columbia, and at San Francisco State College, to name the most widely publicized of possible examples.

These highly dramatic incidents, as unique as each might seem, are the most recent examples of a phenomenon which is *not* new at all, that of students massing to challenge institutional authority with the goal of broadening freedoms, either their own or those of persons or groups whose cause they espouse. In the United States such activism has long been a part of the political culture,[2] and in universities in other countries student activism is not even very unusual.[3]

Among the dramatic aspects of recent student activism in the United States is the fact that relatively large numbers of students are willing to involve themselves. On the basis of survey evidence it appears that only a few of the student participants are highly militant and bent on forcing change,[4] but these few are frequently supported by a larger body of students

---

[2] On March 23, 1904, the first-page headlines of the *San Francisco Bulletin* read, "Riot at the University"; "Twelve Rushers Taken in Hand by State University and Booked for Expulsion"; "Two hundred strong, classmen lined up for battle but were fought back by school faculty and the police." Quoted from Arthur H. Sherry, "Governance of the University: Rules, Rights and Responsibilities," *California Law Review*, 54 (March 1966), 23, 25.

[3] Witness first the involvement of French students in the crisis threatening the De Gaulle regime in 1968. George Mannello, Jr. reports his observation of a 1953 student strike in Burma, focusing especially on the relationship there between students, faculty, and administrators, which is of a different sort than exists in the United States. See his "Student Strike at an Asian University: A Case History," *A.A.U.P. Bulletin*, 43 (June 1957), 249–262. See also Frank C. Newman, "The Berkeley Crisis: Recollections, Overview, and Response to Professor Louisell," *California Law Review*, 44 (March 1966), 118. Newman quotes news stories appearing in the *San Francisco Chronicle* between February 2 and March 14, 1966. Some of them reported, "It was the students' rioting [in Indonesia] which finally resulted in President Sukarno's downfall." "Mobuto [of the Congo] bans 'youth politics'." "Boumedienne's regime [in Algeria] met its first serious challenge . . . by expelling the ten leaders of 8000 striking university students. . . ." "Shutters were clamped across the storefronts [in India] . . . in silent protest against alleged police brutality during this week's student rice demonstration." "Police hurled tear gas [in Belgium] . . . at about 1000 students who massed outside their police barracks and shouted 'Murderers, Murderers'. . . ." "Some 2500 riot police . . . invaded Waseda University [in Tokyo] where students had been barricaded for a month . . . and dismantled the barricades."

[4] A six-year study of students at Stanford and the University of California at Berkeley done by Professor Jacob Katz, a Stanford psychologist, showed that no more than 10 per cent of students were involved in such activities as the civil rights movement, the New Left, or efforts to reform universities through vehicles like the Free Speech Movement. Few of the interviewed students considered themselves radically different from their parents. Between 17 and 25 per cent reported regular church attendance, but only 4 to 7 per cent said they were active in the civil rights movement. Only 2 to 4 per cent acknowledged being involved in national

with more moderate commitments, and by a certain contingent of students who appear to participate in order to provide themselves with entertainment. The number of demonstrators has added up to a minority of the total university enrollment in nearly every reported case, but in several of the recent cases, including Berkeley, the more militant position of the leaders and the "broader-than-usual" scale of student involvement have drawn attention from and startled the outside observer.

The ultimate fame of the Free Speech Movement as the first spark and the shining example of the broader-involvement activism among American university students must be credited to the fact of FSM's success. This too was dramatic. Regulations restricting student speech, association, and political advocacy on campus *were relaxed.* The result of a vote of the Berkeley faculty which the student leaders interpreted to be in favor of their position in the controversy was a signal to them that the strike was over, and most of the demonstrators were convinced that they had won.[5] One apologist-participant has written of the Free Speech Movement, "It was probably the mightiest and most successful single effort of any kind ever made by an American student body in conflict with authorities." [6]

Mass action by students after the order of the civil rights demonstrations in the South has thus in numerous instances had a significant and in certain respects a permanent impact on some of the nation's most prestigious universities. It would seem apparent that successful use of mass demonstrations as a technique in the civil rights movement influenced the choice of the same tactics by student leaders of the FSM and subsequent student demonstrations.

Student activism appears to have been stimulated in part by the attention given the participants by the news media and by the reporters' and photographers' understandable zeal to expose the most extreme and bizarre aspects of the demonstrations. Such attention makes it easier for demon-

---

or community political activities, and from 4 to 8 per cent said they were involved in campus political activities. From a report in *National Observer,* 11 (October 16, 1967), 1, 17. After a sit-in demonstration at Stanford in early May, 1968, the student body voted overwhelmingly by 70 per cent to condemn the sit-in actions that had closed the Old Union for three days and to censure the school's student-body president for participation in it. Reported in the *San Francisco Chronicle,* May 23, 1968.

[5] The importance of the vote by the Academic Senate was great in the eyes of the students who took it as their victory signal. The Academic Senate members, however, had mixed motives in voting to do what appeared to be siding with the students. It seems clear that only a part of the faculty had the sole intention of supporting the student position. For what the students had won, many were to pay a dear price. On June 21, 1967, the first 60 of 556 students arrested during the crisis appeared in Berkeley Municipal Court for sentencing. Fines ranged up to $254.00, and one jail sentence was set at 94 days. Sentencing continued on a small group basis after June 21 until all 556 of those convicted received sentences. Reported in *Santa Barbara News-Press,* June 22, 1967.

[6] Hal Draper, *Berkeley: The New Student Revolt* (New York: Grove Press, Inc., 1965), p. 117.

strators to dramatize any cause to university administrators and to the public, and thus it seems to follow that more demonstrations take place.

A further stimulus to mass student action on the campus is the slow but continual liberalization of the rules governing demonstrations and student use of campus facilities that has occurred rather widely since 1964.[7] The time which administrators have had to reflect on student activism since the events at Berkeley in 1964 has apparently allowed the partial shaping of conflict management strategies in advance of the conflict. The student-body president at Indiana University referred in the spring of 1967 to a change on his campus in "official" responsiveness to student representatives:

> The Free Speech Movement at Berkeley may be one of the best things that ever happened to students. . . . I don't know what it did to the administration at Berkeley, but here it opened the channels of communication like the Red Sea. I was given permission to sit in on the Board of Regents meetings. . . .[8]

An essential question facing administrators concerning the strategy to be used when students demonstrate is the extent to which *university* authority may legitimately be used to control a student's participation in political activities. A simple answer can be suggested: If the student is a United States citizen, his rights to freedom of political expression *begin* at the same points in American culture and constitutional tradition as do the rights of every other citizen. His rights *end*, as do the rights of a nonstudent citizen, at the point where a community law is violated.

University administrators know, however, that the university as an institution with an assigned role in society has certain legally recognized special interests in student conduct, and that they, the administrators, are

---

[7] At Berkeley in 1967, Chancellor Roger Heyns agreed to an anti-Vietnam teach-in as a part of the End the War Movement which later contributed to the mass action at the Oakland Army Induction Center. This administrative approbation would almost certainly not have been forthcoming from Heyn's predecessor in the chancellorship in 1964. Again, in 1968, after considerable controversy and heavy opposition from Governor Ronald Reagan, who called the gathering "obscene," Berkeley students were given permission to stage the "Vietnam Commencement" already mentioned. Nor has the atmosphere changed only at Berkeley. At the University of Wisconsin in February 1967, Chancellor Robben Fleming wrote a personal check in the amount of $1,470.00 to pay bond and secure the release of seventeen students whom he felt were wrongly arrested in connection with an anti-war sit-in demonstration. Reported in *Santa Barbara News-Press*, June 4, 1967. The Northwestern University administration agreed to implement almost completely the demands of sixty black students who occupied the Administration Building in protest over policies regarding housing. This action at Northwestern and similar efforts to maintain restraint in matters of student discipline at San Francisco State College and Columbia University have met with sharp criticism from persons convinced that such "coddling" is harmful to the purposes of higher education.

[8] Dean Aulick, quoted by Gerald Moore in "Who Says College Kids Have Changed?" *Life*, 62 (May 19, 1967), 96.

responsible for utilization of this unique authority. They thus may impose restraints upon student behavior in the event that they feel it constitutes a serious threat to the university's legitimate goals. A *student's* freedoms, therefore, legally end *somewhat short* of the freedoms of the nonstudent citizen.

The issue for administrators and other parties involved, including students, faculty, and community leaders and officials, is the definition of the particular points in the area of freedom of action and expression at which the university's right to maintain the integrity of its special mission conflicts with the individual rights of the student. The issue is highly complex because of the social and political values of the "other parties involved" within the community. Pressures upon administrators emanate from constituent groups within the campus community and in the broader community in which the university is located. The university is "tied by a thousand threads" [9] to the society which surrounds it, and thus community values and demands impose inescapable constraints upon the behavior of administrators, faculty, and students when student demonstrations precipitate a major public crisis. Fortunately, not all student political action is of a negative character, and not all of the negative activism reaches crisis proportions.

Issues which have set off student protest appear to be of two fundamental types. The first set of issues is oriented outward from the university, and includes those relevant to Vietnam, civil rights, and public policy generally. Concern with these issues seems to imply a conception of the university as an instrument to be used in forcing social change. This "revolutionary" philosophy underlies such recent activity as the massive peace vigils, campaigns against military training on university campuses, picket lines opposing the use of campus placement facilities by Dow Chemical and other companies manufacturing war materiel, anti-draft demonstrations (since the draft is an issue which hangs like an omnipresent cloud over the heads of virtually all physically eligible males in the student community), and demonstrations against university decisions regarding the location of new facilities when the consequence of construction involves the loss of living and recreation space by minority groups.

A second set of issues is related to the institution itself and implies that the university's mission may not be the central issue but rather that rules and relationships within the institution need reform in ways which do not affect its mission, or which could provide for greater rationality in seeking to carry out its mission. This "reform" philosophy is expressed when students boycott classes after popular professors are not rehired, when they demonstrate for longer parietal visiting hours in campus housing, or when they voice objections about housing facilities, the racial composition of athletic teams, and the lack of a significant voice in university rule-making,

---

[9] Max Mark, "The Meanings of Academic Freedom," *A.A.U.P. Bulletin*, 43 (September 1957), 505.

application, or adjudication. These feelings are exemplified by the statement of a student leader of the Free Speech Movement who wrote at an early point in the crisis:

> [There is] . . . a chronic condition . . . inherent in the nature of the university's structure as it now exists: absolutist rule by the administration. Whatever the cause of such a development, the fact is that the jurisdiction of the administration is unchallenged by any organized body. The only means of opposing a particular action of the university is through spontaneous organization of those who oppose that action.[10]

Both the "revolutionaries" and the "reformists" (and students as individuals are not easily separable into such groups; many of the same students are active in both types of demonstrations) are capable of and engaged in positive actions as well. In addition to a willingness to debate, demonstrate, and disobey, students in impressive numbers have joined the Peace Corps, tutored children in culturally deprived neighborhoods, joined VISTA projects, or volunteered for summer and part-time service in locally directed projects to alleviate poverty. As early as 1961 (which is only early in the relative sense that it was *before* passage of the major civil rights legislation and poverty program), California's Governor Brown stated:

> Thank God . . . for students protesting and freedom-riding, for students listening to society's dissidents, for students going out into the fields with our migratory workers, and marching off to jail with our segregated Negroes. At last we're getting somewhere. The colleges have become boot camps for citizenship—and citizen leaders are marching out of them.[11]

The deeply felt idealism of many persons with university affiliations, faculty as well as students, has impelled them to seek direct personal experience at the "cutting edges" of social movements, where the needs for change are first highlighted and where pressures for reform take shape. In the direct sense that students and faculty have been aware, committed, and actually involved, universities have provided leadership in the expression of social concern and in the support of a broad liberalization of social attitudes in the United States.

For perspective it must be stated again that even the most massive of the student demonstrations do not appear to have involved majorities of students on any given campus. But militant student leaders have learned well the lessons in social drama taught earlier by the civil rights movement. Whenever it is possible, as it was in Berkeley, to persuade between five

---

[10] Graduate Coordinating Committee, a Free Speech Movement affiliate group, in a leaflet entitled, *Are You All Right, Jack?* The leaflet is reprinted in Draper, *Berkeley*, pp. 196–199.

[11] Quoted from a speech to the graduates of the University of Santa Clara in June, 1961, in Draper, *Berkeley*, p. 103.

and ten thousand interested students from a single campus to rally *en masse*, or to gather between five and six hundred students who are willing to submit to arrest, fines, and imprisonment to dramatize a cause, the students will surely succeed. Student political action is now a highly visible part of the American political culture. It is "bigger," more assertive, and more successful than it has been in the past, and it is more consequential socially as well, not only because of its size and success and the sincerity of its participants, but also because of a broadening and deepening change which seems to be taking place in the social conscience of the whole American people. A broader social awareness contributes increased sensitivity to the issues which student activism spotlights.

In late August 1967, student leaders representing radical viewpoints were invited to the Center for the Study of Democratic Institutions in Santa Barbara, California, to discuss, according to a newspaper report, "the ills of U. S. campuses." [12] An official of the sponsoring Center explained, "The Center's interest was in hearing from representative student dissidents from the major campuses whose basic complaint is that the adult world does not understand them because it doesn't listen to them." [13] More than a dozen conferees represented (unofficially, of course) Harvard, Howard University, Indiana University, Stanford, several branches of the University of California, and Washington University at St. Louis. What resulted was "a far-ranging bull session on radicalism," [14] especially as it was felt to bear on university life.

Some of the student proposals called for the overthrow of the university structure as it now exists, and one student even proposed the overthrow of the U. S. Government. He advocated student terrorism on a scale broad enough to "demoralize and castrate America." Another suggested that the capacity of the university to "prop up our political institutions," especially in the Vietnam War effort, must be attacked. He advocated anti-ROTC demonstrations and student interference with military drills and classes. He suggested hampering defense research on university campuses by massing to block governmental advisers and research faculty from their offices. As a worthwhile off-campus activity the same student suggested that government office staffs could be hampered by the "introduction of a small quantity of LSD in . . . government coffee urns." [15]

Most views were more moderate than these, and the conference produced neither very firm conclusions nor any specific guidelines for radical action on the campus. The expression of the more aggressive attitudes, however, produced the following predictable reactions from the public and the local press. First, a number of editorials appeared locally which

[12] *Los Angeles Times*, August 26, 1967.
[13] Letter to the Editor of the *Santa Barbara News-Press*, from Harry S. Ashmore, Executive Vice President of the Center for the Study of Democratic Institutions; published August 30, 1967.
[14] *Santa Barbara News-Press*, August 25, 1967.
[15] *Ibid.*

were sharply critical of the Center for the Study of Democratic Institutions for gathering radical students together in the first place. Second, the local newspaper printed a series of critical letters to the editor from persons whose perspective appeared to be very conservative. And third, as a direct political result of the conference the local representative to Congress announced he had requested the Internal Revenue Service to "review" the tax-free status granted the Center as an educational institution. The Congressman and the letter writers doubted both the objectivity and the value of the educational contribution made by the Center's personnel and programs.

Public reaction to students' opinions seems to be generally negative. A negative reaction to the extreme student views might well have been expected, but the immediately critical response to the conference was quite typical of public response to student demonstrations as well. It may be that the widely publicized statements of the more militant and socially nonconforming students have misshapen the public's perception of what is happening on the modern campus. Whatever the cause, it seems to be true that the image of today's student held by large numbers of the public is in many respects inaccurate.

The hippie culture has not taken over the modern university campus, nor will it, although some aware administrators would probably prefer dealing with the largely innocent antics of the "peace and love" advocates with long hair, beards, and unconventional dress to dealing with the more threatening actions of the highly militant minority. Experiments with sex and drugs on the campus, though they occupy administrative attention, do not involve large numbers of students. Recent reports from college campuses indicate that student values are largely those held by parents as well, and that frequently the conforming majority of students is as perplexed and unhappy with its nonconformist hippie peers as is the general public.[16]

Nor is the campus filled with "pinkos," or with Communist youth cells whose members' "impressionistic minds" have been poisoned by fuzzy-minded leftist faculty or by the Red-leaning speakers invited to campus. The more rational in the general public would be startled to learn how much of the administrator's attention is absorbed in efforts to reassure indignant citizens. When students demonstrate, a question frequently asked administrators by the public is, "Why do you let them get away with it?" As one commentator put it:

> Public indignation, generated by expressions of protest and dissent by students and faculty members which run counter to popular public feeling, stimulates the urge to punish and suppress by any means readily

[16] See Gerald Moore, "Who Says College Kids Have Changed?"; also "Worried About Today's Young People?" in *U.S. News and World Report*, 63 (October 30, 1967), 44–46, reporting results from campus surveys at Rice University, Allegheny College, University of California at Irvine, Duke University, and Indiana University showing that students' values were essentially the same as those of their parents.

at hand. And what means are more convenient, swift, and effective than the simple expedient of throwing the ungrateful rascals out? [17]

Such an expedient, of course, is too simple. In the first place, administrative problems pushed away are not solved. Secondly, there are counterpressures brought to bear against those of the disquieted general public. Some of these are direct hindrances to arbitrary action like expulsion that grow out of the student's legal position and his individual rights and freedoms. Some other counterpressures are imposed by the university's more obviously "political" public, to whom, in addition to the general public, it must be responsive.

University presidents, according to former University of California President Clark Kerr, are fundamentally "mediators." They play a highly visible mediating role between the public and the university community, and thus they are the focus of much of the indignant public pressure aroused by student activities. Within the campus confines the president mediates between the university's bureaucracy, which he is charged to administer, and the institution's governing body, the members of which are usually called regents or trustees. In an ideal situation his offices provide channels of communication and thus mediation between regents, faculty, and students. If he is effective, the president may mediate between individual members of the board of regents.

Off campus the president may frequently become deeply involved in the ongoing processes of state government and politics. He mediates between regents and state legislators as an official representative of the university. In competition with representatives of other institutions created by the authority of the state, the president and his staff make appeals for state-appropriated money. The most skillful university representatives fulfill roles during the legislative session which are strikingly like those of the pejoratively labeled "lobbyist." In the scramble for state funds a president may find it very helpful, as would any other lobbyist, to seek out privately key legislators to whom detailed information may be provided regarding the vital nature of the need for support of the public university budget.

On other governmental levels the university president may mediate between his institution and the contracting or granting agencies. In Washington he may seek federal funds for a university project, participate in drafting research agreements, or in coordinating other aspects of the growing web of interrelationships between the federal government and the state university. At home the president may deal with officials of local and county governments to coordinate university services provided them. He may further coordinate relationships between the university and representatives of economic interests within the state, many of whom maintain frequent contact, both for philanthropic reasons and for the purpose of

[17] Sherry, "Governance of the University," p. 25.

buying certain university services. A look at the demanding role of the modern university president gives the best indication of how deeply the state university is immersed in political life, and how directly its existence depends upon highly political decisions which may be made at any level of government.[18]

Through it all the university must walk an ideological tightrope of "freedom from political influence"—a way determined by one of the most highly prized principles of the American political culture, that of the separation of education from politics. This principle is sometimes embodied in specific directives from boards of regents limiting the activity of university personnel to supposedly nonpolitical areas.[19] It is supported by the sometimes mistaken notion of faculty and students that freedom from political interference is all that is meant by the concept of academic freedom.

Immersed in politics, but constrained by the ideology of freedom from political influence, the university is in a highly delicate position. In the face of public pressure which mounts in times of crisis, the university administrator is understandably sensitive about the possibility that student action may permanently damage the capacity of the institution to attain its goals. Because of the serious political risks involved, the university can assimilate only with great difficulty incidents in which students openly flaunt social mores, push the laws to their limits, or take actions which threaten to "politicize" the campus by appearing to place it on one side or another of a politically charged issue. It should be no surprise that administrators' responses to student political involvement have been mixed, sometimes indeterminate and uncertain, and further that in times of crisis with students there has been a relatively high turnover rate among administrators.

Public pressure and political risk, however important, are only secondary complicating factors in the determination of when and how university authority may be utilized. The heart of the matter would seem to lie in the meaning of the concept of academic freedom and in a determination of the mission of the university. Before discussing these matters, however, it is essential to establish the extent to which the law restricts administrative impositions upon student conduct.

There *are* legal restrictions upon the university's right to expel or otherwise punish a student. Students *do* have rights as citizens which they do not surrender when they enroll in a university. These include specifically

---

[18] An intensive examination of administration in higher education is reported by Terry F. Lunsford in "Authority and Ideology in the Administered University," *American Behavioral Scientist*, 11 (May–June 1968), 5–13.

[19] According to Clark Kerr, at the University of California, "The regulations make it clear that it is essential that university facilities should not be used in ways which will involve the institution itself in the political, religious, or other controversial issues of the day. Thus they forbid the use of such facilities for the purposes of soliciting political party memberships, or for purposes incompatible with the educational objectives of the institution." From a speech in acceptance of the Seventh Alexander Meiklejohn Award for Contributions to Academic Freedom (*A.A.U.P. Bulletin*, 50 [June 1964], 185).

the right to protection against arbitrary and unreasonable action by university officials, the right to reasonable process of law when action against them is pending, and the right to expect that the university will not act against them for offenses which do not fall within its rightful area of jurisdiction.[20]

What is arbitrary and unreasonable action on the part of the university against a student? This is still a point of some legal dispute. One theory of the legal nature of the university-student relationship revolves around the doctrine of *in loco parentis*, which implies that the university stands in place of the parent and has the same disciplinary authority. The disciplinary prerogatives of the university, including the right to expulsion and some forms of physical punishment, have been upheld by the courts in the past on the basis of this doctrine. *In loco parentis* preserves the right of the university to be somewhat arbitrary, as parents are somewhat arbitrary, and recently its application has been curtailed. Legal experts have noted "the factual demise of *in loco parentis* as an adequate basis for relegating university students to a condition of second-class citizenship." [21]

A competing legal theory of the relationship between university authority and student rights is that which perceives the university to be a service-rendering institution with student constituents. In this view, "students are independent adults, free to behave as they wish subject to rules proscribing only that conduct importantly detrimental to the functioning of the university." [22] This latter view of students as consumers with certain rights appears to be the basis of the more recent formulation and enforcement of student regulation. Frequently both views are embodied in varying gradations in a single university's policies.

The two conceptions pull administrators in opposite directions in establishing rules for student conduct. The *in loco parentis* notion, which stresses the quasi-familial nature of the university-student relationship, calls for informal, perhaps even unwritten rules which are to be administered liberally with the special goal of rehabilitating the offender. Thus, depending on the social costs and possibilities of rehabilitation, the punishment administered might range from the very lenient to the very severe (expulsion). The "constituent" theory, on the other hand, impels rule-makers toward the construction of clearly specified rules with well-defined punishments attached.

[20] For this section of the paper the author relies heavily on a symposium on student rights and campus rules published in the *California Law Review*, 54 (March 1966), 1–178. The papers by Professors Sherry and Newman previously cited are among those included in the symposium.
[21] Edward Van Alstyne, "Student Academic Freedom and the Rule-Making Powers of Public Universities: Some Constitutional Considerations," *Law In Transition Quarterly*, 2 (1965), 1; quoted in Sherry, "Governance of the University," p. 28. On this point see also C. Michael Otten, "Ruling out Paternalism: Students and Administrators at Berkeley," *American Behavioral Scientist*, 11 (May–June 1968), 28–33.
[22] Ira Michael Heyman, "Some Thoughts on University Disciplinary Proceedings," *California Law Review*, 54 (March 1966), 74–75.

These punishments may also range to expulsion, but their formal nature may offer slightly more protection against arbitrary action.

Any rules, however, whether formal or informal, may be arbitrary. They are likely to be less so if careful heed is paid by university officials to obtaining student advice and opinion at the stage when rules are formulated. Student participation in rule formulation is a goal sought on most campuses by students, and normally by administrators and faculty as well. On most campuses it is implemented to some extent but rarely enough to satisfy students. Although students' views are actively sought by deans and university presidents, the recommendations most frequently accepted deal with narrow areas of student social life which are only tangential to the university's academic programs and only minimally threatening to university interests.

The impotence of student government during the Berkeley Free Speech Movement was partially admitted by its duly elected leader in 1964. He stated, "Over-all we've missed the boat. We have in many ways been inadequate in dealing with the free speech problem." [23] The student government found itself shunted aside as the Free Speech Movement picked up momentum. Communication with university authorities through the Associated Student Senate did not appear to the demonstrators as a worthwhile alternative. With meaningful authority largely confined to campus social life, student governments are referred to by students themselves as "sandbox governments," which exist to pacify the students, but not to make important decisions. Naturally, there are some pressures for change.

A student leader at the University of Wisconsin told a newspaper reporter that his followers felt students were a class unto themselves, and that they should be responsible only to themselves.[24] At the radical students' seminar previously mentioned, a participant who was experienced in the civil rights movement proposed a national student activist organization designed to obtain "student power." Specifically he proposed that students and faculty, rather than administrators, be allowed to make decisions jointly about experimental summer sessions, "longer sex hours," admitting "underground" newspapers to campus, free textbooks, and the granting of tenure to faculty members.[25]

The broadest grants of authority to students have been in the area of rule enforcement rather than rule formulation. Some universities, among them the University of Oregon and Indiana University, have successfully granted broader latitude to students.[26] Generally, where more authority has

[23] Charles Powell, Associated Student Senate President, quoted in Draper, *Berkeley: The New Student Revolt*, p. 126.
[24] David Smothers, United Press International, "'Student Power'—Is It a Moving Force on Campus?" *Santa Barbara News-Press*, June 4, 1967.
[25] *Santa Barbara News-Press*, August 25, 1967.
[26] The University of Oregon, according to one of its faculty members, Hans A. Linde, is a "seeming libertarian utopia," where "students collect civil rights funds for Mississippi, and many have gone south themselves; Oregon has Vietnam protests and teach-ins; Oregon has Gus Hall speaking to eleven thousand in the football

been granted it has been used responsibly. Professor Arthur H. Sherry suggests,

> "consent of the governed" represents a primary value in the technique of personnel administration. If those who are bound by the regulations have had some significant voice in shaping them, the task of the administrator is eased immeasurably.

He suggests further that if students are given a stronger, more meaningful voice in rule formulation they will be motivated to act responsibly. Thus they will be "largely freed from compulsions to act like children because of a conviction that they are treated as children." [27]

A student's right to involve himself politically should not be imposed upon unless reasonable precautions to assure due process have been taken by the prosecuting authority. The rights to reasonable process of law mean, in their essence, that a student has a right to fair treatment when any possible harmful action is pending against him. In this sense due process is related closely to an accused person's right to protection against arbitrary action. In the development of the due process concept, however, there are certain specific protections which should be guaranteed.[28] Some of them are summarized below.

Rules: Rules applicable to students must be written clearly and publicized adequately so that knowledge of their content by those students to whom they apply can be reasonably assumed.

Notice: When action is taken against a student, he should be served with adequate and immediate notice, including a full statement of charges made against him, the authority underlying the rules allegedly broken, and the options open, including the time he has to prepare a defense, should he choose to defend himself.

Hearing: A public hearing should be convened (unless the student asks for a closed hearing) by the prosecuting authority. The hearing should be

---

stadium and brings religious speakers to the campus. . . . Oregon has no rules against any of this. The University's president regularly exhorts its students to become committed, *engagé*" ("Campus Law: Berkeley Viewed from Eugene," *California Law Review*, 54 [March 1966], 41). Professor Linde also quotes the following from the University of Oregon policy on off-campus speakers: "Any faculty or recognized student groups may invite to the campus any speaker the group would like to hear; . . . The appearance of an invited speaker on the campus does not involve the endorsement of his views by the faculty." The author of the present paper witnessed peaceful and well-attended speeches by American Nazi leader George Lincoln Rockwell and LSD advocate Timothy Leary on the University of Oregon campus during the academic year, 1966–67. At Indiana University a bill of student rights was accepted by the administration which granted "authoritative or advisory power for students in all decisions which concern them" (Moore, "Who Says College Kids Have Changed?" p. 96).

[27] Sherry, "Governance of the University," pp. 34–35.

[28] The following paragraphs rely heavily on the symposium papers of Professors Sherry (especially pp. 36–38), and Heyman (especially pp. 78–86).

promptly scheduled, and during the course the accused student should be allowed to question witnesses against him and to call witnesses in his own defense. If the hearing is formal (in exceptional circumstances) the accused student should have the right to legal counsel should he desire it. A student's right to protection against self-incrimination should be protected.

Record: A careful record should be kept showing compliance with all requirements of due process and an accurate reporting of the testimony produced at the hearing.

Findings: The prosecuting authority, whether administrators, faculty, or other students, should produce a report of the findings of the hearing in writing, and a copy should be made available to the accused student.

Review: In any case where serious consequences to the accused may result, either through conviction and punishment or as a result of the action of inquiry itself, a review of the entire proceeding by a higher authority and the right to appeal the decision should be granted the accused.

Most administrators experienced in dealing with students will find a formal statement of due process requirements unfamiliar and somewhat unrealistic. The primary tasks of deans of students are not legal or judicial, and most student problems are handled routinely and informally. The exceptional and infrequent case will be the one requiring special attention and close adherence to due process guarantees. Nevertheless, an awareness of student rights is a useful safeguard for administrators. It provides a better guarantee of fair treatment and greater protection against the possibility of arbitrary punishment.

Fairness to students is a highly valued goal of administrators, and it should be attainable. Professor Sherry states that rules and regulations imposed on student conduct by university officials constitute

> in a very real sense the . . . criminal law of the campus. Beyond that, it is a law whose penalties may have an impact upon a student's career, livelihood, or reputation of far more disastrous proportions than conviction for crime. The stigma of expulsion or suspension and even the effect of so minimal a penalty as a recorded reprimand may become a lifelong handicap.[29]

Concern for the protection of the interests of accused students has not always been characteristic of administrative disciplinary actions. Under intense public and political pressures for quick action, and sometimes facing deadlines of their own, it can be a severe strain on administrators to be forced to proceed cautiously. Yet, in an ideal and detached discussion of administrative prerogatives in crisis situations it would never occur to administrators that protection of the rights of a university student would have less importance than would the protection of the rights of a habitual pickpocket.

Regarding jurisdiction the most obvious point to be made is that existing community law enforcement agencies have the primary responsibility

[29] Sherry, "Governance of the University," pp. 36–37.

The Political Involvement of Students

for prosecuting offenders when laws have clearly been violated. The complicating factors for community law enforcement officials are those which crop up when their jurisdiction is questioned because the offender is a student, or because the offense is committed within the boundaries of the campus. A further factor to be considered is the seriousness of the violation. In minor matters where the offense has greater consequence for the university or its constituents than it has for the general community, the university may well be justified in taking jurisdiction away from the community.

If, however, an offense is committed by a nonstudent on campus, or by a student off campus, or if the offense is of a serious nature with implications extending beyond the university community, university officials are well advised to yield jurisdiction and to offer cooperation to regularly established community law enforcement agencies. Even as a student does not surrender his civil rights and liberties when he enrolls at a university, neither does he move within a wall of protection afforded by the university which makes his rights superior to those of the ordinary citizen.[30]

A further point may be made to the effect that courts have recognized that the university has special interests which are to be considered in jurisdictional questions. These interests are of two fundamental types: academic, which relate to improper use of copyrighted materials (plagiarism), cheating on examinations, establishing academic restrictions on degree requirements, and so on; and nonacademic, which include the interest of the university in the proper flow of traffic through the campus, and in the health, morals, and welfare of its student constituents. On the basis of its interest, the university is granted certain authority to regulate hours and standards in fraternity and sorority housing and to protect students from financial fraud and drugs, etc. Courts have interpreted the university's authority rather broadly in the past.

Finally, certain obligations incumbent upon students relate to the question of university jurisdiction. *Obligations* of students are as important as their rights, though obligations are not as easily and specifically defined. They grow out of the right which society grants to the university to fulfill its own mission. It is expected that university constituents willingly obligate themselves to support the university in its basic purpose, and any serious threat to that purpose is illegitimate. What, then, is the mission of the university?

The mission of the university may be broadly stated as "to impart learning and to advance the boundaries of knowledge." [31] Thus the specific

[30] Professor Robert M. O'Neil, another contributor to the *California Law Review* symposium, suggests that there is an artificiality in attempting to distinguish between "on-campus" and "off-campus" activities of students as a primary consideration of how the law applies to them. Legally the distinction is not as clear as it might popularly be believed.

[31] Sherry, "Governance of the University," p. 27. The position taken here is that the mission of the university can be defined *acceptably* in these rather traditional terms. It must be recognized, however, that this point is the crucial one around which a great deal of philosophical and moral discussion revolves. Recent

tasks in which the university community should be engaged include teaching, learning, and research. Faculty members, clearly, are to do the teaching and most of the research. Through research they join the students in learning. The important point to consider is that the primary reason for the student to affiliate with the university is *to learn*. Such a conception of a student's relationship to an educational institution is hardly earthshaking. Its importance at the present time is that no one is quite sure what it means. There are differing interpretations, clear only in the context of meanings which have been attached to the concept of academic freedom.

If the university is to make reasonable progress toward its own goals, it must operate in an atmosphere of reasonable freedom. As freedom applies to those groups directly engaged in pursuit of the university's goals, it is labeled "academic," implying that it is of a special nature. One conception of its nature is elaborated by Arthur O. Lovejoy of the American Association of University Professors, one of the groups which has expressed the most concern about its proper maintenance.

> Academic freedom . . . is the freedom of the teacher or research worker in higher institutions of learning to investigate and discuss the problems of his science and to express his conclusions whether through publication or through the instruction of students, without interference from political or ecclesiastical authority, or from the administrative officials of the institution in which he is employed, unless his methods are found by qualified bodies of his own profession to be clearly incompetent or contrary to professional ethics.[32]

One implication of this definition is that academic freedom has only an indirect meaning for students. As Professor Sidney Hook explains:

> Strictly speaking it is nonsense to speak of "academic freedom" for students. Students have a right to *freedom to learn*. The best guarantee of freedom to learn is the academic freedom of those who teach them. Where teachers are deprived of academic freedom, students are *ipso facto* deprived of the freedom to learn.[33]

That the student's right is to learn further implies that he has attendant obligations which should morally prevent him from actions such as political

---

examples of such discussion include Robert A. Nisbet, "Is There a Crisis of the University?" *The Public Interest*, No. 10 (Winter 1968), pp. 55–64. See also Martin Trow, "Conceptions of the University: The Case of Berkeley," and Troy Duster, "Student Interest, Student Power, and the Swedish Experience," both in *American Behavioral Scientist*, 11 (May–June 1968), 14–27. Clearly, a different notion of the university's mission will provide different parameters within which academic freedom must be defined, and thus a set of rights and responsibilities applying to administration, faculty, and student different from those discussed here.

[32] Quoted in Sidney Hook, "Academic Freedom and the Rights of Students," in Seymour M. Lipset and Sheldon S. Wolin (eds.), *The Berkeley Student Revolt: Facts and Interpretations* (Garden City, N.Y.: Doubleday & Company, Inc., 1965), p. 432.

[33] *Ibid.*, pp. 432–433.

involvement which might limit the academic freedom of the faculty which teaches him. Or, as stated earlier, a student must respect the mission of the university and refrain from hampering its accomplishment. If he does not, he is misperceiving the latitude of his freedom to learn and he justifies action taken against him. Professor Hook continues:

> Students . . . must earn the right to continue as students. Higher education is not a civil right. A person does not have to earn the right to a fair trial or freedom of speech, press or assembly. But he must earn the right to become and remain a university student.[34]

A second implication of the Lovejoy definition of academic freedom is based on the phrases stating that investigation, discussion, and expressed conclusions of teachers and researchers should be free from interference by political, ecclesiastical, or administrative authority. The broad suggestion here is that control of a university's research facilities (for investigation), its library and other facilities, and its student curriculum (for discussing and expressing conclusions) should primarily be in the hands of *faculty* (the teachers and research workers).

A third implication is closely related to the second. Decisions as to the competence of teachers and research workers are to be rendered only by qualified bodies of the relevant profession, who are to base their decisions on the competence of the methods employed and on the ethics of their application.

Both the second and third of these implications have been implemented on most university campuses to some degree. Individual academic departments have been granted broad latitude in curriculum decisions, in the use of facilities, in the control and expenditure of certain funds, and in the establishment of minimum academic requirements for students. Tenure decisions (those providing protection from authority) are frequently made by the collective judgment of peers on recommendation of close faculty associates.

Students are frequently dissatisfied with this interpretation of academic freedom because it restricts both their off-campus activities (because of political threat) and their on-campus demands (when those demands impose on prerogatives that are properly those of the faculty). Students assert that they should be admitted as junior citizens to the community of scholars of the university with certain rights and privileges. They would subscribe to a position such as the following:

> The development of the character and intellect of university students cannot be viewed as a one-way process, in which the university gives and the students take whatever is given. It is a two-way process, in which the students give their time, their energy and their loyalty, and

[34] *Ibid.*, p. 434.

the other members of the academic community give in return. University education, in other words, is not simply a privilege provided by society to those of its children who can benefit from it. University education is a set of mutual obligations, in which society provides the student with certain privileges and opportunities, and he in turn commits a part of himself to society's purposes. His commitment is as important as society's, and must receive equal weight in the thinking of both educators and statesmen.[35]

While recognizing the obligations incumbent upon them, students subscribing to this philosophy feel that academic freedom, and specifically their freedom to learn, should be interpreted broadly enough to allow them to express themselves freely and collectively about social issues, and further to allow them a voice, along with the faculty, in decisions about faculty tenure, establishment of academic requirements, and policy regarding the use of university facilities. Freedom to learn, they feel, is not enhanced by some common requirements for faculty tenure, such as publication and community service, both of which require faculty withdrawal from teaching obligations. In the students' view, good teaching, which brings about good learning, is not adequately compensated.

The issue now being decided is, "What does academic freedom mean, and for whom?" The question is essentially the same as that of where student freedom begins and ends, because the concept of academic freedom is the dynamic base-point for determining the power relationships between students, faculty, and administration. As its interpretation changes, so do the relationships between students, faculty, and administrators. Whatever academic freedom means at a given time, and for whom, will determine the extent of legitimate university authority over student conduct.

At present it may be said that the interpretation of academic freedom seems to be shifting in a liberal direction. Power has moved away from administrators and toward faculty. In small bits some increased voice is being given students. Since Berkeley there has been increased support for the view that universities should be cautious in attempting to regulate student political activity, especially that which occurs off campus. The contrast between the attitude of Chancellor Roger Heyns at Berkeley during the 1967 demonstrations against the Vietnam war and that of Chancellor Edward Strong in 1964 offered clear evidence of greater willingness to support student views. That Heyns defended the students, even in the face of criticism by the Governor and Lieutenant Governor of California, indicates a change in the actual meaning of academic freedom for students.

As the concept of academic freedom is broadened and as university faculties exercise more authority it will be more common for student ac-

---

[35] Jerome C. Byrne, *Report on the University of California and Recommendations to the Special Committee of the Regents of the University of California*, May 2, 1965, p. 2; quoted in Sherry, "Governance of the University," p. 35.

tivism regarding on-campus issues to be directed toward faculties rather than toward university administrators.[36]

New interpretations for the concept of academic freedom will definitely result from the new student activism. As it evolves the concept should place neither students, faculty, nor administrators in any superior position before the law. Its "special" nature should be guarded, and it should serve as a restraining influence on the behavior of all three groups.

Administrative policy should be carefully directed toward maintaining academic freedom. Most administrators have already come to recognize that universities do not necessarily "endorse" student viewpoints, and thus "politicize" the university, when they defend the rights of students to express themselves.

Faculties should be conscious, as their prerogatives increase, of the need to protect against the misuse or misapplication of academic freedom. They should at the same time be actively concerned with the definition of the university's mission and purpose in society.

Students must exercise restraint in their attempts to broaden their freedom to learn. They need to recognize the visible and highly sensitive position of the university in society and the very real potential that their actions, if they exceed certain limits, as they seem to have done in a number of recent instances, may help to destroy the university as we now know it, and with it, whatever part of academic freedom the students now share.

[36] Dr. William E. Boyd, who reportedly was "brought to Berkeley from Ohio State University . . . to be the administration's trouble shooter on student problems," stated recently that campus radicals have already shifted their attention from the administration to the faculty and curriculum. He implied that in some noticable measure, "the heat was off" the administrators when he said that there were considerably fewer student-administrator problems in November of 1967 than there had been when he was hired in August 1966. Reported in *Santa Barbara News-Press*, November 2, 1967. An interesting analysis of the changing relationships between constituent groups on the university campus is available in Burton R. Clark, "The New University," *American Behavioral Scientist*, 11 (May–June 1968), 1–5.

LOUIS C. VACCARO
THOMAS E. WOLF

Student Rights
and
Academic Due Process

Louis C. Vaccaro is Vice President for Academic Affairs at the University of Portland. Thomas E. Wolf, formerly a member of the faculty of Gonzaga University, received his J.D. degree in 1967 and is presently a practicing attorney in Portland, Oregon.

The current interest in problems relating to the governance of academic institutions has occasioned a whole host of questions about the settlement of conflict in the university: How much of a voice, if any, should students have in establishing and administering regulations pertaining to student affairs on campus? What procedures ought to be followed in adjudicating differences that arise among various individuals in the same academic institution? Does a person surrender his constitutional rights when he enters a university, public or private, as a student?

Although there has been an increasing amount of interest in the conflict which has erupted on campuses over the past five years, little substantial study has been made of the issue of student rights and freedoms as they relate to the legal principle of "due process of the law." [1] It is not the purpose of this essay to provide an exhaustive analysis of this subject, but rather to provide an overview of the topic as it relates to student rights and a reasonable discussion of how the principle of due process relates to the larger issue of conflict settlement within the American university. We are of the opinion that the major issue for the campus political activists during the next two to

---

[1] James A. Perkins, "The University and Due Process" (Washington, D.C.: American Council on Education, 1967); and Clark Byse, "The University and Due Process: A Somewhat Different View," *The Chronicle of Higher Education*, May 6, 1968, p. 6.

three years will be *how* individual and group grievances can best be settled.[2] We believe, further, that this will involve, to an increasing degree, application of the principle of due process.

Many of the problems of student discontent and alienation on campus have been attributed to the impersonal, bureaucratic nature of present-day institutions of higher education. Students claim—with increasing support from faculty and others—that many of the rules and regulations developed and applied by university administrators are archaic and insensitive. Moreover, the claim is made that many of these rules are also an abridgement of their rights as citizens—rights guaranteed by the First and Fourteenth Amendments of the United States Constitution.

In his speech, "The University and Due Process," President James Perkins of Cornell University referred to a number of problem areas that have already emerged as a result of recent student interest in challenging the heretofore uncontested rights and authority of the university in setting and administering regulations affecting student life on campus. Instances reflecting these problem areas include a U. S. Merchant Marine Academy student's bringing suit against his being expelled from the Academy on the grounds that the Academy's rules and the procedures for their enforcement violated his constitutional rights of due process and a suit challenging the right of the State University of Iowa to impose higher tuition rates on out-of-state students. The basis of the latter case is that such discrimination between residents and nonresidents threatens to deprive nonresident students of equal protection of the law.[3]

The implication is clear—those persons in the university who claim abridgement of their rights are no longer content to accept the judgment of university committees and administrators and appeal their cases from one level of authority to another. Rather, they show increasing willingness to take their cases to the civil courts. To be sure, many of the more forward thinking universities are planning ahead to avoid such civil action by developing elaborate and effective systems of campus adjudication. In such cases, however, the principle of due process is also involved.[4]

When it comes to guaranteeing rights within an academic institution, careful thought must be given to guaranteeing the rights of *all* individuals. Specifically, to guarantee the students' rights within the university calls for guaranteeing the rights of others at the same time. In doing this, the university must be careful to protect the students' rights as citizens as well as their rights as students. The following paragraphs reflect the concern of the faculty of Michigan State University with these principles as they attempted to work out a system of student rights on campus:

[2] L. C. Vaccaro, "Power and Conflict in the University—A Search for Solutions," *College and University* (Fall 1968).
[3] Perkins, "The University and Due Process," p. 2.
[4] "A Report of the Faculty Committee on Student Affairs to the Academic Council," *Academic Freedom for Students at Michigan State University* (East Lansing, Mich.: Michigan State University, 1967).

1.2 Each right of an individual places a reciprocal duty upon others: the duty to permit the individual to exercise the right. The student, in his status as a member of the academic community, has both rights and duties. Within that community, the student's most essential right is the right to learn. The University has a duty to provide for the student those privileges, opportunities and protections which best promote the learning process in all its aspects. The student, for his part, has duties to other members of the academic community, the most important of which is to refrain from interference with those rights of others which are equally essential to the purposes and processes of the University.
1.4 The student is not only a member of the academic community; he is also a citizen of the larger society. As a citizen, he retains those rights, protections and guarantees of fair treatment which are held by all citizens, and the University may not deny them to him. The enforcement of the student's duties to the larger society is, however, the responsibility of the legal and judicial authorities duly established for that purpose.[5]

It is clear that such a system has been well thought out and that genuine concern exists for establishing or maintaining procedural safeguards to insure those rights. However, many university administrators, regents, faculty, and parents have little understanding or toleration of the principle of due process (increasingly referred to on campus as "academic due process" or "procedural due process"). They do not see why an individual is not content to accept decisions within the university by those in authority. This is understandable since the leading advocate of academic freedom itself—The American Association of University Professors—has only recently begun to seriously discuss the concept of due process and its application within the academic community. Furthermore, there is little understanding of the idea outside the legal profession.

Professor Louis Joughin, writing in a recently published handbook of the A.A.U.P., states in this regard:

> Academic due process is brand new as a term, young as an idea having formal dimensions, but of venerable antiquity in some elements of its practice. The difference in age among these aspects is obvious when one considers the sparse use which has thus far been made of the chief approaches commonly applied to the study of a socially operative principle:
> 1. The concept of academic due process does not appear as yet to have received preliminary attention by writers on the history of ideas.
> 2. In the growing literature of academic freedom, reference is customarily made to academic due process as a chief instrument, but there is little critical analysis.
> 3. Studies of the college or university as an institution sometimes refer to the procedures which constitute due process, but these are not

[5] *Ibid.*, pp. 1–2.

subjected to much scrutiny. Social studies of a more general kind, such as those dealing with the major forces at work in human arrangements, do not deal especially with academic due process.[6]

As Professor Joughin has pointed out, there has been little attention devoted to the concept of academic due process and how it fits into the history of ideas in the United States and, more specifically, how it relates to our concepts of justice and equity. If one is to understand the full implications of this concept and how it might apply in the university, a thorough knowledge of its origin and use is necessary.

The principle of due process of the law is a broad one. Its guarantee that no person shall be deprived of life, liberty, or property without due process of the law was intended by the framers of our Constitution to encompass a great variety of situations. It would have been less imaginative of them to set out in great specificity their views of due process, for by that very act they could have destroyed the timelessness of the principle. The Forefathers were farsighted; but they could never have foreseen every problem which would arise after their time. They never dreamed of the problems we face today—such as civil disobedience in our urban areas and student unrest which rages across the great campuses of the world—from Columbia to Berkeley, and from Paris to Tokyo.

The concept of due process dates to ancient Greece, where it was said that reason was supreme. Reasonableness was essential, because by its very definition reason provides order. The concept of "due process," like that of "reason," provides for order, and order in turn is necessary to insure a structure within which individuals are able to properly realize and fulfill their aims, ideals, and goals.

Student unrest has caused very serious problems. In its severest form it not only can destroy man's precious property but it also deeply disturbs the roots of what man has come to know as law and order. On the heels of the assassination of Senator Robert F. Kennedy, the very foundations of our sense of reason and order have been badly shaken. Why the unrest? What are its causes? And what can be done to reestablish a reasoned and orderly society?

The unrest is in great extent due to our contemporary questioning of the so-called eternal values—those truths which for so long had been considered self-evident. The result of our challenging some of these truths has been rebellion, disorder, and dissatisfaction with present university policies.

It is this situation which has brought about a need for an adjudication of rights. In fact, the situation has developed to the point where on a number of our college campuses today students pay a fee for legal services they may incur while a student at the university. It is in this adjudicative procedure that the requirement of due process is most imperative, for it is the backbone of American justice.

[6] Louis Joughin (ed.), "Academic Due Process," *Academic Freedom and Tenure* (Madison: University of Wisconsin Press, 1967), p. 264.

Since law must provide the structure, the law must be "above all men." But there is always the possibility that in the administration of law by men there will result arbitrary and capricious infringements and violations of individuals' rights. Thus it is that we have the broad and general principle of due process of law guaranteed to all our citizens.

Due process is basically a guarantee that certain procedural steps will be taken prior to denying to a person certain of his individual liberties and rights. For example, before it can take a man's property, the State must apply to the courts and pay the property owner a just compensation for the condemnation of his property. An individual may express whatever ideas he wishes, except in those situations where his speech incites others to riot. In both of these situations and in many others too numerous to discuss here, two points come to light: Where there is a right there is also a corresponding duty, and in an effort to enforce those duties, it is necessary that a procedural "due process" be employed, in the event individuals fail to act fairly and in order to keep the legal structure of our society from breaking down.

The university is a special place. It is here that men's minds have pondered the great issues and, in many instances, discovered solutions to the great problems. It is in the university that there is the spirit of inquiry, that freedom of thought exists. The function of a university is, as Cardinal Newman put it, "intellectual culture . . . it educates the intellect to reason well in all matters, to reach out towards truth, and to grasp it." The very position of a university in our society demands that its thinkers be allowed to continue to inquire into practical as well as theoretical problems—that they have the right to speculate, as the Greeks did, about the Universe and Man. Restrictions on free inquiry are anathema.

But, as we are beginning to discover, maintaining the university's spirit becomes difficult, if not in some cases impossible, in these times of reevaluation and reanalysis. We cannot expect that our students will remain complacent and docile in the face of serious problems. Rather, as new ideas and discoveries unfold, the student has an obligation and a duty to view, review, and analyze in the spirit of free inquiry those truths which so many of us take for granted as unshakeable. But we should not have to expect that if university administrators do not knuckle under to militant demands our universities will be burned to the ground.

The problem which arises is that a university, like any society of individuals, must have its rules, its orders, its structure; otherwise the achievement of its goals becomes impossible. Without such structure, the whole concept of freedom to investigate and reevaluate becomes meaningless in the midst of an anarchical and undisciplined mass. Here there can be no real freedom. Meaningful and knowledgeable insights do not grow out of chaos. Due process provides the broad scheme within which the administration of university rules shall take place.

There are those who criticize the administration of the law in the courts, which is due process exemplified, as being too expensive, too technical, and too slow. On the other hand, there are those who press at every moment to insure a strict and usually burdensome procedure, which at times moves so cumbersomely that one could hardly say that it moves at all.

We cannot escape the fact that we face a dilemma. On the one hand, we must make every effort to insure an orderly disposition of those cases where university administrators have found a violation of the university regulations. And by an orderly disposition, we must not allow a summary dismissal of those who did not agree with the university administration. And on the other hand, we cannot tolerate a full-blown hearing, with long and elaborate notices to the violators for every small and relatively insignificant infringement of the rules. Where might the line be drawn?

One of the interesting points we might consider is why it has taken until this time in our history for the question of academic due process to arise. Or, perhaps in similar terminology, why does academe, which follows in the tradition of the great schools of Greece, fail in achieving substantial due process in the administration of its law? Perhaps one answer is that universities have until recently been administered by a very conservative element. Although it is true that university leaders have often been thought to be the great liberals of the country, it is also true that in the administration of their own internal affairs they have been slow to recognize new procedures in dealing with their problems.

One would not have to interview a great number of people familiar with academic institutions to find that more than a few of our citizens continue to believe that university attendance is a privilege, and that if the student does not want to submit to whatever the university administration may dictate he should merely pack his bags and leave. The idea of forcing students to follow university mandates, not because they are reasonable but because failure to follow them will result in expulsion, probation, or some other socially undesirable punishment, is no longer applicable to the present state of affairs. The very nature of a university fosters the attitude that those rules and regulations should be questioned. Even though we may feel that the values we live by are true and eternal, these values should at all points be questioned, dissected, and reanalyzed.

To merely say that the student should submit to the professor is to impose upon higher education in this country a method which is at best suitable only for grammar school. The old adage, "if a student doesn't like our rules, let him go elsewhere," is no longer acceptable as a solution. The situation in which the teacher pours out the material and the student writes it down is a passing method of pedagogy. And the student who accepts all rules that are handed down by the administration as the law of his university life is a passing phenomenon. Dialogue is now the method, with teacher and student searching together for new insights. This is what is most productive, we feel, and what brings about the greater development of a growing mind. Yet this is also what brings about requests for greater freedom on college campuses.

Having broadly discussed the place of due process in our academic institutions, let us look at what due process actually consists of. When a person in our society, for example, is charged with a crime, there are certain protections which are guaranteed him by the Constitution. These protections insure that the citizen will not be punished or incarcerated until there has been proof, beyond a reasonable doubt, that he has committed the crime. The reason for adhering to this time-honored proposition is that in many situations if such a great burden of proof were not required, innocent individuals might be punished for crimes they had not committed. In addition to the prosecuting attorney's being required to present evidence which might convince twelve jurors that the defendant committed the crime, certain other safeguards are found in our Constitution. These safeguards make up other aspects of due process. First is the right to a preliminary hearing and to refuse to testify against oneself. Second, the right to counsel. Third, the right to have one's accusers confront him and make charges in open court. Fourth, the right to object to certain evidence which does not meet the tests of relevancy, materiality, and competency and to introduce evidence which has a direct value toward proving the issues of the case. Fifth, the right to present witnesses in one's own defense and to cross-examine those witnessing against you. And finally, the guarantee that some sort of record of the proceedings will be made and that an appellate machinery exists.

Although legal due process by its very definition is not academic due process, nevertheless many of the aspects of legal due process are exemplary. For serious offenses which may result in punishment, such as expulsion, the guarantees of legal due process seem appropriate. Expulsion casts a stigma upon the student; it affects his future employment or the possibility of entering graduate school; it affects his psychological as well as his economic life. Because an act such as expulsion carries with it these consequences, the due process safeguards appear to be a necessity.

For smaller or lesser offenses, such elaborate machinery would not be necessary. It is the same with the courts. Lesser crimes require less in the way of procedural machinery; and though this has been criticized, it seems that elaborate constitutional machinery for every offense, no matter how small, would not be practicable. It would merely overburden already crowded judicial machinery and affect everyone's rights adversely.

Is it justifiable to deny these same rights to an individual because he happens to be a student in the university? We believe not. Yet, this is exactly what many people have traditionally argued when they contend that a student must accept the rules of a university when he or she enters as a student (particularly as it pertains to the private university). Recently, however, Professor Clark Byse, retiring President of the A.A.U.P., speculated that the present-day due process limitations employed by so-called private universities will soon be removed.[7]

Although the cases Professor Byse cites run counter to his plea, he makes an interesting point in his argument that "although adherence to precedence

[7] Byse, "The University and Due Process: A Somewhat Different View," p. 6.

should be the rule, when a legal doctrine has been found to be inconsistent with the sense of justice or with the social welfare, it may appropriately be abandoned."[8] He then goes on to cite two relevant cases, and continues by saying, "I do not invite your attention to those two cases in order to convince you that one was right and the other was wrong. The purpose, rather, is to urge that questions of this character may appropriately be presented to the judiciary for resolution."[9]

At a conference held at the University of Denver Law School recently, a number of legal educators and university administrators expressed their candid views about the present state and direction of student rights and the courts' jurisdiction. The concepts of *in loco parentis* and contract theory were but two notions discussed extensively by those presenting papers at this conference. Of course, there was not complete unanimity by all conference participants about what should be done to prevent campus conflict while at the same time guaranteeing individual student rights. However, there was general agreement regarding the belief that a student should not be required to give up his constitutional rights when he enters the university and that universities ought to be expending more thought and effort in developing "an internal order that takes into account the legitimate claims of students, one that makes provision for internal justice and that recognizes the rights and obligations of students should be defined after long and searching deliberation, and not dismissed simply because the law, at present, provides no compulsion to act differently, . . ."[10]

As we have stated earlier, we believe the campus activists will be increasingly inclined to take their cases to the courts if the university does not insure careful handling of their grievances. It would be tragic indeed if cases involving course grading and the like had to be reviewed by the courts, but we have no doubts whatsoever that this is what will happen if colleges and universities persist in circumventing due process in their dealings with students. As Professor Phillip Monypenny of the University of Illinois recently said, "If the agencies of education act justly, and seem to act justly, the courts will find very few occasions to inflict a judicially imposed view of justice on them."[11]

As the university increases in importance as an institution in American society, we believe that the courts will be more concerned about individual rights, particularly as they relate to the university's role as opinion-shaper, social critic, political catalyst, and the like. This means that those responsible for formulating policy within the university—faculty, administrator, and regent—will need to apprise themselves of the import and applicability of due process and take the time to develop well-thought-out systems of administration which will insure fairness and justice for all.

[8] *Ibid.*, p. 4.
[9] *Ibid.*
[10] "Colleges and the Courts: Advice from Four Legal Scholars," *The Chronicle of Higher Education*, June 10, 1968, p. 3.
[11] Ian E. McNett, "Courts Will Not Inflict Justice, Colleges Told," *The Chronicle of Higher Education*, June 10, 1968, p. 1.

In the last analysis this means that we need to realize that due process, in the words of Mr. Justice Robert H. Jackson, "is not for the sole benefit of an accused. It is the best insurance . . . against those blunders which leave lasting strains on a system of Justice but which are bound to occur on *ex parte* consideration." We plead with those responsible for policy formulation in colleges and universities to consider the consequences of failing to follow due process in adjudicating the grievances that regularly arise within their academic community.

SHERIDAN P. McCABE

Religious Commitment and Student Freedom on the Church-Related Campus

Sheridan P. McCabe, formerly Chairman of the Department of Psychology at the University of Portland, recently accepted the Directorship of the Counseling Center at the University of Notre Dame.

A growing concern of college faculty members and administrators is the unrest which appears to typify the current generation of college undergraduates. An account of some student demonstration or protest can be found in almost every daily newspaper. Ten years ago such stories were rare and usually dealt with an innocuous student prank, such as a panty raid. Such evidences of student unrest were regarded as possibly troublesome, but certainly innocent. Today, the news stories must be taken seriously. These demonstrations are not undertaken in a spirit of good, clean fun by the students, but as thoughtful and usually responsible reactions to the deep-seated ills of contemporary society.

One cannot listen to the students who come to a student counseling center to discuss their anxieties and conflicts and come away with any impression other than that these conflicts are rooted in their value orientation and religious commitments. The serious student of today is in search of meaning. Many times we have brought him to this search through our teaching, and then we respond with chagrin and confusion when he takes us seriously. Sometimes the college students of today are referred to as the "Now" generation. They are not satisfied with a "pie-in-the-sky" approach to values. They demand a serious attempt to implement these values today. This situation is described by Daniel Callahan:

> Though there may be exceptions in every college, few students want to waste their time. They do not appreciate, and for very good reasons,

having silly and wasteful requirements imposed upon them. They do not appreciate dull courses, poor teaching, dictatorial deans, petty professors. More than anything else, they value their dignity. If their university is any good at all, they will hear much about human freedom. They want to see some of it in their own lives. They will also hear much about the need for "maturity," "responsibility," "community," "service," and "personal relationships." Again, they would like to see some of these values realized in their own lives. Not their lives after college, or their lives at home on vacations, or their lives from two to four in the afternoon, but in everyday campus life, inside the classroom and outside, within the dormitory and off the campus.[1]

We are currently witnessing the powerful manifestations of students' preoccupation with freedom and concern for moral and spiritual values. The phenomena of student protest groups and student participation in social action movements are evidence of this. There is a sort of paradoxical linking of a movement toward spiritual values with a dissatisfaction with traditional or institutionalized mores and morals. A good example of this can be found in the Berkeley demonstrations of the Free Speech Movement. Here the basic complaint of the student appeared to be the lack of concern of the university and of society with the dignity of the human person, and yet the protest took the form of a flaunting of propriety through the public utterance of obscenities. A more recent example is the series of events that occurred at the Pentagon in October 1967 when students were protesting against what they considered to be the immorality of the war in Vietnam. This demonstration for peace was characterized by violence, and students attempted to demonstrate their idealistic concerns by manifesting an open contempt for authority and order.

By the spring of 1968 the campus problem had reached such monumental proportions that it became a major national problem, one which captured front-page headlines on an almost daily basis. The most serious incident was the student demonstration at Columbia University, which resulted in a complete shutdown of the university for a period of time. The interesting point is that the students were not demonstrating for benefits for themselves but rather for what they saw as important moral issues; they protested the university's involvement in military-related research which might contribute to the nation's participation in the Vietnam conflict. The students also objected to the university's taking property from a nearby park in Harlem because it would be at variance with the best interests of the Negro poor who live in that area. Another important incident occurred at Marquette University, where a direct confrontation between administration and students took place over the student's charge that the university was not doing enough to serve the Negro community.

[1] Daniel Callahan, "Student Freedom," in Edward Manier and John W. Houck (eds.), *Academic Freedom and the Catholic University* (Notre Dame, Ind.: Fides Publishers, 1967), p. 129.

In a sense, the students felt that this Catholic university was not being Christian enough, and they made their feelings known.

Many other incidents could be cited and described in detail, but one more dealing with finance illustrates the extent of the pressure students can bring to bear on a university administration. Because the source of the money for a major financial contribution was rental income in a slum area, students were instrumental in encouraging the university to refuse the donation. This, it seems, is evidence that students are not only aware of but effectively articulating what they see as significant and relevant values. Thus we find in the contemporary college student an almost violent preoccupation with freedom and a deeply-felt concern for spiritual and human values. Yet these are manifested in a manner which is difficult to reconcile with highly institutionalized religion or morality.

Another manifestation of the involvement of students with idealistic principles and religious-like values is the great interest shown today in existentialism. This interest is reflected not only in the beatnik and hippie movements, but also in their academic interests as well. Professor J. G. Gray points out the great popularity of existential philosophy courses on many college campuses.[2] He describes students' genuine involvement with the ideas and theories discussed in these courses.

This complex situation poses a serious problem for the church-related campus, for the concerns and activities of the student challenge the very reason for the existence of colleges and universities of this type. The conflict between communicating the traditional ecclesiastical structures and teachings on the one hand and developing the student's own religious commitment and maturity as a religious person on the other will be the concern in this article.

Controversy over the compatibility of religion and a creative intellectual life is hardly new. Throughout the history of ideas this struggle between the leaders of established religion and the intellectuals is evident. It is typified by the death of Socrates and characterizes the Renaissance period. This conflict between a commitment to organized religion and the freedom necessary for the intellectual life is coming into focus with an even greater intensity today. Some educators, including Catholics, have termed the Catholic university a contradiction in terms. On some well-established Catholic campuses it is reported that more than half of the students fail to practice even the minimum requirements of their religion.

The problem of the possible relationship of religious commitment to intellectual freedom can be approached in two ways. One of these is to consider the external restraints on freedom effected by the regulations and practices of the religion along with the authority exercised through ecclesiastical structures. The other is to consider the internalized restraints associated with one's commitment to a particular religion.

[2] J. G. Gray, "Salvation on the Campus: Why Existentialism is Capturing the Students," *Harper's*, 215, 5 (1965), 55–59.

The most obvious limitations that a church-related college can exercise over the intellectual freedom of the student are those which are imposed through external restraints. Denominations, religious orders, and other ecclesiastical institutions created and maintain colleges at considerable expense and effort in order to produce leaders whose influence will be specifically religious. The energy expended in running institutions of higher learning is felt to be a worthwhile investment inasmuch as it furthers the mission of the Church. It can hardly be surprising, therefore, that these institutions develop academic and student life programs that tend to produce alumni who fit neatly into these projected roles. Deviations from orthodoxy cannot be tolerated, for they are inimical to the overall objectives which are being pursued. This is particularly true in what are considered sensitive areas of the curriculum, such as theology, philosophy, and sometimes the social and behavioral sciences. Church-related colleges are often torn between the horns of a dilemma—i.e., the achievement of academic excellence on the one hand and the preservation of their unique identity and mission on the other. It is difficult to preserve and hand on a particular tradition at the same time that a spirit of criticism challenging this tradition is encouraged in the student.

This is not to suggest that the church-related colleges are not facing up to these problems. Assiduous efforts are being made to examine and resolve them. The role of the church-related campus is being critically reviewed. Modes of preserving a unique and valuable heritage while communicating it in a genuinely intellectual and scholarly atmosphere are being sought.[3] In recent years there have been many efforts to implement this goal. Control of church-related colleges is being transferred to boards of trustees which are not under the control of the institutional church. Faculty members who represent a wide range of viewpoints and religious commitments, including atheism and agnosticism, are being recruited. Scholarly productivity rather than religious orthodoxy is becoming the basis for promotion and tenure. Even the sacrosanct areas of theology and philosophy are gradually being taught from a variety of points of view rather than from that confined to a particular ideology. The question remains, however, whether these efforts will be enough to resolve the basic issues.

The area of student life is also a very important consideration. Many students on the church-related campus are there because their parents want them to be educated within a specifically religious framework. Parents desire that the faith which they have fostered in their children will be reinforced and not threatened as it could be on a secular campus. Parents desire the protective influence of the campus life of the church-related college. They expect the college authorities to monitor the activities of their sons and daughters and to provide the necessary discipline conducive to the

[3] M. M. Pattillo, Jr. and D. M. Mackenzie, *Eight Hundred Colleges Face the Future: A Preliminary Report of the Danforth Commission on Church Colleges and Universities* (St. Louis: Danforth Foundation, 1965).

leading of a good Christian life. John Gardner points out that growing up themselves during the Depression has made the parents of today's college students profoundly and incurably unadventurous for their children:

> They do not want their children to suffer as they did. They hope that somehow they can save them all the foolish mistakes, the blind alleys, the regrets and detours that characterized their lives. Faced with decisions for their children, they favor the conventional over the unconventional, the easy over the difficult, the secure over the risky.[4]

Thus many of the restrictions imposed on the student are not only in keeping with the religious commitment of the school but also reflect a real concern to meet the expectations of the students and their parents.

This approach may well have been effective in past generations. However, the college student today is often more sophisticated than the student of past generations. Certainly the student today is more sensitive to his need to experiment in living, to test his ideals and commitments against reality. He feels keenly the need to be free to determine himself, to make his own mistakes if need be in order to learn from them. He cannot accept uncritically the values and ideals of others, no matter how time-honored they may be.

The structure imposed upon student life with the aim of encouraging development of habits of Christian behavior is often ineffective and self-defeating. This is aptly pointed out by Daniel Callahan:

> Many Catholic colleges and universities complain that they cannot get good students, or at least not the best students. But why should a man or woman go to a college where he or she will have to fight tooth and nail for freedoms long taken for granted elsewhere? Why should he go to a college where the administration looks upon him as a child, a potential usurper of the throne, an incipient enemy? Why should he go to a college where he is treated as if he were a latent alcoholic from whom all intoxicating beverages should be kept? Why should he go to a college where he is supposed to play the dead, dead game of being Victorian Christian gentleman, resplendent at all times in suitable apparel?[5]

We can further ask, Why, if he is asked to play these games in the name of a religious tradition and obligation, should he accept that tradition as meaningful and follow that authority?

One of the crises faced by the church-related campus today is that in order to be effective in its very mission—to preserve its religious traditions and produce leaders in that tradition—it must abandon its restrictive and authority-oriented approach. It is not until the student has the freedom

---

[4] John W. Gardner, "How to Choose a College, If Any," *Harper's*, 216 (February 1958), 53.
[5] Callahan, "Student Freedom," pp. 139–140.

to challenge and question the very bases of his religion that he can truly and honestly accept it. Not until he takes the risk of losing his faith will he finally find and totally embrace it. Not until he is given responsibility for his own Christian life can he accept it and exercise it.

> If we really believe in man's basic freedom and that we commit men more deeply to truth by incorporating this freedom into the search, then we must accept the fact that this questioning spirit prompts him to probe the mystery of faith. Only a belief that our faith contains no mystery and is rather presented to us in neat packets of knowledge would stifle the attempt to explore.[6]

Of far greater importance than freedom from external surveillance and restraints is internal or personal freedom. This is the freedom that springs from within the individual. No man is free, no matter what political system or set of social structures surround him, unless he has faced and accepted himself. Many psychologists have pointed out that religion can serve as a defense against reality. Rather than face up to one's self, one can pursue elaborate rituals and religious theorizing. We can use religion to allay our anxieties, to avoid our responsibilities, and to maintain our dependency on external authority. Many college students, sensitive to this, often reject institutional religion as irrelevant. They point to the failure of the church to assume its responsibility for leadership, to its apparent lack of sensitivity to the major problems in the world today in the form of social injustice, to man's inhumanity to man. Such students often abandon their formal religion in order to embrace a commitment to what they consider meaningful human values in the civil rights or peace movements.

In his search for meaning, the student is reaching out for a sense of personal identity. He is caught up in the process and struggle of becoming himself. He looks to the interpersonal relationships of his daily life to contribute to the development of his self-definition. He feels an acute need to engage in meaningful relationships with others, to communicate and to share in a very personal way with others. He needs to experiment with various roles and the values implicit in them. This process cannot take place in a stifling structure or repressive atmosphere. It requires a climate of freedom in which his growth and independence is nurtured and encouraged. Given this he can form and develop stable value commitments, commitments that will endure and form the basis for creative expression throughout his life.

A true religious commitment presupposes and is based on the attainment of a sense of personal identity and an openness to truly human experiences. Without this sort of personal integration and interpersonal sensitivity, religion lacks authenticity. It is reduced to a kind of role-playing. Faith is basically a quest for meaning. The Christian life should involve the

[6] Joseph B. Simons, *Retreat Dynamics* (Notre Dame, Ind.: Fides Publishers, 1967), p. 41.

experience of the meaningfulness of our lives and should supply the energy and motivation for our activities; otherwise, it is a superficial intellectual and social exercise. This basically human dimension of religion is explained by Michael Novak:

> Religion can thrive only in a personal universe; religious faith, hope and love are personal responses to a personal God. But how can the immense questions of a personal God even be posed and made relevant when fundamental questions about the meaning and limits of personal experience are evaded? . . . God, if there is a God, is not dead. He will come back to the colleges, when man comes back.[7]

The church-related campus can foster this process by providing a climate of freedom. It can set up an open environment that will provide not only the opportunity but also the encouragement to test one's roles, ideas, and values. It will be free of repressive regulations and restrictions. It will not present theology and philosophy in a doctrinaire fashion, as though afraid of the consequences of admitting the existence of alternative points of view, let alone discussing their merits. Its unique contribution as a church-related campus will be the availability of individuals—faculty and fellow students—who by their lives and their integrity as scholars give witness to true Christian values.

Students themselves point out the need for and the value of the availability of this form of witness. Robert Hassenger and Gerald Rauch provide verbatim responses of students at Notre Dame who were asked to react to problems inherent in the dilemma between academic excellence and the Christian mission of the Catholic university. Two brief excerpts will illustrate the perspective of the students. A senior history major said:

> Theology here doesn't rise above the level of an intellectual game. I think about Christianity but who can I turn to to witness to me how to live it? Certain priests can teach me to lose my childhood faith but there is very limited witness to the life that you live after you pass through this stage. Notre Dame offers a large quantity of religious services. It is the super welfare state for Christian consumers. But running through the rituals is not sufficient. We want quality. A depth of meaning. Intellectual quality is coming. But the quality of pastoral work is very low. I see priests doing all sorts of things but not what is expected of them as priests.[8]

A junior philosophy major said:

> Witness is paramount. Theology classes and theological talk don't help. There has to be witness. The priest has to be Christian manifestly. He

---

[7] Michael Novak, "God in the Colleges," *Harper's*, 223 (October 1961), 178.

[8] Robert Hassenger and Gerald Rauch, "Some Problem Areas in Catholic Higher Education: C. The Student," in Robert Hassenger (ed.), *The Shape of Catholic Higher Education* (Chicago: University of Chicago Press, 1967), p. 218.

has to have willingness to give of himself. Of the chaplains in the halls how many do the students even feel are approachable? The priest would have to go out to the students.[9]

These students single out the priest in their criticism of the lack of Christian witness on campus. I feel that perhaps the nonclerical faculty should share in this responsibility, or, even further, should have the lion's share, since as laymen they can constitute a more effective role model of Christian living for the student who will leave the college to live in the world.

This Christian witness, which should pervade and characterize the church-related campus, must be integrated with the climate of freedom that leads the student into meaningful relationships. There should be a consistency in the college experience which is focused on development of mature and creative Christian leaders. Michael Novak says that "the greatest contribution to the religious life of the university could come from teachers and scholars—formally religious or not—who could lead the student to the profound human experience lying below the surface of the academic curriculum." [10]

The college or university is typically conceptualized as a community of scholars. This community is united in the pursuit of truth. On a church-related campus, it is to be uniquely Christian; that is, it is to be united not only in the scholarly pursuit of truth, but also in giving witness to the risen Christ, incarnate in our contemporary world.

Thus we are confronted with the two essential considerations: the importance of the individual and the significance of the community. We have, in the Christian context, always recognized, at least intellectually, the dignity of the individual. Practice, however, does not always reflect this recognition. Persons need to have the freedom to become themselves, with all their differences and uniqueness. They must be given the opportunity to develop into mature and responsible human beings. However, this is not at the expense of the community, for it is precisely within the community that persons can become fully themselves. Modern psychology has shown the devastating effects of isolation on the person. Studies of infants who have been institutionalized for long periods of time, of children separated from their parents during war, and of experimental subjects who have undergone periods of sensory deprivation all show how vitally dependent all of us are on our environment, particularly our interpersonal environment, for the maintenance of our personalities. Yet in modern society, particularly in the age group of the college student, individuals experience a deep sense of isolation. If the college is to provide the basis for true personal freedom, it must provide a climate of love and acceptance, a situation in which persons can find meaningful relationships with others. The college must provide a truly human community. It is precisely by living and working and loving and praying as a community that we become truly

[9] *Ibid.*, p. 219.
[10] Novak, "God in the Colleges," p. 176.

human, truly ourselves. It is from this community that we draw the vital force and direction of our own unique religious commitment. It is this very community itself that constitutes a witness to the living, incarnate Christ.

It is not meaningful to conceptualize religious commitment in terms of dogmatic or moral checklists or inventories of religious practices. Religious commitment is much deeper than that. It is a vital and creative force that gives meaning to the experiences of the individual. It gives him a perspective on reality. It expands rather than beclouds his sensitivity to truth. Since it finds its source and grows out of freedom, it is anything but inimical to freedom. Today, when almost every aspect of our lives is a matter of free choice and responsibility, it is impossible to view religion as a matter to be left to higher authorities.

Traditionally, church-related campuses have not been uniquely characterized by an atmosphere of freedom. Quite the contrary; the path of academic freedom has been blazed by the nonsectarian colleges and universities. The church-related colleges have been runners-up at best. They have been too caught up in the structures of their tradition and insensitive to the spirit of those traditions. They have been too involved in protecting their students from reality to expose them to meaningful experiences. In their fear of communicating wrong meanings, they have run the risk of communicating no meaning at all.

The mission of the church-related college is the mission of Christ. It hopes to supply Christian leaders who are both truly Christian and truly leaders. Its students must grow and become truly human in order to become effective. The path of the future is not clear, but need for decision and action is immediate and pressing. The objectives, structures, and practices of church-related colleges are being critically reviewed. Many changes and innovations are being made. But the burning question remains: Will they change fast enough to keep up with the demand for change?

ROBERT HASSENGER

A Campus Sexual Revolution?

Robert Hassenger is Assistant Professor in the Department of Sociology and Director of the Office for Educational Research at the University of Notre Dame. He recently edited *The Shape of Catholic Higher Education*.

"The Inheritor," *Time* labeled him, naming the Under-25er its collective Man of the Year for 1967.[1] It was not clear whether the successors of Mr. Luce intended an allusion to William Golding's saga of our distant ancestors, portending a future human as different from the present as Golding's "proto-humans" were from their former comrades. What is clear is that Americans under twenty-five will soon be a majority: by 1970, 100 million of them will be around. Most will be in college.

Immediately after the return of U.S. servicemen at the close of World War II, the birth rate jumped considerably; from 2.8 million births in the twelve months ending June 30, 1946, there was a sharp increase to almost 4 million births in the next year. And the rate stayed up during the postwar boom. The result: 12,090,000 young Americans between 18 and 21 in 1965, with a projected 15,768,000 in this age bracket by 1975. These potential undergraduates are *already born*.

At the same time, the percentage of young adults intent on embellishing themselves with what Irving Howe has called the great American tatoo of a college degree has steadily increased. From the fourteen per cent of college-age Americans going on for higher education in 1940, through the twenty-nine per cent in 1955, to the approximately forty per cent in 1965, the trend has been ever upward. It is estimated that almost half the college-age young adults will be enrolled by 1970, and sixty per cent by 1980. So the peculiar kind of multiplier effect sending

* © 1967 by Robert Hassenger. Reprinted with permission.
[1] "The Inheritor," *Time*, 89 (January 6, 1967), 18–23.

increased percentages of an ever larger pool of potential students to college is expected to result in ten or eleven million attempting to elbow into the classroom by 1980, little more than a decade hence.[2]

It is a safe bet that these legions will continue to make waves for college and university administrators. When those presently presiding over student populations were in college, only about one in seven of their age-mates were there, typically in rather pastoral settings. Now, as presidents and deans, they are faced with demonstrations, sit-ins, and lie-ins, which, even if they draw but 1 per cent of the students in a multiversity, may involve 250 to 300 people. Consequently, administrators are finding they have their hands full—and, with miniskirts and sitars, often their eyes and ears, as well.

In one of the most useful discussions of the phenomenon which has come to be called the "generation gap," Christopher Jencks and David Riesman sketch some of the forces that have made the college "both a battlefield and a negotiating table in the ceaseless war between the generations." [3] The increase in overall student age distributions caused by escalating graduate school enrollment is one of the factors contributing to whatever gap separates students entering college from their parents. Although some of the graduate students are themselves over thirty, they remain trustable, and even the married ones are often more in tune with undergraduates' lives than with those of their age-grade counterparts outside the university. Jencks and Riesman estimate that approximately one-third of all undergraduates now attend universities with large graduate school enrollments. While not always in the same classrooms, there is a variety of opportunities for interaction, including exposure to thoughts and behavior patterns that once were considered private. Such influence often only exacerbates already existing tendencies of students toward change.[4]

A great deal is being written and broadcast about today's youth, much of it fatuous. Probably the most trustworthy guide through the mini-society of today's Under-25er is Kenneth Keniston. The brief sketch which follows

[2] Robert Hassenger (ed.), *The Shape of Catholic Higher Education* (Chicago: University of Chicago Press, 1967), pp. 295–296.

[3] Christopher Jencks and David Riesman, "The War Between the Generations," *The Academic Revolution* (Garden City, N.Y.: Doubleday & Company, Inc., 1968), Chap. 2. An excerpt also appeared in *The Record*, Teachers College, Columbia University, 69 (October 1967), 1–21.

[4] One of the perennial issues among those who study students is the extent to which changes in values, attitudes, and behavior really occur during the college years. We cannot resurrect this issue here; the reader is referred to my "The Impact of Catholic Colleges," in Hassenger, *The Shape of Catholic Higher Education*, pp. 103–161; and "A Rationale for Changing Student Values," *Educational Record*, 48 (Winter 1967), 61–67; and to Kenneth Feldman and Theodore Newcomb, *The Impacts of Colleges Upon Their Students*, a forthcoming volume summarizing all the available research on this problem. One of the most useful summaries of studies on student development is the contribution of Susan Singer to the volume edited by Joseph Katz, *Growth and Constraint in College Students* (Stanford, Calif.: Institute for the Study of Human Problems, 1967).

leans heavily on Keniston's work.[5] What *Time* called the "Now Generation" has also been termed "The Hungry Generation," and another calls them "The Restless Believers."[6] And anyone who has paid attention to what's happening can only agree. I suppose I have been most helped to understand what *is* happening—the new sound, the psychedelic experience, the "mod look," the Dylan and Paul Simon lyrics, the sound of The Doors—by reading Keniston and Marshall McLuhan. Throughout his work, McLuhan illustrates how the new electronic communication media of our time have shaped both modern culture and individual psyche. Electricity has made things instant, and the structural assumptions of the Gutenberg world of print are no longer viable. The result has been a stylistic revolution, most manifest in the postwar babies who have experienced the new media from their earliest days.

At the same time, we have witnessed the loss of what Keniston calls "positive myths." The frantic flux we are all caught up in has generated a disenchantment, a quite literal loss of enchantment with the simple things an earlier generation may have been more attuned to. Many young adults have seen such dramatic transformations that they seem unable to believe in the permanance of anything. The majority of today's students will work at jobs which did not exist when they were born. And, of course, many of the jobs for which people are now preparing will not exist when they are fifty. This is not only the problem of the Job Corps—training people for positions which are being phased out—but of the college campus as well.

Perhaps this is one of the reasons for the cult of the present, exemplified in such things as the drug "trip" and "total environment" discotheques. Timothy Leary urges the young to "turn on, tune in, drop out," to "kiss off" middle-class values. The bother is that many who purport to have a substitute offer only a different cult. One of these is a kind of teenybopper subculture which provides a means of suspending commitment for at least a time—while, as Keniston shows, continuing to apply one's self to acquiring the skills and attitudes that will be required if society's demands are to be met. Certainly college serves both purposes at once, or seems to. As Keniston puts it:

> By "taking off the pressure" for a period ranging from five to fifteen years, the youth culture permits most youths to remain uninvolved in the adult world without having to take an open stand against it. By sanctioning and *even requiring* de facto alienation, it removes the need in most youths for a more focused and articulated alienation from adult-

[5] See particularly Kenneth Keniston, *The Uncommitted: Alienated Youth in American Society* (New York: Harcourt, Brace & World, Inc., 1966); and "The Faces in the Lecture Room," in Robert S. Morison (ed.), *The Contemporary University: U.S.A.* (Boston: Houghton Mifflin Company, 1966), pp. 315-349; "The Sources of Student Dissent," *Journal of Social Issues*, 23 (July 1967), 108-137; and *Young Radicals* (New York: Harcourt, Brace & World, Inc., 1968).

[6] John Hardon, S.J., *The Hungry Generation* (Baltimore: Newman Press, 1967); John Kirvan, C.S.P., *The Restless Believers* (New York: Paulist Press, 1966).

hood. And it takes the pressure off longest for those on whom adult pressures will eventually be greatest: the highly educated, of whom most will be later required.[7]

Yet even after such a massive put down of middle-class values, the young still sense their collective loss; the cult of the present does not really eliminate the sense of homelessness, of estrangement. The "historical dislocation," as Keniston calls it,

> can bring an enormous sense of freedom, of not being bound by the past, of creating oneself at each moment of one's existence. Yet characteristically a philosophy of absolute freedom, based on a denial of any necessary relationship with the past, is usually a philosophy of the absurd; the signs of this freedom are not joy and triumph, but nausea and dread; and its possessors are not the creators but the Strangers and Outsiders of the universe.[8]

David Riesman has often pointed out the absence of any clear feedback to young adults in our culture, of appraisals by others in light of some clear standard. The *rites de passage* of the primitive tribe which connect the individual with others through common experiences are lacking.[9] Such pale replicas as drivers' licenses and draft cards do little to publicly confirm one's adult status. (That is, if one even *wants* adult status: Americans tend to cling to a romanticized vision of childhood, about which they are nostalgic.) With the lack of any institutionalized means to clarify one's identity, it is not surprising that sexual conquest is accepted by many as a kind of quasi-official initiation rite. When the young grow up in a milieu characterized by sexual overkill, this is perhaps inevitable.

There is no need to rehearse in detail the changes making for an apparent sexual revolution in our time. Virtually every form of the mass media has run cover stories and special reports on the current sexual situation. It is, of course, difficult to know to what extent behavioral changes have accompanied new standards in picture and print. Some observers believe that the sound and fury betoken a kind of spectator sex, but very little real action. They point to such things as the growth of a new kind of pornography, with its overtones of sadomasochism, and suggest this is directly linked to the new sexual role prescribed for women, with a concomitant decline in wide-scale prostitution;[10] and to the phenomenal rise of the Playboy Clubs. There *is* something rather ingenious in the Playboy Club set-up, where the pudgy and balding codger, for whom the term "playboy"

---

[7] Keniston, *The Uncommitted*, p. 404. (Italics added.)
[8] *Ibid.*, p. 238.
[9] See, for example, David Riesman, "The Search for Challenge," *Abundance for What?* (Garden City, N.Y.: Doubleday & Company, Inc., 1965), pp. 331–348.
[10] See the work of my colleague Peter Michelson, "An Apology for Pornography," *New Republic*, 155 (December 10, 1966), 21–24; and the more sociological interpretation of Ned Polsky, *Hustlers, Beats and Others* (Chicago: Aldine Publishing Company, 1967).

is a ludicrous misnomer, can look but not touch, and where the rules of the game actually *prevent* any testing of the masculinity he so safely wallows in. Those who teach in all-male schools know the less obvious forms this can take on their campuses, with myths about the nearby women's college designed to bolster the egos of insecure males who need never go near the place since everyone over there is frigid. Writing about such phenomena, and the rise of the super-cool, highly trained automaton in the spy stories, who can make love and leave without feeling, Eugene Kennedy said this:

> He has mastered wine-lists, wenching, and witty remarks. He utters throwaway lines that say life really doesn't matter, that authority is for assaulting, that death is just the big sleep, and that the capital sin is really compassion. It is all deft capework on endless afternoons of hot sun and cool wine . . . splendidly skilled passes that lead to animal conquering. It is so defensive, so overcontrolled and casual that one hardly notices the urgent pulse of these anxious heroes as they fruitlessly try to allay their hours of fear through repeated superficial moments of truth. . . . There is something almost unbearably sad about the aging playboys who think it is the height of manhood to nurse themselves at the breasts so bountifully proferred to them in the topless topography of the twentieth century. Bunny turns out to be a mother comforting and reassuring them that it is all right to be boys forever. The sadness lies, not in that anyone would call this sin, but that anyone would call this sophistication.[11]

The overexposure and overkill notwithstanding, there are a number of indications that the sexual changes in our time are somewhat short of revolutionary. It is, of course, clear that the Puritan and Victorian heritage has in large measure succumbed to the assaults of Freud and the new romanticism of our time.[12] Whether the approach is a literary one with Henry Miller, a popular mechanics one with Albert Ellis, or a commercial one with Hugh Hefner, these moderns and their imitators have made a difference. The effects show up in countless dramatic and more subtle ways. Only three will be mentioned here, for these seem to have the most direct relevance to the discussion of campus sexual behavior which follows.

The first is the redefinition of women's sexual role. It would be astounding if the greater equality and visibility of twentieth-century women did not lead to drastic modifications in their self-concepts and life styles. No longer is it expected that desire, not fulfillment, should be the best part of love. Further, women are expected to go after what they want, not only

---

[11] Eugene Kennedy, "Sexual and Emotional Maturity," *The Critic*, 25 (April–May 1967), 15–16. See also, Kennedy, "The Male Mystique," *The Critic*, 24 (April–May 1966), 26–31. See also Harvey Cox's devastating critique of the "Playboy Philosophy," in *The Secular City* (New York: The Macmillan Company, 1965), Chap. 9.

[12] For an illuminating discussion of the parallels between the old and new romanticism, see Philip Gleason, "Our New Age of Romanticism," *America*, 117 (October 7, 1967), 372–375.

educationally and in career-terms, but in sexual matters as well. The second effect is directly related: with the move away from a traditionalist, guilt-centered ethic to one stressing personalism and trust, the standard for evaluating sexual behavior has become not "is it wrong?" but "is it meaningful?" Thus, the word "virgin" comes to take on a revised meaning, applicable to the girl who has had sexual experience with only her husband before marriage, or with others, as part of a "meaningful relationship." A third change which must be mentioned because of its ramifications on the campus is the greater tolerance for sexual "deviancy," particularly homosexuality. This is not the place to enter the discussion about the homosexual's influence on modern society, in women's clothes, in the theatre, and in pop art, particularly "camp." This influence can also be expected to show itself in collegiate life.

What do we know about the sexual attitudes and behavior of today's collegians? How do these compare to those of their predecessors? There are less data available than might be expected. The first systematic attempts to study sexual behavior in this country were, of course, the investigations of Alfred Kinsey and his collaborators at the Institute for Sex Research at Indiana University.[13] Although it is likely that Kinsey had a biased sample since he obtained subjects by asking for volunteers, and the considerably stricter standards of the time would undoubtedly have meant that primarily the less inhibited volunteered, this work still provides the best available base point in our attempt to get some sense of what changes have occurred. Since his results are referred to several times in the discussion below, it is best to present some of the Kinsey data here.

About three-fourths of the girls twenty and older in the Kinsey sample reported having been aroused by some form of kissing and petting during adolescence, and about one-fifth to one-fourth had petted to orgasm. Of those born before 1900, only 10 per cent had petted to orgasm during adolescence, compared to almost a third of those born in the 1920's. About 20 per cent of the college women in the Kinsey sample were nonvirgins. This is comparable to the results for college women found a decade earlier,[14] but considerably higher than the 7 per cent Katherine Davis found in the early 1900's.[15] Looking at the data available in 1938, Louis Terman predicted the disappearance of the female unmarried virgin by 1960;[16] but Mervin Freedman, whose own work will be discussed below, suggests that

[13] Alfred C. Kinsey and Paul H. Gebhard, *Sexual Behavior in the Human Female* (Philadelphia: W. B. Saunders Company, 1953); Alfred C. Kinsey, Wardell B. Pomeroy, and Clyde E. Martin, *Sexual Behavior in the Human Male* (Philadelphia: W. B. Saunders Company, 1948).

[14] Dorothy D. Bromley and Florence H. Britten, *Youth and Sex* (New York: Harper & Row, 1938).

[15] Katherine Davis, *Factors in the Sex Life of Twenty-Two Hundred Women* (New York: Harper & Row, 1929).

[16] Louis M. Terman, *Psychological Factors in Marital Happiness* (New York: McGraw-Hill Book Company, 1938).

the percentage of college women having premarital intercourse was stabilized by the 1930's.[17]

The data Kinsey provided for males support the conventional wisdom that males are more active sexually. For example, whereas about one-third of the women in his sample masturbated to orgasm in their adolescence, over 90 per cent of the men did so. Further, Kinsey found that more than half of the males he studied had coitus before age twenty. Males of upper economic strata typically had less sexual experience of all kinds except masturbation.[18] The work of Winston Ehrmann at about the same time found comparable male-female differences.[19]

Further data on the sexual activity of college women are found in the research of Mervin Freedman, who carried out his studies at Vassar in the 1950's.[20] Questionnaire results were available for students from three Vassar classes, and forty-nine girls were interviewed throughout their college careers. Of the forty-nine, five (10 per cent) had limited sexual experience, thirteen (27 per cent) had done restricted petting ("above the waist"), twenty (41 per cent) had petted extensively ("genital involvement but not intercourse"), eight (16 per cent) had engaged in intercourse in a relationship of emotional intimacy, and three (6 per cent) were "uninhibited." Only four of the eleven nonvirgins had intercourse prior to college; three of these four were in the "uninhibited" group.[21] All of the Vassar girls who had intercourse as part of a close emotional relationship reported they enjoyed it,

---

[17] Mervin Freedman, "Sex and Society," *The College Experience* (San Francisco: Jossey-Bass, Inc., Publishers, 1967), p. 108. As Kinsey and his collaborators emphasized, there are a number of factors in the culture making for stability in the rate of premarital and extramarital sexual intercourse, so it may well be that a plateau has been reached. On the other hand, Kinsey was writing before the widespread availability and convenience of some of the newer birth control techniques.

[18] Kinsey et al., *Sexual Behavior in the Human Male*, p. 550. There was an interesting inverse relationship between education and sexual experience, so that about half of the college-bound males had coitus in their teens, compared to three-fourths of the high school educated, and more than 80 per cent of the grade school educated. Girls were also differentially experienced at various educational levels, but religiousness was an even more important predictor, for girls more so than for boys, in the Kinsey data. Masturbation was the *main* source of sexual "outlet" for two-thirds of the college males in Kinsey's sample; but this was the chief "outlet" for only two-fifths of the same age males with only a high school education, and for less than a third of the same age with only a grade school education.

[19] Winston Ehrmann, *Premarital Dating Behavior* (New York: Holt, Rinehart, & Winston, Inc., 1959). Only 13 per cent of the girls in Ehrmann's study of 1000 college students were not virgins, but his sample was of eighteen to twenty-two years olds, and cannot be compared directly to Kinsey's sample of women at age 20.

[20] See, for example, "The Passage Through College," in the issue of the *Journal of Social Issues* entitled "Personality Development During the College Years," Vol. 12 (1956), edited by Nevitt Sanford; and Freedman's contributions to Sanford (ed.), *The American College* (New York: John Wiley & Sons, Inc., 1962); as well as Freedman, *The College Experience*.

[21] See Freedman, *The College Experience*, p. 85.

while two of the three "uninhibiteds" expressed some dissatisfaction.[22] But none of the eleven felt that she had done anything sinful or wrong. Data from the questionnaire study showed a considerable "liberalizing" of sexual attitudes (e.g., about "temptations," homosexuality, and abortion) between freshman and senior year at Vassar. Most of the changes were in attitudes and judgments about behavior, not in behavior itself. Although most were themselves virgins, virginity in the abstract had little meaning for the majority. Of concern was not whether religious or social standards were transgressed, but whether personal integrity was preserved, which meant primarily that sexual expression should take place within the context of a "meaningful relationship." More will be said about this below.

It is clear that there has been, if not a revolution, at least an evolution—some will prefer to describe it as a devolution—in the standards of sexual behavior among college women. In an earlier time, fidelity within marriage was considered the duty of the wife but not necessarily of the husband, who often had at least tacit approval for his visits to a brothel. But since the 1930's, the sexual behavior of college women has become less different from that of college men.[23] When the mothers of today's adolescent and college-age girls were themselves "bobby-soxers," about seven in each thousand had babies outside of wedlock; today, about seventeen out of a thousand of their daughters are having illegitimate children, about one hundred thousand a year. It is estimated that somewhere between one hundred and two hundred thousand more are conceived and aborted.[24] In 1957, about 40 per cent of the country's unwed mothers were teenagers, but in 1940, the figure was 46 per cent.[25] Indications are that no dramatic changes are taking place in the number of teenage unwed mothers.

Changes in attitudes toward sex are more striking, however. Ira L. Reiss has presented some interesting data comparing the attitudes of high school

---

[22] Kinsey and Gebhard reported that "69 per cent of the still unmarried females in the sample who had had premarital coitus insisted they did not regret their experiences. Another 13 per cent recorded some minor regrets" (Kinsey, *Sexual Behavior in the Human Female*, p. 316). They also found that "77 per cent of the married females, looking back from the vantage point of their more mature experience, saw no reason to regret their premarital coitus" (*ibid.*).

[23] Numerous studies show that men and women become more like each other with greater education, the women losing some of the more stereotyped forms of femininity, and men sloughing off some of their compulsive masculinity.

[24] Susan Strom, "The Schools and the Pregnant Teen-Ager," *Saturday Review*, 50 (September 16, 1967), 80–81, 97. At the present rate, there will be about 30,000 additional pregnant girls each year for the next decade. Improved contraceptive techniques and their increasing acceptability may change this, of course.

[25] Ira L. Reiss, "Sexual Codes in Teen-Age Culture," *The Annals*, 338 (November 1961), 53–62. Reiss also notes that although a slight rise in the rate of venereal disease has been reported for teenagers, it is "quite likely that this slight increase is due to the greater number of teenagers today. More than 80 per cent of the venereal disease reported is from older groups of people" (*ibid.*). The pregnancies of teenagers are concentrated in the lower class (although it should be noted that the upper classes are more favorably disposed toward—and can better afford—abortion). See also Ira L. Reiss, *Premarital Sexual Standards in America* (New York: The Free Press, 1960).

A Campus Sexual Revolution? 133

and college students with those of adults. For example, 85 per cent of the students felt that petting was acceptable for engaged men, and 82 per cent for engaged women; the figures for the adult sample were: 61 per cent for the male and 56 per cent for the female.[26] Fifty-two per cent of the students approved of intercourse for the engaged male, and 44 per cent for the engaged female. Only 20 and 17 per cent, respectively, of the adults would allow intercourse for the engaged male and female.

Additional data can be found in the study of Bell and Buerkle comparing the attitudes of 217 college females with those of their mothers.[27] Eighty-eight per cent of the mothers thought it "very important" for a girl to be a virgin when she married, and the remaining 12 per cent judged this "generally important." But only 55 per cent of the daughters felt it "very important," 34 per cent thought it "generally important," and 13 per cent replied that it was "unimportant." Further, more than four-fifths of the mothers thought intercourse during engagement was "very wrong," compared to slightly more than a third of the daughters. It is perhaps not surprising, then, that only 37 per cent of the daughters believed they should answer freely their mothers' questions about their sexual behavior, while 83 per cent of the mothers expected such answers. In the Bell and Buerkle data, it also appeared that freshman and sophomore girls did not yet diverge greatly from their mothers' attitudes, but around age twenty there emerged "sharp differences between mothers and daughters in regard to premarital sexual attitudes." [28]

Regarding the sexual behavior of college women, Freedman concluded after a review of the available data that, unlike attitudinal changes, behavioral changes since World War I have not been great. Kinsey, after all, reported that nearly two-fifths of the unmarried women who were college graduates were not virgins at age twenty-five. There is little doubt that sexual experience increases during college, but most begin higher education with extremely limited experience. Freedman suggests that "various degrees of petting are the norm" for college students and believes that between half and three-fourths of the women in college will refuse to have intercourse, except "perhaps on the brink of marriage."

What of college men? We are prepared to expect greater sexual activity from men than women, if only due to the vestiges of the double standard. Joseph Katz, whose own research is discussed below, notes that sexual interest does not correlate with the onset of puberty: some do not show any such interest until some time between seventeen and twenty-one. But only about a third of the boys in his Berkeley and Stanford sample reported an absence of sexual interest until after seventeen, compared to three-fifths of the girls.[29]

---

[26] Reiss, "Sexual Codes in Teen-age Culture."
[27] Robert R. Bell and Jack V. Buerkle, "Mother and Daughter Attitudes to Premarital Sexual Behavior," *Marriage and Family Living*, 23 (1961), 390–392.
[28] *Ibid.*, p. 392.
[29] Joseph Katz, "A Portrait of Two Classes: The Undegraduate Students at Berkeley and Stanford From Entrance to Exit," in Katz, *Growth and Constraint in College Students*, p. 60.

Freedman pointed out that although few women are nonvirgins at college entrance, about one-fourth of the men had experienced intercourse. By senior year, about half of the men have had intercourse, compared to about a fourth of the women.[30] At San Francisco State, Freedman found that 19 per cent of the women he sampled, and 61 per cent of the men, had engaged in intercourse. About half of the men and virtually all of the women had done so within the context of a serious emotional relationship. Perhaps one quarter of the college men differed substantially from most of the college women in that they had experienced intercourse with six or eight girls, often beginning in high school. The majority of these men seemed to hold something of a double standard, classifying women as either "good" and inviolable, or as objects to be exploited. There is little support, however, in the Freedman data for charges of campus promiscuity.

There is evidence that males in colleges and universities with religious affiliations have less sexual experience than those in secular schools. The writer collected some data from a sample of fifty freshmen entering Notre Dame in 1967 with a view to looking especially at the differences between students' own sexual experience and what they believed to be the experience of others. An attempt was made to discover the extent of several kinds of sexual behavior. Forty-four per cent of the sample had "french-kissed" ("deep" or "tongue" kissed) very little or not at all, and less than a third had done so "quite a bit," "very much," or "very, very much." But their perception was that only 10 per cent of their student colleagues had little or no experience in this regard, and they believed that more than a third had french-kissed considerably. Only slightly more than half had petted "above the waist," about a fourth considerably, but their perception was that more than 90 per cent of their colleagues were experienced in this regard, half of them considerably. Less than half had petted "below the waist," less than a fifth considerably. But they believed that about 85 per cent of the others had done this and that two-thirds had done so considerably. Less than a third had "petted to emission," about 20 per cent considerably. They expected that about four-fifths would have done so, and that more than a third would have done so considerably. About the same percentage (32 per cent) had experienced intercourse—20 per cent with one girl, 2 per cent with two girls, 8 per cent with several, and 2 per cent with many. The students in the sample thought, however, that about two-thirds of the others had had intercourse and that nearly a third would have done so considerably.

The range of experience was even more limited. Only 60 per cent had "necked" with more than two girls, about a third with several, the remainder with many. Less than half had french-kissed with more than two girls, 29 per cent with several, 15 per cent with many. The petting was done for the most part with one or two girls, and most of those who had experienced intercourse had not only done so with only one girl, but had done little

[30] Freedman, *The College Experience.*

french-kissing or petting with anyone else. There was a strong suggestion of the long-term dating of one person, which had led to intercourse once or twice, perhaps during the summer before they came to college, both out of sentiment that "parting was near," and perhaps to stake out a claim, or "obligate" the other to "faithfulness." The majority, of course, were relatively inexperienced. Certainly these Notre Dame freshmen were far from promiscuous.[31] After studying behavior at thirty-seven representative institutions, the Committee on the College Student of the Group for the Advancement of Psychiatry (G.A.P.) also concluded that the charge of collegiate promiscuity was entirely unfounded.[32]

Not only are orgies uncommon, but even satisfactory social life is hard to find. The recent data collected by Katz and his associates at two of the country's leading universities will surprise many, although probably few who are close to life on the campus.[33] Students at both Stanford and Berkeley clearly agreed that the freshman year was the worst for them socially: 51 per cent of the Stanford men and 39 per cent of the women said this; at Berkeley, 43 and 42 per cent of the men and women, respectively, said so. More even results at Berkeley may reflect the nearly one-to-one sex ratio there, compared to two and a half boys per girl at Stanford. The men's situation at both schools improves more than the women's: whereas more than half of the Stanford and Berkeley men reported having *no* evening dates in an average week during their freshman year, only a third of the seniors were without evening dates in an average week. About a fourth of the Stanford and Berkeley freshman women had no evening dates in an average week and the proportion was just as high for seniors. Even with the favorable male-female ratio at Stanford, over a fifth of the women appeared to have no dates in an average week in any of the four college years, according to Katz.[34]

One-third of the Stanford men in Katz's sample, and half of those at

---

[31] In fact, it may well be that an over-concern with relatively harmless forms of adolescent sexual expression (especially masturbation) is common among a fairly large number of students. Riffel reports that a study in the late 1950's at Catholic Fordham showed that somewhere between a fourth and a third of the students who came for counseling to the Fordham Psychological Services were troubled by excessive guilt about sexual matters. While such a sample is not representative, it was surprising to find percentages as high for boys as for girls, although scruples in both declined from freshman to senior year. See F. A. Riffel, S.J., "Sex and Scrupulosity," in W. Bier, S.J. (ed.), *The Adolescent and His Search for Understanding* (New York: Fordham University Press, 1963), pp. 39–51.
[32] Group for the Advancement of Psychiatry, *Sex and the College Student*, GAP Report No. 60 (November 1965).
[33] Katz, *Growth and Constraint in College Students*.
[34] *Ibid.*, pp. 58–61. Perhaps this helps explain the popularity of the lyrics in a recent Beatles' song: "All the lonely people, where do they all come from?" It may also help explain why Katz found that entering college freshmen, ranking the periods of life according to when they thought people were "most happy," put the period from thirteen to sixteen near the bottom, but expected the period from seventeen to twenty-one to be near the top. As seniors, the years from seventeen to twenty-one ranked lower. College turned out to be not exactly the "ball" the slick magazines promised.

Berkeley, reported they did not think they had experienced a meaningful relationship with a girl; nor did roughly a third and a quarter of the Stanford and Berkeley men, respectively, have any close ties to other men. Women were somewhat less isolated, although about one-quarter at both schools reported they had no close friendships with any men; but less than a fifth of the Berkeley women and an eighth of those at Stanford had no real relationships with other girls. It is interesting that people who have close friendships with members of their own sex, according to the Katz research, tend to have deeper relationships with members of the opposite sex as well.[35]

Less than a third of the senior men and women at both schools reported they had reached a high degree of physical intimacy with another. In a smaller interview sample of 166 juniors, about a third of the men and a quarter of the women had experienced sexual intercourse. These students typically had known each other for a considerable period of time before physical intimacy occurred. As in much of the other research, Katz found less behavioral than attitudinal change between freshman and senior years. It is interesting to compare the freshman and senior responses to three items inquiring directly into attitudes toward sexual behavior:

RESPONSES TO THREE SEXUAL ITEMS BY SCHOOL, SEX, AND CLASS
(After Katz, *Growth and Constraint in College Students*)

	\multicolumn{4}{c}{Percentage Answering "True"}
	Stanford		Berkeley	
	Men (N=185)	Women (N=148)	Men (N=286)	Women (N=265)
	Fr Sr	Fr Sr	Fr Sr	Fr Sr
"No man of character would ask his fiancee to have sexual intercourse with him before marriage."	52 11	52 11	47 13	54 21
"People would be happier if sex experience before marriage were taken for granted in both men and women."	33 60	18 45	41 63	18 51
"I believe women ought to have as much sexual freedom as men."	61 77	32 57	59 76	35 60

By senior year, less than a third of the Berkeley and Stanford men and women opposed sexual relations for the male before marriage. Three-fourths of the men and three-fifths of the women agreed that women ought to have as much freedom as men. Women endorse sexual intercourse and even sexual

[35] *Ibid.*, p. 50.

equality less strongly than men, although clearly more strongly as seniors than as freshmen. But it is significant that extramarital intercourse is apparently considered an altogether different matter by students of both sexes at both universities: only 11 per cent of the Stanford men and 3 per cent of the women condoned extramarital intercourse; at Berkeley the figures were 13 per cent of the men and 10 per cent of the women.

Some comparable data are available from the writer's sample at Notre Dame. Asked how important it was that their wives be virgins, 36 per cent of the freshmen responded that it was "very important," 24 per cent that it was "fairly important," 17 per cent that it was "somewhat important," another 17 per cent that it was "not at all important," and 4 per cent did not know. Only 8 per cent of the 36 per cent who deemed virginity "very important" had had intercourse, all but one with one girl only; of the 24 per cent who said it was "fairly important," only 4 per cent had had intercourse; of the "somewhat important" group, 10 of the 17 per cent had had intercourse; and of those who considered virginity "not at all important," all but one had had intercourse, although most had done so with only one girl. A large number of those who did not insist on virginity for their wives, then, seemed to have had intercourse with one girl only, and it is not clear whether or not they were thinking of her when responding that it was "fairly" or "somewhat" or "not at all important." Considerably different responses might have been given to an item asking about feelings regarding marriage to a girl who had previously had intercourse with someone else.

I suggest this because of the clear indications in the available data of the importance of "real relationships" to the contemporary collegian. Some link this concern to the broader social and political forces making for instability in our time. Those now in college are, of course, the only generation yet born into a world where someone an ocean away can push a button sending all of us up in smoke. If the angst of the present had its counterpart in the acedia of the Middle Ages, the formerly prescribed cure of hard and unremitting prayer is unlikely to be successful in a post-death-of-God age. These people have seen, as Martin Marty put it, "the exhaustion of a tradition: Western, production-directed, problem-solving, goal-oriented and compulsive in its way of thinking." [36] Acknowledging this bankruptcy, the more sensitive of the young seek alternatives; they grope toward a new ethic. This, Freedman points out, "means, among other things, a resurgence of the impulse life, of instincts or biology. . . . This is sexual, although not sexual in a narrow sense." [37] They follow such mentors as Paul Goodman, Norman O. Brown, Erich Fromm, Herbert Marcuse, and even—for the less sophisticated—Hugh Hefner. And this leads to mistakes, as well as new identities.

One of the dangers is what Rollo May recently called the "New Puritanism," the search for sex as a means to "fulfillment," but not involving

[36] Quoted in *Time*, 90 (July 7, 1967), 19.
[37] Freedman, *The College Experience*, p. 126.

love and commitment.[38] Those who need to prove their acceptability or desirability often seem hooked on a kind of compulsive sexuality which appears rather joyless. There seems to be so much concentration on proving one can "make it" sexually that the whole experience seems grim and urgent.[39]

Another danger is entrapment in homosexuality. It is difficult to know the prevalence of homosexual behavior on the campus. Impressionistic reports indicate that homosexual exploration is more common than is usually believed, particularly at all-male schools. What proportion of these lead to persistent homosexuality is unknown. Abram Kardiner states that "male homosexuality has had a tremendous increase in the last three decades," [40] and Freedman also believes it is fairly common, although not necessarily on the increase.[41] It does not seem to be declining.[42]

Among women, however, homosexual involvements may be decreasing, primarily because of the new-found heterosexual freedom in the last quarter-century. In 1929, Katherine Davis reported that nearly a fifth of the women in her sample had engaged in homosexual activity with other women.[43] This is much higher than the 4 per cent found by Bromley and Britten in the 1930's, but perhaps the samples differed considerably. Freedman discovered no overt homosexuality in his sample of forty-nine Vassar students.

One other danger which should be mentioned briefly here is that of pregnancy. It may seem that the dangers of unwanted pregnancy are virtually eliminated with the easy availability of condoms, diaphragms, IUD's, foams, pills for women *and* (soon) men, and all the rest. But with "authenticity" a cornerstone of the new morality, some students are insistent that sex must occur spontaneously, without taking precautions, which not only dampens desire but also seems to build a limitation into the relationship. There are those, of course, who seem to desire a pregnancy as punishment for behavior about which they have been unable to avoid feeling guilt.

---

[38] Rollo May, "Antidotes for the New Puritanism," *Saturday Review*, 39 (March 26, 1966), 19–43.

[39] Some of the mood of this sexual athleticism has been well caught by Marlene Nadle in her "Larger than Life, Less than Human," *Village Voice*, February 24, 1966. She quotes a touching statement about the New Puritanism from a University of Connecticut coed: "And so I yield myself completely to him. Society says I should. Damn society!" Girls are probably more sensitive to such social pressures, and feel more cheated by them. Both Ehrmann and Katz found sex and affection more closely associated for girls than boys: 48 per cent of the Stanford men felt that sex had to be accompanied by affection, compared to 86 per cent of the women, in the Katz data; 32 per cent of Berkeley men felt this, as compared to 63 per cent of the women.

[40] Abram Kardiner, "The Flight from Masculinity," in Hans Ruitenbeek (ed.), *The Problem of Homosexuality in Modern Society* (New York: E. P. Dutton & Co., Inc., 1963), p. 18.

[41] Freedman, *The College Experience*, pp. 104–105.

[42] McLuhanists contend that the psychic mobility and heightened intuition the new media require of us all will lead to accelerating sensitivity and tenderness in men, with accompanying homosexuality.

[43] Davis, *Factors in the Sex Life of Twenty-Two Hundred Women*, p. 245.

Therefore pregnancies do occur, and some marriages are still precipitated by them.

Part of the cause for such problems is the inadequacy of sexual instruction students receive.[44] This is beyond our present concern. It is important to mention here the insistence of the G.A.P.'s Committee on the College Student that even unfortunate sexual experiences can be the occasion of individual growth. The same behavior that may precipitate despair, frigidity, and inhibiting guilt in one person may lead to personality growth in another. Although some sexual activity represents the attempt to work out hang-ups, the preponderance of the evidence from such recent research as that of Freedman and Katz is that sexual intimacy takes place within the context of a serious relationship. It is interesting that both Ehrmann, nearly a decade ago, and Katz, in the mid-1960's, found that both sexes are more lenient about what is permissible for their peers than for themselves. The high marriage rate for students is another indication of their basic seriousness; one in ten of Katz's student sample was married, and other studies have found rates as high as one in six.[45] The great majority of college alumni are married by the time of their fifth homecoming after graduation.

There are solid reasons to suggest, then, that there has been no sexual revolution on the campus.[46] As a number of studies have shown, college students are in large part like their parents; they reflect the conservatism of the American middle classes.[47] If some of the brightest and most autonomous

[44] The Kronhausens discovered that only about half of the two hundred male students they studied had any adequate sexual instruction, even at home. See Phyllis and Eberhard Kronhausen, *Sex Histories of American College Men* (New York: Ballantine Books, Inc., 1960), p. 29.

[45] See Freedman, *The College Experience*, pp. 114–115.

[46] Just as this chapter was completed, a similar review of the available evidence resulted in the same conclusion; see Robert B. Sherwin and George C. Keller, "Sex on the Campus," *Columbia College Today*, 15 (Fall 1967), 22–34. But in late summer 1968, Vance Packard's *The Sexual Wilderness* (New York: David McKay Co., Inc., 1968) presented some different findings. Based on the questionnaire returns from 1393 juniors and seniors in twenty-one U.S. colleges and universities, Packard concluded that the proportion of nonvirgins among college women had more than doubled during the 1960's. About two-fifths of the women who responded to his questionnaire reported having experienced intercourse, compared to three-fifths of the college males. Increases in pre-coital sexual experience seemed also to have occurred. Students from the East and Far West were the most permissive; Southern males reported the greatest experience of any group, but Southern females were among the least experienced. Other results support the general conclusions of this chapter: there was little evidence of promiscuity, and considerable emphasis upon the "serious emotional relationship" ethic described above.

[47] Several of the research ventures summarized in the Katz volume indicate this; see also the research on student political and social attitudes in Seymour Lipset (ed.), *Student Politics* (New York: Basic Books, Inc., 1967), particularly the comprehensive chapter of Lipset and Philip Altbach, "Student Politics and Higher Education in the United States," pp. 199–252. Further evidence that there are typically few dramatic personality changes in college can be found in Katz, *Growth and Constraint in College Students*, and in Stanley King, "Personality Stability: Early Findings of the Harvard Student Study," a paper read at the American College Personnel Association Conference, Dallas, March 21, 1967 (mimeographed).

students are highly vocal and visible in their petitions for contraceptive information and freer dormitory visiting policies, this is but a manifestation of their more comprehensive demand for a reexamination of a value system which allows the wholesale destruction of a small agricultural country and the systematic exploitation of our own minorities, including children. What are we to respond to them when they ask about the expenditure of $78,030,661 on Barbie dolls in 1962–1963? [48] Or about the $40-a-day spent in frantic search for Mr. or Miss Right at Grossinger's during "Singles Week"? [49] How can a society which condones this—let alone elects one governor who is said to have suggested North Vietnam be "turned into a parking lot" and another who wielded axe handles to chase Negroes from his restaurant—worry about what happens to collegians in fraternity houses and motels? It is difficult to answer such questions.

One of the things it is especially important to point out is that the students who are most permissive about such things as sexual relations before marriage—at least attitudinally—are those who have the strongest intellectual interests and who in other ways more closely approximate the ideal student that faculty and administration say they want.[50] Other research has shown that the college dropout is often too mature and complex to fit readily into the docile role expected of him on some college and university campuses.[51] There is, after all, much that is wrong with college life today.

Katz has some data bearing on the artificiality of the campus and its discontinuity with "the real world." For example, only 4 per cent of the students at Stanford and Berkeley expected sports or athletics to be important in their lives after graduation, yet about half the men and a third of the women spent considerable time playing and attending sports while in college.[52] It is ironic that this unreality persists (although the more radical students say faculty and administrations encourage it) at the same time that students are coming to college more ready than ever to break with their families—if they have not already done so through a strong high school subculture—and to play a more mature role. Jencks and Riesman

[48] Donovan Bess, "Barbie and Her Friends," *Ramparts*, 3 (April 1965), 25–30. Gael Greene reports that $25,000,000 is spent by teenage girls on deodorants each year, $20,000,000 on lipstick, and $9,000,000 on home permanents; see *Sex and the College Girl* (New York: Dell Publishing Co., Inc., 1965), p. 87.

[49] *The New York Times*, August 28, 1967.

[50] Joseph Katz et al., "Stress and Development During the College Years" (Stanford, Calif.: Institute for the Study of Human Problems, no date; mimeographed). Further evidence for this statement can be found in the Katz volume, *Growth and Constraint in College Students*. See W. Watts and D. Whittaker, "Free Speech Advocates at Berkeley," *Journal of Applied Behavioral Science*, 2 (1966), 41–62; and "Profile of a Non-Conformist Youth Culture: A Study of the Berkeley Non-Students," *Sociology of Education*, 41 (Spring 1968), 178–200.

[51] R. F. Suczek and Elizabeth Alfert, "Personality Characteristics of College Dropouts" (Berkeley: Student Health Service, 1965; mimeographed); L. Pervin, L. Reik, and W. Dalrymple, *The College Dropout and the Utilization of Talent* (Princeton: Princeton University Press, 1966).

[52] Katz, *Growth and Constraint in College Students*, p. 40.

sketch some of the forces that make college come later today, psychologically, if not chronologically, in the overall life cycle, leading to greater frustration if a series of "mickey mouse" course requirements and social regulations are encountered.[53] One result for the students who do not leave—and some of the most creative and talented do—is that they are forced to turn to each other for the acceptance they so desperately crave. Often this means either victimization by peer pressure, especially for men, that forces them to prove that they can "make it" sexually (in large measure because of the pluralistic ignorance which makes each think everyone else has had more experience than he); or escape into the fraternity-sorority world of compulsive sociability.[54] Little wonder that the more sensitive tend either to challenge the legitimacy of the whole system or to seek intimacy—psychological and physical—with another.[55] The former style leads to demonstrations and teach-ins, the latter to agitation over drinking and parietal hours. Both cause grief for administrators.

Some of the other contributors to this volume have addressed the problems arising from student discontent. I shall not rehearse these matters here. It is difficult not to agree with the insightful metaphor of Jencks and Riesman in this regard: attempts to enforce the doctrine of *in loco parentis* have "little more chance of success than a colonial administration confronted with a determined guerilla movement. . . . The occupying powers may win all the battles while gradually losing the war." [56] The nurturant approach of custodial arrangements will not work. Nor will the faculty-administration "cop-out" that would allow complete student autonomy, which, if less dangerous than most seem to believe, would be distinctly threatening to many undergraduates. What is the right mix? There are no a priori answers; they differ from campus to campus, perhaps from subculture to subculture, even from student to student. But what students, faculty, and administrators might first do, before sitting down together, as they must, to work it out on their own campus, is to consider how to best create a Zima Junction, a place where each can confront the child in himself, and consider the kind of adult he wants to become:

> I scarcely had one single care in the world,
> my life, presenting no big obstacles,
> seemed to have few or simple complications—
> life solved itself without my contributions.
> I had no doubts about harmonious answers
> which could and would be given to every question.

[53] Jencks and Riesman, "The War Between the Generations."
[54] See the contribution of Marjorie Lozoff to Katz, *Growth and Constraint in College Students*, pp. 294–372; and J. F. Scott, "Sororities and the Husband Game," *Trans-Action*, 2 (September–October 1965), 10–14.
[55] Jencks and Riesman rightly note that the proto-marital relationships which are increasingly common on the campus consume "far more time and emotional energy" than casual and exploitative ones ("The War Between the Generations").
[56] *Ibid.*, pp. 19–20.

But suddenly this felt necessity
of answering these questions for myself.
So I shall go on where I started from,
sudden complexity, self-generated,
disturbed by which I started on this journey.

Into my native forest among those
long-trodden roads I took this complication
to take stock of that old simplicity,
—like bride and groom, a country matchmaking.
So there stood youth and there childhood together,
trying to look into each other's eyes
and each offending, but not equally.
Each wanted the other to start talking.
Childhood spoke first, "Hullo then.
It's your fault if I hardly recognized you.
I thought you'd be quite different from this.
I'll tell you honestly, you worry me.
You're still in very heavy debt to me."
So youth asked if childhood would help,
and childhood smiled and promised it would help.
They said good-bye, and, walking attentively,
watching the passers-by and the houses,
I stepped happily, uneasily out
through Zima Junction, that important town.[57]

[57] From "Zima Junction," by Y. A. Yevtushenko, in *Selected Poems* (Baltimore: Penguin Books, 1964).

SELECTED BIBLIOGRAPHY

Astin, Alexander. "Trends in the Characteristics of Entering College Students, 1961–76," *American Council on Education Research Reports*, 1, 4 (1966).

Bell, Robert R. *Marriage and Family Interaction*. Homewood, Ill.: Dorsey Press, 1963.

Bell, Robert R. "Parent-Child Conflict in Sexual Values," *Journal of Social Issues*, 22 (1966), 34–44.

Bell, Robert R., and Buerkle, Jack V. "Mother and Daughter Attitudes to Premarital Sexual Behavior," *Marriage and Family Living*, 23 (1961), 390–392.

Bell, Robert R., and Buerkle, Jack V. "Mother-Daughter Conflict During the 'Launching Stage,'" *Marriage and Family Living*, 24 (1962), 384–388.

Bernard, Jessie (ed.). "Teen-Age Culture," *The Annals of the American Academy of Political and Social Science*, 338 (November 1961), 1–12.

Bier, W. (ed.). *The Adolescent: His Search for Understanding*. New York: Fordham University Press, 1963.

Bromley, Dorothy D., and Britten, Florence H. *Youth and Sex*. New York: Harper & Row, Publishers, 1938.

Brown, Norman O. *Life Against Death*. Middletown, Conn.: Wesleyan University Press, 1959.

Brown, Norman O. *Love's Body*. New York: Random House, Inc., 1966.

Davis, Katherine B. *Factors in the Sex Life of Twenty-Two Hundred Women*. New York: Harper & Row, Publishers, 1929.

Ehrmann, Winston. *Premarital Dating Behavior*. New York: Holt, Rinehart and Winston, Inc., 1959.

Ellis, Albert. *Sex and the Single Man*. New York: Lyle Stuart, Inc., 1963.

Ellis, Albert. *Sex Without Guilt*. New York: Lyle Stuart, Inc., 1958.

Ford, Clellan S., and Beach, Frank A. *Patterns of Sexual Behavior*. New York: Harper & Row, Publishers, 1954.

Freedman, Mervin. *The College Experience*. San Francisco: Jossey-Bass, Inc., Publishers, 1967.

Fromm, Erich. *The Art of Loving*. New York: Bantam Books, Inc., 1963.

Ginzberg, Eli. *Values and Ideals of American Youth*. New York: Columbia University Press, 1962.

Goodman, Paul. *Growing Up Absurd*. New York: Random House, Inc., 1962.

Goodman, Paul. *Hawkweed*. New York: Random House, Inc., 1967.

Gornick, Vivian. "It's a Queer Hand Stoking the Campfire," *The Village Voice*, April 7, 1966.

Gorovitz, Samuel (ed.). *Freedom and Order in the University*. Cleveland: Western Reserve University Press, 1967.

Gottlieb, David, and Ramsey, Charles. *The American Adolescent*. Homewood, Ill.: Dorsey Press, 1964.

Greene, Gael. *Sex and the College Girl*. New York: Dell Publishing Co., 1964.

Group for the Advancement of Psychiatry. *The College Experience: A Focus for Psychiatric Research*. GAP Report No. 52 (May 1962).

Group for the Advancement of Psychiatry. *Sex and the College Student*. GAP Report No. 60 (November 1965).

Hagmaier, G., C.S.P., and Gleason, R. W., S.J. *Counselling the Catholic*. New York: Sheed and Ward, 1959.

Hassenger, Robert. "Freedom and the Quality of Student Life," in E. Manier and J. Houck (eds.), *Academic Freedom and the Catholic University*, Notre Dame, Ind.: Fides Publishers, 1967.

Hassenger, Robert. "A Rationale for Changing Student Values," *Educational Record*, 48 (Winter 1967), 61–67.

Hassenger, Robert (ed.). *The Shape of Catholic Higher Education*. Chicago: University of Chicago Press, 1967.

Hassenger, Robert. "Values and Social Change," *The Barat Review*, 2 (June 1967), 124–136.

Hettlinger, Richard F. *Living with Sex: The Student's Dilemma*. New York: Seabury Press, 1966.

Jencks, Christopher, and Riesman, David. *The Academic Revolution*. Garden City, N.Y.: Doubleday & Company, Inc., 1968.

Katz, Joseph (ed.). *Growth and Constraint in College Students*. Stanford: Institute for the Study of Human Problems, 1967.

Kennedy, Eugene. *Fashion Me a People: Man, Woman and the Church*. New York: Sheed and Ward, 1967.

Kinsey, Alfred C., and Gebhard, Paul. *Sexual Behavior in the Human Female*. Philadelphia: W. B. Saunders Company, 1953.

Kinsey, Alfred C., Pomeroy, Wardell B., and Martin, Clyde E. *Sexual Behavior in the Human Male*. Philadelphia: W. B. Saunders Company, 1948.

Knorr, Owen A., and Minter, W. John (eds.). *Order and Freedom on Campus: The Rights and Responsibilities of Faculty and Students*. Boulder, Colo.: Western Interstate Commission for Higher Education, 1965.

Kronhausen, Phyllis and Eberhard. *Sex Histories of American College Men.* New York: Ballantine Books, Inc., 1960.

Marcuse, Herbert. *Eros and Civilization.* Boston: Beacon Press, Inc., 1955.

Maslow, Abraham H., and Sakoda, James M. "Volunteer-Error in the Kinsey Study," *Journal of Abnormal and Social Psychology,* 47 (1952), 252–267.

Reiss, Ira L. "How and Why America's Sex Standards Are Changing." *Trans-Action,* 5 (March 1968), 26–32.

Reiss, Ira L. *Premarital Sexual Standards in America.* New York: The Free Press, 1960.

Reiss, Ira L. "Sexual Codes in the Teen-Age Culture," *The Annals of the American Academy of Political and Social Science,* 338 (November 1961), 53–62.

Rubin, Isador. "Sex and the College Student: A Bibliography of New Findings and Insights," *Journal of the National Association of Women Deans and Counselors,* 26 (1963), 34–39.

Ruitenbeek, Hans (ed.). *The Problem of Homosexuality in Modern Society.* New York: E. P. Dutton & Co., Inc., 1963.

Sanford, Nevitt. "The Developmental Status of the Entering College Freshman," in N. Sanford (ed.), *The American College,* New York: John Wiley & Sons, Inc., 1962.

Sanford, Nevitt. *Why Colleges Fail.* San Francisco: Jossey-Bass, Inc., Publishers, 1968.

Sanford, Nevitt (ed.). *The American College.* New York: John Wiley & Sons, Inc., 1962.

Smith, Ernest A. *American Youth Culture.* New York: The Free Press, 1963.

Sontag, Susan. "Notes on Camp," *Against Interpretation.* New York: Random House, Inc., 1966.

Vincent, Clark. *Unmarried Mothers.* New York: The Free Press, 1961.

DOUGLAS KENT HALL

Student Freedom and the Development of Creative Education

Douglas Kent Hall, Northwest author and poet, and former Instructor at the University of Portland, has had numerous short stories published.

One of the most promising advances for fostering creativity in higher education in a long while seems to be growing out of the present unrest among students on the college campuses across this nation. In assessing the positive value of this movement, two things stand out above everything else—its scope and the consistency of the demands students are making of faculties and administrative bodies. If the revolt in particular areas has not been large enough or ugly enough to attract national news coverage, we can see it clearly by quickly reviewing campus newspapers from Columbia to Berkeley and from the University of Montana to the University of Texas. The movement is, happily, both social and intellectual. Students are crying out for change: they want a place on the floodgate and not merely to remain an anonymous part of the flow that gushes through it. They are demanding a stronger voice (or, on some campuses, simply *a* voice) in the governing of their affairs, which they feel—and rightly so—have been badly neglected in the past few years. They are now asking for some sensible revisions in the archaic codes that have made the possibility of obtaining an education, in the real sense of the word, almost obsolete. And most important, they want to participate in the restructuring of an educational system that will put a measure of integrity back into the business of learning, a commodity sadly lacking in our present system.

What I foresee as a probable outcome of this student discontent is the promise in the not too distant future of a secure place for creativity in higher education. The advantages of developing creativity in education are not limited to any particular type of student. The creative approach would mean an improvement in two broad areas of education. The first of these would be the creative education of the general student, which would constitute a major advance over what the present system is offering him; for the most part, our universities provide students with a kind of advanced training, with emphasis on acquiring skills and learning to respond, instead of education, or the development of independent thinking. The second would be the education of the creative student—the poet, the musician, the painter, the sculptor, the actor, the film-maker—which, as a total concept, is almost nonexistent in the present system. Under a plan based on fostering creativity the artistic individual would not be required, as he now is, to exist on one plane as an artist and on another as a student. My belief is that through this kind of education we could not only help the general student discover in himself a thinking human being instead of a machine, but that we could also help the creative student realize his full artistic potentialities.

At the core of most of the student discontent is a drive for more freedom. And this is, I think, basic to making creative education a reality. The students want to be freer socially, intellectually, and personally. But these ends are difficult to achieve. Part of the students' problem is to somehow prove to the establishment that there is some positive value in what they seek. What they are encountering in their fight is the old misconception that the freedom of which they speak is synonymous with capriciousness, disregard for established codes of morality, and lack of proper respect for law; in short, the conservative attitude is that, if they had what they wanted, the end would be utter chaos. The students' immediate reaction to this opposition is to brand it as being the senile judgment of an old-fashioned conformist regime. But the misconception of freedom did not come into being out of idle fears. In his book *Escape From Freedom*, Erich Fromm explores the dual nature of freedom in a way that seems extremely meaningful to an understanding of its values and drawbacks:

> . . . freedom has a twofold meaning for modern man: that he has been freed from traditional authorities and has become an "individual," but that at the same time he has become isolated, powerless, and an instrument of purposes outside of himself, alienated from himself and others; furthermore, that this state undermines his self, weakens and frightens him, and makes him ready for submission to new kinds of bondage. Positive freedom on the other hand is identical with the full realization of the individual's potentialities, together with his ability to live actively and spontaneously. Freedom has reached a critical point where, driven by the logic of its own dynamism, it threatens to change into its opposite. The future of democracy depends on the realization of the individualism that has been the ideological aim of modern thought since the Renaissance. The cultural and political crisis of our day is not due to the fact that there is too much individualism but that what we believe to be individualism has become an empty shell. The victory of freedom is possible only if democracy develops into a society in which the individual is not subordinated to or manipulated by any power outside of himself, be it the State or the economic machine;

finally, a society in which his conscience and ideals are not the internalization of external demands, but are really *his* and his self. These aims could not be fully realized in any previous period of modern history; they had to remain largely ideological aims, because the material basis for the development of genuine individualism was lacking. Capitalism has created this premise. The problem of production is solved—in principle at least—and we can visualize a future of abundance, in which the fight for economic privileges is no longer necessitated by economic scarcity. The problem we are faced with today is that of the organization of social and economic forces, so that man—as a member of organized society—may be the master of these forces and cease to be their slave.[1]

The aim of democracy and of the unique society that has grown out of it is to safeguard our freedom; and very often in achieving this end it does not allow us enough freedom. We find that, as Fromm points out, freedom is mercurial and can almost without our realizing it become its opposite, a bondage. As most of us know, *freedom* is a magical word that can mean everything and nothing; it can all too easily become a mere fetish for an emotionally overloaded, intellectually empty movement. History has proved this. And people are justifiably suspicious of it.

The kind of freedom being sought by the students in today's campus revolution is not, I think, empty freedom. In many ways it closely parallels the personal inner freedom that allows the artist to proceed creatively. Since the artist's task is a selective restructuring of the mass of unrelated images he sees in the world around him into some kind of meaningful statement, he must by necessity be of the world but not in it. That is to say, the artist must be familiar with the workings of the world in the practical sense, he must be a participant in the action of living, but he must not be a slave to the world. In his discussion of the responsibility of the writer—and this could be extended to the artistic person in general—Sartre goes one step further to state: "If the writer is a maker of literature; in other words, if he writes—it is because he is assuming the function of perpetuating, in a world where freedom is always threatened, the assertion of freedom and the appeal to freedom." [2] So in this sense the artist, if he is completely honest, is constantly engaged in creating his own freedom by actively having to exercise and assert it. The same thing, then, is applicable to the student; his freedom, which has not only been threatened but has to a large extent been denied, can only be maintained through his will to create it.

Sartre's idea, although specifically about writers and writing, is a simple key to a more general concept of freedom and creative thinking and can easily be extended to test the validity of the student revolt in respect to an

---

[1] Erich Fromm, *Escape From Freedom* (New York: Holt, Rinehart & Winston, Inc., 1941), pp. 270–271.
[2] Jean-Paul Sartre, "The Responsibility of the Writer," in Haskell M. Block and Herman Salinger (eds.), *The Creative Vision* (New York: Grove Press, Inc., 1960).

ultimate concept of creative education. The promise this revolt gives for a better system is clearly manifest in the interest students are taking in the future of their own education. Further, to justify the students' right to revolt—indeed, their duty to revolt—Sartre adds the following indictment of someone not totally committed to his or her cause: "A writer who does not take his stand on this ground is guilty; not only is he guilty, but he soon ceases to be a writer." [3]

What does a person do when his freedom is repeatedly denied? I think there are two answers to this question. He may very easily fall under the pressures around him and accept the bondage they offer. Or he may, if he is more forthright and values his individuality, seek another kind of freedom, an artificial or fantasy freedom. Because the person has been forced into it, artificial freedom is usually exhibitionistic in nature.

Today the thwarted student is finding his artificial freedom either by "dropping out" or "turning on," or both. In the face of current publicity and polls, we cannot possibly say this is not happening; nor can we say that these same students would have dropped out and turned on no matter what we did for them or allowed them to do for themselves. Parents are concerned; authorities are concerned. And we hear a great deal of discussion about the use of drugs; most of it recommends education against their use, but this is only our Thou-shalt-not approach, which has little effect when it is made with no attractive or practical alternatives. We know, of course, that conscience-expanding drugs produce artificially a condition that can be achieved naturally through education. But at the present time we do not have a conscience-expanding educational system. We cannot offer new horizons. So the student seeks them elsewhere.

I believe an attractive alternative to student discontent can be found in the education that emphasizes creativity. The education of a creative person is largely practical; the creative person gains his proficiency through practice, trial, and error. A writer or a painter or a musician cannot simply be isolated from the world, be taught principles and methods for four years or more, and then be told to return to the world and put them to use. Generally, the creative student begins to work through imitation or out of an impulse that has struck him in a meaningful way. He makes his attempt and then measures its effect on himself, his models, and the people with whom he is in contact. From that point on, whatever progress he makes is by accrual; he discovers his faults and deficiencies and seeks methods to repair them: it is a natural process of growing, as natural as learning to walk or speak. For the finest artists, this growth through attrition never ceases. By the very nature of his work, which is interpreting the world around him in meaningful images, the artist is forced constantly to move ahead.

The creative student, because he learns early in his career that he must relate his studies to himself and the world in which he lives, finds the university to be an impractical place for getting the education he wants. The

[3] *Ibid.*

reason for this is that the university, as it now exists in America, presents the student with a hybrid, phony situation and therefore cannot provide the stimulation and atmosphere conducive to the honest continuation of his creative pursuits. Because of a growing awareness of his inner self and his possibilities, the potential artist is in a sense already free; he is becoming an individual; and he thrives on this new concept of himself. But when he enrolls in the university, where he believes he will have a chance to develop his particular talent, he finds himself in a vast melting pot. He is numbered and forced into a pre-established pattern designed to "round-him-off"; he is put into large lecture classes where there is little if any opportunity to discuss even briefly the material being presented, let alone to test it in some practical way. And he discovers that what he actually knows or what he can put to use is deemed less important than his performance on exams, what his final grade is, and how this ultimately affects the decimals in his G.P.A.

The history of how our universities fell into such a deplorable state is doubtless long and intricate. Although recently conditions in education have improved, the improvements have not come fast enough or been far-reaching enough to accommodate the increasing needs of greater numbers of students and the resultant larger and more complex educational systems.

In the university a student ought to be free to find a new kind of education and not simply a continuation of the training he took in primary and secondary schools; here, important seeds ought to be planted, he ought to be directed toward models that will help him develop his own way of thinking, and—most important—he ought to be stimulated and encouraged. Instead, he is thrown into a vastly impersonal situation where, partly as a result of the size of his classes and modern testing devices designed to facilitate grading, he is required not to learn but to memorize. In short, he is programmed to fit certain answers to certain questions. And there are few rewards for him if he attempts, even out of sheer boredom, to push beyond this and take a new look at his materials.

Some of the blame in this area lies with teachers. Admittedly, they are overloaded with classes, they have far too many students to allow personal interest and contact, and they are inevitably involved in too many meaningless faculty tasks. Given these obstacles a teacher often becomes overly concerned with his students in a purely superficial way. He places major emphasis on responses to discipline and on his students' proficiency with a skill and overlooks the fact that they are there to learn, to be taught.

A good example of this nearsightedness on the part of a teacher occurred a few weeks ago. A student I was assigned to as an adviser brought me a paper to read. Her Freshman English instructor had marked it with an "F" and written at the bottom of the last page: "Not on assigned topic." The girl was particularly upset because she had worked hard on the paper and had expected to do well. When I read the paper I thought it was in some respects exceptionally well done for a student in her class. She was obviously interested in the subject (which, by the way, was not entirely unrelated to the topic her instructor had assigned) and that made her paper readable, far more readable than those void assignment fillers submitted by students who spend the first two weeks of a term trying to "psych-out" the instructor so they can feed back what they think he wants. This particular instructor had failed to mention that the paper was interesting. And, even more shameful, he had failed to read the paper carefully enough to point out to the girl that there was a serious error in logic in the central paragraphs, as well as two or three minor mistakes in sentence mechanics. Had he done these things, he might very well have helped this girl learn something about writing. Technically, that was his job. But he simply wanted to discipline her. And naturally, since she wanted a grade out of his class, her reaction was: "All right, I'll give him what he wants."

The conclusion we must draw from the above story is applicable to a wider area than we would like to admit. That is not education; it is hardly training. In great numbers of classes in our universities the student has to warp himself to fit the thinking of his teacher, when, instead, the teacher should be working to help the student realize his individual potentialities. Parading under the guise of education we have a glorified system of training and indoctrination. Our students are required to satisfy the demands of an impersonal system instead of working to achieve self-fulfillment.

These, then, are some of the problems with the university system as it exists today. They are serious. But there is evidence of imminent change. The most propitious is rooted in the student revolt. (I am not saying faculties do not recognize these faults; they just seem reluctant, for reasons of time and security, to do anything about them.) We might well ask what might come of this rebellion among students. Camus, with his own particular kind of terse accuracy, answers us in *The Rebel*: "With rebellion, awareness is born." [4] If we can accept his premise, then we can see the reason why the growing discontent among students has not merely flared up and then died out. As Camus writes near the end of Part One of *The Rebel*: "In order to exist, man must rebel, but rebellion must respect the limit it discovers in itself—a limit where minds meet and, in meeting, begin to exist." [5]

In America, we should not find rebellion a difficult concept to accept; the history of this country is based largely on rebellion. It was populated out of numerous small rebellions and became autonomous through one large, unified rebellion. We should realize that rebellion is, in itself, a strong manifestation of the creative impulse; its purpose is to reshape and redefine incompatible parts into a more consonant whole. And its emergence as a tactic in the student movement speaks favorably for the eventual existence of creative education.

What the students ultimately hope to achieve through their rebellion is, then, the positive freedom Fromm discussed: "the full realization of the individual's potentialities, together with his ability to live actively and spontaneously." Their positive freedom in the university must come with a

---

[4] Albert Camus, *The Rebel* (New York: Random House, Inc., 1956), p. 15.
[5] *Ibid.*

realistic, practical application of the material they are studying to their lives; without this kind of assimilation the student is left, as many students now are, with a catalogue of facts, theories, and data that have little meaning outside of the context of school. These students do not have an education. An education is a preparation for coping with reality. Being able to meet oneself in the world on one's own terms is essential to a rich and happy life. The values of such an encounter are pointed out by Karl Jaspers in *Man in the Modern Age*:

> The reality of the world cannot be evaded. Experience of the harshness of the real is the only way a man can come to his own self. To play an active part in the world, even though one aims at an impossible, an unattainable goal, is the necessary precondition to one's own being. What we have to endeavour, therefore, is to live at harmony with the powers of this world without being absorbed by them.[6]

What can the university do about making the student more aware of his responsibiliy to himself—as opposed to the empty responsibility to requirements of an impersonal university system? How can it help him to come to a full realization of his individuality and bring that into a meaningful conjunction with the world around him? How, in fact, can the university be changed from a system of training to a place of education?

The basic answer to all these questions lies in rehumanizing the university. We need to create for the student a situation in which he can learn to visualize himself as an individual and recognize that the people around him are human beings and not mere machines designed either to give out or to receive back information. He should be able to look at the people about him not as competitors for a grade but as individuals with whom he can freely exchange ideas and thereby measure his own progress.

Probably the logical place to begin in transforming the existing university into this kind of desirable environment is with the faculty. They ought to be hired for a specific purpose and then not pressured into other areas. They should not be asked to be baby-sitters; they should not be looked down upon if they are not active committeemen; and if they are not sincerely engaged in writing they should not be forced into publishing vapid articles for the sake of keeping up their credentials. Their class loads should be lightened. They should be put into direct personal contact with a small number of students. Each member of the faculty ought to have his own unique contribution to make to the university community as a whole; he ought to be allowed that and not put into competition with his fellows. If these changes could be made, the university would be moving in the general direction of creative education.

Continuing in this direction, I think the next place for a major overhaul would be in curriculum. With the exception of a few basic skills

---

[6] Karl Jaspers, *Man in the Modern Age* (New York: Doubleday & Company, Inc., 1957), p. 197. Reprinted by permission of Routledge & Kegan Paul Ltd.

courses that would help the student achieve his ends, the general requirements for all students—which in many institutions are so all-encompassing and rigid that the student is left with almost no time to take the classes he is genuinely interested in or curious about—should be dropped completely. Instead, the faculty member assigned to work with the student should design a schedule to fit this student's own specific needs and personality. The student's schedule should be left flexible enough to allow him to pursue, under the close supervision of his faculty advisor, the courses of study that interest him most and are most likely to benefit him in his quest for identity and individuality.

Next, for all practical purposes, grades ought to be abolished—pass/fail or satisfactory/unsatisfactory would be sufficient to indicate to the student how he was doing (indeed, the majority of students know this without being told). I feel that such a move would eliminate a great deal of the undesirable competition that forces students to work toward artificial goals. Without competition for grades students would be encouraged to be more open with one another and would therefore discuss freely the information they get through lectures and independent study. And this would certainly be one more giant step in the direction of a more human university environment.

As I see it, these changes, if carried to their proper ends, would serve to rejuvenate our ailing system of higher education. It would satisfy a great many of the demands of the protesting students and bring them back to more serviceable pursuits; and it would offer the dropout who has left the university in search of the "real" something challenging to which he might return. It would be unrealistic to maintain that anything as brief and incomplete as what I have here outlined is not without flaws; but using these proposed changes as a starting point, an ideal college system could be devised. What it might become is encouraging. Its major promise would be the revival of integrity, which is nearly absent from our present, extremely corrupt system of university education. It might not be capitalistic, but it would be democratic; and certainly it would be humanistic. It would, in short, produce a student better prepared to go out and meet the world on its own terms than the student we are turning out today. And with this kind of education behind him, he would be better able to utilize his talents, no matter how inconsiderable, in living creatively and realizing his place and worth in his society.

JOHN BLEWETT, S.J.

Student Movements: East Asian and American Patterns*

John Blewett, S.J., until recently the Academic Dean of Sophia University, Tokyo, Japan, is now Secretariat for the worldwide system of Jesuit education.

I will state forthrightly that I am an agitator. I am an agitator because I am a priest, a teacher, and, of recent years, one condemned to the coal mines of administration. As a priest, I must protest vocally and through action against the lethargy, the smugness, the self-centeredness in myself and others that dull our wits to the things that are. As a teacher, especially in Comparative Education and in Sociology of Education, in my adopted country of Japan, I remind my students of the truth of the proverb that the "frog at the bottom of the well is ignorant of the vast ocean" (*ido no kawazu taikai wo shirazu*) and ask them to join me in dispelling our prejudices as we tackle complex social questions. As an administrator, I must exhort professors to remember their responsibilities to their students; and students to remember that although professors are cursed in not being so young and brilliant as themselves, they have at least survived and consequently deserve a hearing. Further, far more often than I would like, I must cudgel the consciences and appeal to the generosity of men with power and coin to support the university ever more fully.

* Editors' Note: This essay is a revised version of an address delivered at Marquette University on November 17, 1965. The author has recently indicated to the editors that "the antics of the Red Guards or the broadening of the peace movement among American students" has not substantially changed the nature of student movements in China and the United States. Furthermore, he asserts that where major social institutions allow a significant degree of freedom, as they do in Japan and the United States, the "concluding, unorthodox recommendations" of this essay "swing in the right direction." It is the author's opinion that "where unfreedom prevails, students can be manipulated as adroitly as their elders."

With these few words of introduction it is now necessary to survey briefly some of the essential points in the student movements of three of the mighty countries of the Pacific: China, Japan, and the United States. Some readers may be advanced enough in years to remember newspaper accounts of what history has come to know as the "Double Tenth," the beginning on October 10, 1911, of the revolution in China against the decadent Manchu dynasty, the revolution that led on February 12 of the following year to the formal abdication of the dynasty and the beginning of China's political struggle to become strong, respected in the council of nations, modern. This whirlwind, which was finally taken over and guided by the present rulers of China, was more wind than power from 1912 until another eventful day in modern history—May 4, 1919. On that day, some three thousand students in Peking, from thirteen universities and colleges, incensed at what they considered to be weakness and conniving on the part of their government vis-à-vis Japan and palpable unfairness on the part of England, France, Italy, and the United States in their treatment of China at the Versailles Peace Conference, opened a series of demonstrations. The students were indignantly earnest, as the burned home of one of their targets (Ts'ao Ju-lin) and the maimed body of another (Chang Tsung-hiang) made abundantly clear. For more than a month following this first outburst, students organized boycotts against Japan, and protests demanding that the Chinese delegation at Versailles be instructed by Peking not to sign the Treaty. On July 10, 1919, China did refuse to sign the Treaty, claiming that its interests had been sold out to Japan by compliant Western powers.[1]

The May Fourth Movement, partially organized and guided by student activists, marked the renewal in China of a national consciousness. Although the Chinese Communist Party was not formally established until July 1, 1921, May 4, 1919, is looked upon by the Party today "as marking the birth of contemporary revolutionary nationalism in China. It constituted a break with the old-style anti-foreignism centered on 'sea-devils' and 'the hairy ones' and the beginning of a new impulse, modern 'anti-imperialism.'"[2] When the Party was founded in 1921 in the French Concession in Shanghai, three of its prime movers, Li Ta-chao, Ch'en Tu-hsiu, and the absent Mao Tse-tung, saw in the action the natural culmination of the May Fourth Movement.

Another landmark in the history of the student movement in modern China is May 30, 1925. An overanxious British officer in the Shanghai International Settlement ordered his men to fire at a crowd of demonstrators. When the smoke cleared, twelve Chinese students were dead. Their deaths intensified anti-foreign feelings of the Chinese intellectuals and political leaders. A boycott of British goods ensued, extending all the way to Hong Kong. Who was right and who was wrong is still disputed, but the student-

[1] T. T. Chow, *The May Fourth Movement* (Cambridge, Mass.: Harvard University Press, 1960), *passim*.
[2] O. Edmund Clubb, *Twentieth Century China* (New York: Columbia University Press, 1964), p. 87.

martyrs became a symbol for China's demands that Western powers and Japan respect her right to self-government and forego the concessions they had wrung from her in former days of weakness.

Through the late twenties, the thirties, and the early forties, the student movement in China continued although it reached no dramatic levels of intensity such as those of May 4, 1919, and May 30, 1925. Resentment against the Western powers and Japan formed one of the main themes for writing and other activities. With the resumed attacks on China by Japan in 1937, thousands of students joined their professors in transplanting their universities from the Japanese-held sections to the western part of China. Young urbanites from Shanghai and Peking, in their trek across central China, saw at firsthand the labors of the peasant, heard stories of the effective resistance to the Japanese by the growing Communist centers under Mao Tse-tung, and looked forward to the end of war when they could use their talents to make China once again the "middle kingdom," the center of Asia.

Today, once again, China is the "middle kingdom." A breath in Peking can stir a storm in Indonesia, cause the dissolution of a scheduled Afro-Asian conference in Algeria, or keep the corridors of the U.N. alive with fearful and frightened conversations. And the students now in mainland China—how do they prosper? Have they entered into the promised land?

It is not easy to present a balanced picture of higher education in China today, for foreign observers rarely enjoy the freedom necessary to study what is going on by survey, questionnaire, and interview. Even reliable statistics on the numbers of institutions of higher education and of students have been hard to come by since 1960. Two points, however, are clear: First, student protests *against* the government are unthinkable. In the spring of 1957 Mao Tse-tung, in an effort perhaps to smoke out latent opposition to his Communist rule, called for open discussion in the words: "Let the hundred flowers all bloom; let the hundred schools contend with and emulate one another." The voices of teachers and university students were quickly heard in loud complaints about the anti-intellectualism of the regime, the excessive political indoctrination required of every university student, the inadequate opportunities for real schooling, etc. By early June, enough flowers had bloomed—and many weeds along with them, which Communist Party officials energetically set to work to pull out. Students and teachers who had criticized were led to repent of their ideological sins through endless group meetings, through hard labor, and occasionally through a bullet in the head. Perhaps one of the best summaries of the present method of government in China and of the amount of freedom it allows students for unorthodox activities was written by a Chinese-born intellectual after a visit of nearly a year in that country:

> In the last analysis the Communist method is government by organized intimidation. Rebellion is prevented not by satisfying the people, but by destroying the germs of resistance and what looks like them. This is

why the power to suppress open opposition, the army and the police, need never be activated. Government "by ideology" is really government by bullying the people to join the bullies.[3]

A few years ago I was watching a Japanese documentary on the higher education system of China. (The Japanese are able to travel to China without too much difficulty; in fact, a sizeable number of opinion-makers are invited every year by the Chinese government to visit.) I sat directly behind a Japanese Jesuit about my age who had received most of his university education in the late thirties and early forties when the militarists controlled Japan. The commentator, after guiding us through some university classrooms, remarked that all students are expected to work about three months annually on projects determined by the government. "Would Japanese university students of today accept such dictation?" he asked of his television audience. The Japanese Jesuit in front of me, quite a mild man by nature, slapped his hand hard on his chair and fairly shouted back: "No. That *was* the system in Japan. But never again." So the second point we can affirm about the Chinese student movement is that, under the guidance of Communist cadres, it must persuade students that they *want* to spend three months annually in manual labor. Since in schools students are divided into small groups in which everybody is morally responsible for what everybody else does, a large range of methods of group persuasion is available to stifle reluctance. If the reader is interested in a survey of the frightful forms of "togetherness" used in China to insure the happiness of all the inhabitants of that vast Animal Farm, it is recommended that one read the chapter "The Chinese Communists: What They Do" in Mu Fu-sheng's *The Wilting of the Hundred Flowers*.

Happily separated by a considerable stretch of water from China, Japan is another East Asian country whose student movement can be briefly examined. Perhaps many will recall that the activist units of the student movement in Tokyo made the front page of *The New York Times* of November 7, 1965. The occasion was a protest against the Japanese government attempting to terrorize it into refusing the ratification of a treaty with South Korea and the resumption of full diplomatic relations. Many of the students wore helmets, ski boots, and heavy windbreakers as they paraded beneath red flags to the Diet building for a show of strength. Long-term residents of Tokyo probably recalled similar demonstrations by the young bloods of the world's largest city: in 1952, on the occasion of the signing of the peace treaty between Japan and the Allied Powers, apart from Russia, and in May and June 1960, on the occasion of the revision of the Treaty of Mutual Cooperation and Security between Japan and the United States and the projected visit of President Eisenhower. Those with even longer memories may recall a similar demonstration in February 1936

---

[3] Mu Fu-sheng, *The Wilting of the Hundred Flowers* (New York: Frederick A. Praeger, Inc., 1962), pp. 176–177.

of young military officers against what they considered the excessively dilatory way the older military men were bending China to her knees.

Unlike China, Japan is free. Hence, although Japanese students too must live a life of some order, restrictions on their freedom are few indeed. In comparison with China, where perhaps one of every 700 people attends a college or university, in Japan one out of every 100 does. (In the United States, roughly speaking, one of forty in the total population attends college or university.) Unlike the United States where major university centers can be found in all parts of the country and the university population is diffused, in Japan university life is heavily concentrated in the Tokyo area. Approximately one out of every two Japanese collegians is in Tokyo— some 450,000, a little less than 5 per cent of the total population of Tokyo. (I believe the total college-university population of Tokyo is equivalent to that of New York City, London, and Moscow combined.)

A further feature favoring the development of the student movement in Japan is that, although there are some regulations governing class attendance, students can spend much more of their time in nonacademic activities than would be tolerated in almost any university in this country. A student at the Jesuit Sophia University in Tokyo, for example, has the legal right to take final examinations even though he has been absent from one-third of his classes. Sophia, in this respect, is considered to be quite strict. (I should add, however, that professors do not enjoy the option of dropping one-third of their classes.)

After this brief review of a few features of the university system in Japan, the origin of the *Zengakuren*, the National Federation of Students, can be examined in order to see why its political activities have become so prominent. It should be clear from the outset, of course, that the *Zengakuren* is very different from, and much less significant than, the literally hundreds of clubs and associations within individual universities. At Sophia University, for example, with a full-time student body of around 6,000, more than ninety clubs ranging in interest from archery to international tourism keep the campus humming.

To trace the history of the *Zengakuren*, it is necessary to go back to the days of spiritual and material confusion which followed upon the bitter experience of defeat in war. From 1945 to 1952 Japan was governed by the Allied Forces—effectively, under American control. In an effort to establish democracy in Japan, General Douglas MacArthur's headquarters instituted a series of far-ranging reforms, including abolition of the secret police, release of political prisoners, encouragement of the labor movement, dissolution of the *Zaibatsu* or large financial holding companies, redistribution of land, and guarantees of freedom of speech, publication, and assembly. The educational system was changed into a single track 6-3-3-4 system, and its administration was placed more in the hands of the people. Among the political prisoners released from prison were many Communists, men who quickly moved into the spiritual vacuum brought about by the defeat in war. Their work among students began. The move for student self-government organizations on university campuses quickly reflected their influence. They had been jailed for allegedly unpatriotic activities, but they now found themselves regarded by many students as the true patriots. "Democracy" was the slogan on everybody's lips, but its meaning was rarely grasped, more often than not being understood as a philosophy of "do as you please." Students began calling for autonomy for self-governing organizations. Re-examining those days of confusion, one can say that the idea of the self-governing association and many of the democratic reforms begun were all to the good, but the fact that they were manipulated by the Communists was, and is, regrettable.

In 1947 social and economic conditions in Japan were very unsettled, and students in universities were experiencing real hardships. The student self-government organizations on university campuses spearheaded the students' belief that they, the students, must solve the many problems of Japan. For greater effectiveness, more unity was needed among the self-governing organizations. To bring about this unity the National Federation of Students, *Zangakuren*, was formally organized on September 18, 1948, with a stated membership of some 220,000 students. The principles it advocated were the following: (a) Equal opportunity for education and increasing stability for students; (b) Freedom within the university and protection of the national culture; (c) Complete democratization of the educational system; (d) National independence and peace and defense of democracy; (e) Fostering of good living conditions for teaching staffs.

On the face of it, these principles are all very reasonable, but one must not forget that the leadership of the movement was Communist. The thinking behind them was that a revolution would be necessary to establish a new social order; but, under the American occupation a revolution was impossible; hence, Japan must work for her independence. Whatever one thinks of the principles and their ideological background, it is clear that, with the formation of the *Zengakuren*, all the self-government organizations on university campuses in Japan were united in one federation.

The subsequent history of *Zengakuren* has involved almost constant opposition to major legislative efforts by the Japanese government—to nuclear testing, especially as carried out by the United States and the Soviet Union, to continued occupation by the United States of Okinawa, and to the lingering presence within Japan itself of American military groups. It has been a history, too, of fission and factionalism. In January 1950, when the Japan Communist Party was severely criticized by the Cominform, the Communist Party and the *Zengakuren* expelled from their membership those considered to be excessively internationalistic. In May 1958, the leaders of the *Zengakuren* were denounced as Trotskyites by the Japan Communist Party, and they along with the entire membership were expelled from the Party. In late 1960, after its failure to prevent ratification by the Japanese Diet of the security pact with the United States, the *Zengakuren* experienced even more bitter days, with one faction after another claiming leadership. Efforts to unify the different factions are still being made, but the increasing differences between the Communist parties of Russia and China, personal ambitions of individual student leaders, and bitter memories of intrigue and denunciation make reunification very difficult, if not impossible.

To explain why the *Zengakuren* has been as successful as it has, it is necessary to emphasize that what it purports to be doing is working for peace. Since the Japanese people are united in their desire for peace if in nothing else; since students judge that they represent one of the most articulate voices of the people; since, finally, their distrust of the post-thirty generation is abysmally deep, the astute leaders of the *Zengakuren* are easily able to persuade the activist sections of the student groups to march in the name of peace.[4]

Turning now to the student movement in the United States, one should begin where all intelligent discussion begins—with the obvious. First, whereas both China and Japan have suffered defeat in war and the humiliation of foreign occupations, the United States, protected in part by the oceans cutting her off from Europe and Asia, has not. Second, the college-university system in this country was burgeoning into maturity in the 1860's, a decade before the first modern university in Japan was established. It was healthily adult in the 1890's when the substructure of the later University of Peking opened its doors. Third, students of any single generation in the United States, including the present one, face the fact that a fairly sizeable segment of the immediately preceding generation has also received a university education, and thus it becomes difficult to sustain the argument that they, the students, must provide the intelligent energy for social change. Fourth, the curricula of most students are sufficiently geared to their post-university life, and professors so persist in bedeviling them with quizzes, tests, and written assignments that time for outside activities is quite limited. Finally, the academic traditions of separation of "town and gown," of the university as a center apart from the frets and frolics of political life, of administrators and teachers acting as parents vis-à-vis their students: these and others have all worked until recently to keep the American student comparatively free from preoccupation with direct political activity, and even with sociocultural activity expanding beyond the campus.

It would be false, of course, to conclude that American campuses have not had their share of trouble, largely triggered until recently by discontent with local campus conditions. Students of higher education in this country can regale you with tale upon tale of student riots and demonstrations through the eighteenth and nineteenth centuries at our most revered centers of learning. The regimentation of student life in pre-Civil War days was so strict that in protest windows of classrooms were often broken, furniture

[4] Philip Altbach, "Japanese Students and Japanese Politics," *Comparative Education Review*, 7, 2 (October 1963), 181–188.

burned, animals led into the classrooms, professors occasionally pelted with eggs and vegetables, and some few even maimed and killed. So common were such extracurricular activities that one of the first great American psychologists, G. Stanley Hall,

> saw the history of early student life as one of the richest possible sources for the illustration of parallelism and recapitulation in human cultural development. Here was an authentic counterpart of the savage life studied by the anthropologist. Here the rigors of overwork and excessive restraint unrelieved by a vent for superabounding animal spirits in athleticism, led to exhorbitant license, rioting, dissipation, vandalism, and even personal assaults. Here were illustrations of all phases of sub-civilized existence, complete even to the secret association so characteristic of savagery; the elaborate initiations, the abuses perpetrated on newcomers, and the personal encounters.[5]

In post-Civil War days, campus riots and rebellions almost disappeared. Among the reasons for this change were: revisions of curricula away from the Latin-Greek-Philosophy matrix; willingness on the part of educators to view their students as closer to responsible adulthood than had been the practice; the development of coeducation; and the rise of college athletics and the spread of the fraternity system, with all the implications these two symbols of youthful prowess and meaningfulness contain.[6]

Although the economy of the United States during the hundred years since the end of the Civil War did not always provide abundance for all, starvation and deep-seated unrest were not problems. Wars there were, but in the two major encounters the right of the American battalions to make the world safe for democracy or to save a tottering world from Nazism did not have to be argued on college campuses. It was, by and large, clearly obvious.

It was only in 1947 that the United States National Student Association was founded at Madison, Wisconsin. It has been largely since 1960 that the nation's attention has been fastened from time to time on students as activists outside of their own campuses. What is one to make of this new phenomenon? an older generation is asking. What mean the sit-ins, the teach-ins, the loud calls for free speech unfettered by any campus rules or regulations, the concern with the civil rights and peace movements? It is not only an older generation of Americans and news-hungry editors that are asking this question. Foreign observers, including men in government and education, are also wondering. I will never forget the remark of a Japanese student when he learned of the demonstration at Berkeley in late 1964; "American student movement is no longer underdeveloped."

Whatever the meaning of the protests, one cannot overlook the fact that student activists on every campus are almost without exception a

[5] John S. Brubacher and Willis Rudy, *Higher Education in Transition: An American History, 1636–1956* (New York: Harper & Row, 1958), p. 50.
[6] Ibid., p. 54.

post-World War II group. They are the first generation to face as young adults man's power for total destructiveness as concretized in the Bomb. They are, too, as Rev. Joseph Walsh, Newman Apostolate director at Wayne State, points out,

> the first human results of a life of affluence and suburbia. They are the children of organization men, or at least their neighbors. Their lives are the products of the most organized, technologized and bureaucratized society the world has ever known. Quite possibly they are sensitive to the blight of that system in a way that adults who remember only pre-planning days cannot be.[7]

They have been schooled in the values of group decision-making and the virtues of the outer-directed man. Both at Berkeley and at Selma, Mario Savio pointed out, the same battle was being fought: for the right of those affected by decisions, educational or civic, to participate in decision-making; the enemy in both places was the same: "a depersonalized, unresponsive bureaucracy." [8]

If, after this rapid survey of student movements in three countries, I am asked for my evaluation of them, I fear that my response will produce disappointment. I think that the crucial question about student movements, especially in a stable but flexible society, concerns the participants in it *after* they have graduated and settled into their vocations. The phenomenon of the radical student of today changing into the reactionary alumnus of tomorrow is very common. It leads to the suspicion that a certain type of student wins a role of leadership on campus chiefly because he is voicing what other students in his group want to hear and that, further, when he is comfortably settled in white-collar suburbia he quickly adjusts to the naked reasonableness of not "bucking the system," even if the system needs to be bucked. It is informative to recall that some of the most vocal critics of the Chinese government in the student movement of 1919, Mao Tse-tung, Chou En-lai, and Lin Piao, are today strangely silent about the rights of a new generation of students to criticize. It is informative, too, that the torches of hope which began to flare in this decade were lit by a humble old man in Rome throwing open the windows of the Vatican to the world and by a young Harvard graduate who combined the knowledge garnered during college days with the power which his fellow-citizens voted to him in order to arouse those same citizens to their responsibilities to the unfed, the naked, the poor of the world. In their university years, neither had been active in a student movement.

I do not, emphatically do not, advocate apathy as a stance for today's student. I do advocate agitation, especially the agitation in the mind and the heart of the individual student as he faces the vast stretch of waste that his life may be if he merely and always conforms to the wisdom of his

[7] Rev. Joseph Walsh, *Commonweal*, 83 (November 19, 1965), 209.
[8] *Ibid.*, p. 207.

peer group. I think, for example, of a young Austrian woman doctor who some forty years ago practiced medicine for a time in India. Her heart seared by the awful misery of fellow-humans deprived of medical care, she returned to the West and after much consultation and prayer decided to act. She founded the Society of the Medical Missions, a group of women that now operates hospitals, nursing schools, and smaller medical centers in Asia, Africa, and Latin America. In 1960 it opened a hospital in Quinhon, Vietnam, then a peaceful fishing village. Last year it brought loving hands and understanding eyes to forty thousand Vietnamese. As refugee camps swell around it, the nuns respond, concernedly engaged in a war which only recently has been recognized by American government officials as of equal importance with the bullet-war—that against poverty, suffering, and disease. When some three years ago I visited one of the centers of the Medical Missionaries, I learned that they had more than one hundred requests from underdeveloped areas to open hospitals and training centers for nurses—requests they could not fill for lack of resources, human and financial. I wonder how many of today's activists are planning for a *lifelong* dedication of their talents to those in need.

I think, too, of one of my Jesuit classmates of twenty years ago. He was that quiet type of activist who always seemed to have time to use his brilliant mind and clear understanding to tutor those in greatest need. After finishing a doctorate in economics at Columbia University, he asked, long before Peace Corps days, to be sent to India. As coordinator now of a widespread educational and social program largely financed by the German Catholic bishops, he is raising hopes in village after village in that country. His name, like that of the hospital at Quinhon, has, to my knowledge, never appeared in *Time* or *Life*; nor will it. But he is at work where the action is and always has been: in the hearts and attitudes of men.

I would like to conclude this essay with a few recommendations for students engaged in activism on today's campuses in this country. The recommendations are the same I offer to Japanese students, and would offer to Chinese students, if I could.

1. Remember that now as never before the world needs men and women competent in their profession, wise in their understanding of life, compassionate in their reaching out to the voiceless destitute of our planet. To develop competence, study; to learn wisdom, burn out through reflection, prayer, and fasting the petty resentments that in later life make it so easy to become callous to the social injustices that should be changed; to feel and keep feeling compassion, allow yourselves from time to time, if not systematically, to experience suffering. Have we ever really been cold? Have our stomachs ever really needed food? Have we ever voluntarily lived, if only for a time, the way one-third of mankind has been condemned by social necessity to live?

2. Your world and that of tomorrow is a world, not so much of independent, as of interdependent nations and peoples. Try, I would recommend, to plan your college program so that at some time or other you study

outside the United States. To illustrate my reason for stressing this point, let me relate what happened recently when some Korean and American students in friendly, if at times tense, discussion made it clear to some Japanese that they were not impressed with the Japanese students' claim to be spearheading movements for peace. "Why is it," they asked, "that though you remind the world of Hiroshima and Nagasaki you do not remind your own people of the way Korea was enslaved by Japan?" American students at Sophia's summer program in Asian studies were taken aback when at a high school social science class they visited they were asked by the students: "Why does your country keep Okinawa for war purposes?" "Why do you threaten world peace by sending soldiers to Vietnam?" This type of question leads to an understanding of the complexity of issues that classroom study can rarely bring; for the questions are those of young idealists like ourselves—different though their understanding of world events be.

3. Remember, finally, that a skirmish lost with college administrators does not mean that the battle for a better world must be given up. Every Franny and Zooey among us misses the real point of things, the secret that unhinges the doors of the draughty cells we lock ourselves into—the secret that every person in every crowd is Seymours' Fat Lady. "And don't you know—listen to me, now—*don't you know who that Fat Lady really is?* . . . Ah, buddy, ah, buddy. It's Christ Himself, Christ Himself, buddy."

4. Finally, in every situation, although it may be grim as a Communist meeting in China held to "persuade" me that I've never had it better; although it may be as ponderously important as a jostle with police in Tokyo with the conviction that unless *this* demonstration topples the government the world moves one step further toward war; although it may be as boring as a protracted or disjointed lecture, the ability to laugh is what separates man from the beasts.